Betty Crocker
baking basics

Recipes and Tips to Bake with Confidence

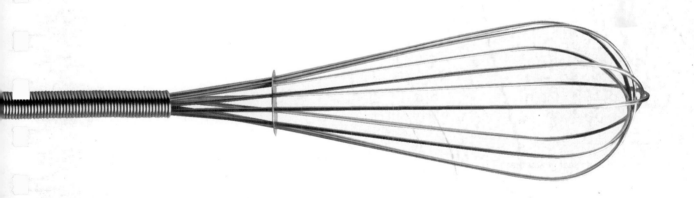

WILEY

Wiley Publishing, Inc.

General Mills

Betty Crocker Kitchens

Editorial Director: Jeff Nowak

Manager and Editor, Cookbooks:
Lois Tlusty

Recipe Development and Testing:
Betty Crocker Kitchens

Photography:
General Mills Photography Studios
and Image Library

Photographer: Chuck Nields

Food Stylists: Carol Grones,
Susan Brosius, Will Knuth and
Amy Peterson

Wiley Publishing, Inc.

Publisher: Natalie Chapman

Executive Editor: Anne Ficklen

Editor: Adam Kowit

Senior Production Editor: Amy Zarkos

Cover Design: Suzanne Sunwoo

Art Director: Tai Blanche

Layout: Holly Wittenberg

Photography Art Direction:
Judy Meyer and Lori Fox

Prop Stylist: Veronica Smith

Manufacturing Manager: Kevin Watt

The Betty Crocker Kitchens seal guarantees
success in your kitchen. Every recipe has been
tested in America's Most Trusted Kitchens™
to meet our high standards of reliability, easy
preparation and great taste.

FIND MORE GREAT IDEAS AT
BettyCrocker.com

For general information on our other products and services or for technical
support, please contact our Customer Care Department within the United States
at (800) 762-2974, outside the United States at (317) 572-3993 or fax (317) 572-4002.

Wiley also publishes its books in a variety of electronic formats. Some content
that appears in print may not be available in electronic books. For more
information about Wiley products, visit our web site at www.wiley.com.

Library of Congress Cataloging-in-Publication Data:

Crocker, Betty.

  Betty Crocker baking basics / Betty Crocker.

    p. cm.

  Includes index.

  ISBN 978-0-470-28661-6 (cloth : alk. paper)

  1. Baking. I. Title. II. Title: Baking basics.

  TX765.C87 2008

  641.8'15—dc22

                                2008009428

Printed in China

10 9 8 7 6 5 4 3 2 1

Photo credits: Sticks of chocolate bar photo on page 9 © Berit Myrekrok/
Digital Vision/Getty Images; bottle of olive oil photo on page 10 © Thomas
Pullicino/istockphoto.com; milk and eggs photo on page 12 © PhotoDisc,
Inc./Getty Images.

Dear Friends,

Remember the wonderful feeling of satisfaction you had the first time you baked cookies as a kid? You can have that feeling again by honing your baking skills and gaining the confidence to bake fruit-filled pies, luscious desserts or crusty breads to enhance any meal!

If you feel a little apprehensive about baking beyond cookies, relax. With the help of *Betty Crocker Baking Basics* cookbook, and some patience and practice, you will be baking like a pro in no time.

Check out the 101 section at the beginning of each chapter to learn about ingredients, selecting pans and making the ideal baked item using the recipes in that chapter. A helpful tip, how-to photo and photo of the finished recipe will assist you through each recipe. You'll also find basic information for stocking your kitchen with baking equipment, as well as baking terms and techniques.

Do you already have the confidence to bake muffins for a brunch, a cake for a birthday party or a pumpkin pie to serve at Thanksgiving? If the answer is yes, it's time to move to the last chapter of learning, You Can Bake It! You've just begun to impress your family and friends with your baking talents. Now you can put the techniques you have learned to the real test by baking a foolproof lemon meringue pie or a crown-topped chocolate soufflé for dessert.

Baking—the true meaning of satisfaction and pleasure!

Warmly,

Betty Crocker

CONTENTS

LET'S START BAKING

Understanding the Recipe

It is important to read all the way through the recipe before you do anything else. It sounds like a no-brainer, but when you're eager to get baking, it's easy to start measuring and then realize you don't have an ingredient you need. Or the cake batter is ready to pour into the pan and you don't have the correct size pan. Before you start, ask yourself:

- Do I have all the ingredients I need to make the recipe?
- Do I have all the gadgets, equipment and correct-size pans I need to make the recipe?
- Do I understand the directions and techniques within the recipe?
- Do I have the time it takes to make the recipe?

Now is the time, before you begin following the recipe directions, to get the ingredients ready. Doing things like chopping nuts, shredding carrots or draining the liquid from a can of pineapple slices will help you assemble the recipe without interruption.

Check your oven and make sure the racks are where you need them to be. If the rack shouldn't be in the middle of the oven, the recipe will tell you where to place it. It's always best to use an oven thermometer to be sure the temperature is accurate.

Because baking is a science, it's best to follow the directions and ingredients exactly. Don't be afraid to make notes on the page as you go.

It's a lot easier to wash utensils and equipment or rinse and put them in the dishwasher as you use them. That way, when you get to the end of the recipe and pop the pan into the oven, your kitchen will be clean.

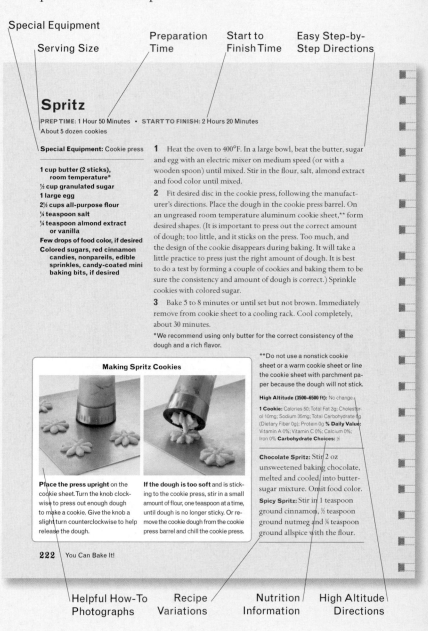

Special Equipment

Serving Size

Preparation Time

Start to Finish Time

Easy Step-by-Step Directions

Spritz

PREP TIME: 1 Hour 50 Minutes • START TO FINISH: 2 Hours 20 Minutes
About 5 dozen cookies

Special Equipment: Cookie press

1 cup butter (2 sticks),
    room temperature*
½ cup granulated sugar
1 large egg
2½ cups all-purpose flour
¼ teaspoon salt
¼ teaspoon almond extract
    or vanilla
Few drops of food color, if desired
Colored sugars, red cinnamon
    candies, nonpareils, edible
    sprinkles, candy-coated mini
    baking bits, if desired

1 Heat the oven to 400°F. In a large bowl, beat the butter, sugar and egg with an electric mixer on medium speed (or with a wooden spoon) until mixed. Stir in the flour, salt, almond extract and food color until mixed.

2 Fit desired disc in the cookie press, following the manufacturer's directions. Place the dough in the cookie press barrel. On an ungreased room temperature aluminum cookie sheet,** form desired shapes. (It is important to press out the correct amount of dough; too little, and it sticks on the press. Too much, and the design of the cookie disappears during baking. It will take a little practice to press just the right amount of dough. It is best to do a test by forming a couple of cookies and baking them to be sure the consistency and amount of dough is correct.) Sprinkle cookies with colored sugar.

3 Bake 5 to 8 minutes or until set but not brown. Immediately remove from cookie sheet to a cooling rack. Cool completely, about 30 minutes.

*We recommend using only butter for the correct consistency of the dough and a rich flavor.

**Do not use a nonstick cookie sheet or a warm cookie sheet or line the cookie sheet with parchment paper because the dough will not stick.

High Altitude (3500–6500 ft): No change.

1 Cookie: Calories 50; Total Fat 3g; Cholesterol 10mg; Sodium 35mg; Total Carbohydrate 6g (Dietary Fiber 0g); Protein 0g **% Daily Value:** Vitamin A 0%; Vitamin C 0%; Calcium 0%; Iron 0% **Carbohydrate Choices:** ½

Chocolate Spritz: Stir 2 oz unsweetened baking chocolate, melted and cooled, into butter-sugar mixture. Omit food color.

Spicy Spritz: Stir in 1 teaspoon ground cinnamon, ½ teaspoon ground nutmeg and ¼ teaspoon ground allspice with the flour.

Making Spritz Cookies

Place the press upright on the cookie sheet. Turn the knob clockwise to press out enough dough to make a cookie. Give the knob a slight turn counterclockwise to help release the dough.

If the dough is too soft and is sticking to the cookie press, stir in a small amount of flour, one teaspoon at a time, until dough is no longer sticky. Or remove the cookie dough from the cookie press barrel and chill the cookie press.

222   You Can Bake It!

Helpful How-To Photographs

Recipe Variations

Nutrition Information

High Altitude Directions

Know Your Baking Ingredients

Understanding ingredients used for baking is important for successful results. Here are some ingredients that you will find in recipes in this cookbook, as well as other common ingredients.

BAKING POWDER: Leavening mixture made from baking soda, an acid and a moisture absorber. Do not substitute baking powder for baking soda because acid proportions in the recipe may be unbalanced.

BAKING SODA: Leavening known as bicarbonate of soda. Must be mixed with an acid ingredient (such as lemon juice, buttermilk or molasses) to release carbon dioxide gas bubbles.

CHOCOLATE: Cocoa beans are shelled, roasted and ground to make a thick paste called *chocolate liquor*. Cocoa butter is the fat or oil from the cocoa bean. Chocolate liquor is processed to make:

Semisweet, Bittersweet, Sweet and Milk Chocolate: Contain from 10 to 35 percent chocolate liquor, varying amounts of cocoa butter, sugar and, for some, milk and flavorings. Available in bars and chips for baking or eating.

Unsweetened Baking Cocoa: Dried chocolate liquor, with the cocoa butter removed, is ground into unsweetened cocoa. Cocoa drink mixes contain milk powder and sugar and are not a direct substitution for baking cocoa.

Unsweetened Chocolate: Contains 50 to 58 percent cocoa butter. Bitter in flavor, it's used primarily in baking.

"White" Chocolate: Is not true chocolate because it doesn't contain chocolate liquor. Made from cocoa butter, sugar, milk solids and vanilla. Often called white baking chips or vanilla baking bar.

COCONUT: Firm, creamy-white meat of the coconut fruit. Available shredded or flaked, either sweetened or unsweetened, in cans or plastic bags.

COFFEE: Use brewed coffee or instant coffee granules or crystals as an ingredient.

CORN SYRUP: Clear, thick liquid made from corn sugar mixed with acid. Available either dark or light, which are interchangeable in most recipes.

CORNSTARCH: White, powdery "flour" made from a portion of the corn kernel and is used to thicken puddings, sauces, gravies and soups and stews. To substitute for all-purpose flour, use half as much cornstarch.

CREAM: Made by separating butterfat from the liquid in whole milk. It is pasteurized and processed into several forms:

Crème Fraîche: Very thick cream often served with fresh fruit and cobblers. Unlike sour cream, it does not curdle when heated.

Half-and-Half: Blend of milk and cream containing 10 to 12 percent butterfat. It won't whip, but you can use it in place of light or heavy cream in many recipes.

Sour Cream: Commercially cultured with lactic acid to give it a tangy flavor. Regular sour cream is 18 to 20 percent butterfat, and light sour cream is made from half-and-half and can be substituted for regular sour cream in most recipes. Fat-free sour cream has all the fat removed and may not work well in all recipes that call for regular sour cream.

Ultra-Pasteurized Whipping Cream: Has been heated briefly to kill microorganisms that cause milk products to sour. It has a longer shelf life than regular cream.

Heavy Whipping Cream: The richest cream and contains 36 to 40 percent butterfat. It doubles in volume when whipped.

Light Whipping Cream: The most common form contains 30 to 36 percent butterfat. It doubles in volume when whipped.

CREAM OF TARTAR: Acids left in wine barrels after wine is made are processed into cream of tartar. Add cream of tartar to egg whites before beating for more stability and volume. Also added as an acid ingredient to most baking powder.

EGGS: Used as an ingredient in cakes and breads as a leavener, and adds structure to other baked goods. An egg with a brown or white shell has the same flavor and nutritive value.

EGGS, PASTEURIZED: Also called fat-free egg product, is liquid eggs, found in cartons in the refrigeration section. The white and yolks are mixed together and then pasteurized at a heat level that kills any bacteria without cooking the eggs. Pasteurized eggs are used as an ingredient in recipes when the mixture will not be cooked or baked.

FATS AND OILS: Add richness and flavor to food, aid in browning, help bind ingredients together, tenderize baked goods and are used for frying.

Butter: Saturated fat made from cream that must be at least 80 percent butterfat by USDA standards. It is high in flavor and has a melt-in-your-mouth texture. Butter is sold in lightly salted and unsalted (also known as sweet butter) sticks, whipped in tubs and as butter-flavored granules.

Butter-Margarine Blends: Available in sticks and tubs, blends usually are a combination of 60 percent margarine and 40 percent butter and are interchangeable with butter or margarine.

Lard: A saturated fat made from rendered and refined pork fat, lard is not used as much now as in the past. Lard makes very tender, flaky biscuits and pastry.

Margarine: An unsaturated butter substitute made with at least 80 percent fat by weight and flavoring from dairy products. Most margarine uses vegetable oils made from soybeans, cottonseed and corn. It's sold in sticks and as soft spreads in tubs. Soft spread margarine in tubs is not recommended for baking because it has more water and less fat.

Oils: Liquid fats used for baking and cooking.

- **Baking Spray with Flour:** For baking, combines unflavored cooking oil with real flour and is used for spraying baking pans.

- **Cooking Spray:** Available in regular (unflavored), butter and olive oil varieties. It can be used to spray baking pans to prevent food from sticking.

- **Olive Oil:** Olive oil is made from pressed olives and classified in several ways: extra virgin, virgin, olive oil and light olive oil.

- **Vegetable Oil:** Blend of oils from various vegetables, such as corn, cottonseed, peanut, safflower, canola and soybean.

- **Reduced-Calorie (or Light) Butter or Margarine:** Water and air have been added to these products, and they contain at least 20 percent less fat than regular butter or margarine. We do not recommend them for baking due to the higher water content.

- **Shortening:** Vegetable oils that are hydrogenated so they'll be solid at room temperature. Use butter-flavored and regular shortening interchangeably. Sold in sticks and cans.

- **Vegetable Oil Spreads:** Margarine products with less than 80 percent fat (vegetable oil) by weight usually are labeled as vegetable oil spreads. They're sold in sticks for all-purpose use, including some baking if they contain more than 65 percent fat, so check the label. Also sold in tubs and in squeeze bottles but these should not be used for baking.

FLOUR: Primary ingredient in breads, cakes, cookies and quick breads.

All-Purpose Flour: Selected wheats blended for all kinds of baking. Available both bleached and unbleached.

Bread Flour: Made from wheat higher in gluten-forming protein, which gives more structure and volume to bread, than all-purpose flour. It's the best choice for making yeast breads and bread-machine breads. It isn't recommended for cakes, cookies, pastries or quick breads.

Cake Flour: Milled from soft wheat, it makes tender, fine-textured cakes.

Quick-Mixing Flour: Enriched, all-purpose flour that's granular and processed to blend easily with liquid to make gravies and sauces.

Rye Flour: Milled from rye grain and low in gluten-forming protein, it is usually combined with wheat flour to increase gluten-forming capabilities.

Self-Rising Flour: Made from a blend of hard and soft wheats that includes baking powder and salt. For best results, don't substitute self-rising flour for other kinds, unless directed in a recipe because the leavening and salt proportions will be out of balance.

Whole Wheat Flour: Ground from the entire wheat kernel, whole wheat flour gives breads and other baked goods a nutty flavor and dense texture. **White whole wheat flour** is made with the whole grain and has the same nutritional benefits as whole wheat flour. Whole wheat flour is made with red wheat, which is darker in color and has a stronger, nuttier flavor. White whole wheat flour is made from an albino variety of wheat, which is lighter in color and has a sweeter, milder flavor. **Stone-ground whole wheat flour**

has a coarser texture than roller-milled whole wheat flour. **Graham flour** is a slightly different grind of whole wheat flour but can be used interchangeably with whole wheat flour. Store whole wheat flour in the freezer or refrigerator to keep the fat in the wheat germ from becoming rancid. Always bring flour to room temperature before using.

HERBS: Leaves of plants without woody stems that have distinctive fragrances and flavors—from savory to sweet—and are available fresh and dried.

SWEETENERS: In addition to adding sweetness to baked goods, sweeteners also help brown and add tenderness. Most recipes call for granulated sugar, brown sugar or both, but other types of sweeteners like honey and maple syrup are called for in specific recipes.

Artificial Sweeteners: Also called sugar substitutes, are used instead of sucrose (table sugar) to sweeten foods and beverages. Many are not recommended for baking so check the label carefully.

Honey: Natural sweetener produced by bees. Honey is safe for persons one year of age and older. Store honey at room temperature.

Maple Syrup: Golden brown to amber-colored sweetener made by boiling down the sap of sugar maple trees. Refrigerate after opening. Maple-flavored syrup usually is corn syrup combined with a little pure maple syrup.

Molasses: Dark thick syrup from the sugar-refining process. Molasses is available in light (mild flavor) and dark (full flavor) varieties.

Sugar: Sweetener produced from sugar beets or cane sugar. Available in several forms: **Brown sugar** is made by mixing white sugar with molasses. Available in light and dark varieties; dark brown sugar has more molasses added and a stronger flavor. If brown sugar hardens, store it in a closed container with a slice of apple or a slice of fresh bread for one to two days to soften.

Granulated sugar is white, granular sugar that should be used when recipes call for just "sugar." It's available in boxes and bags, as well as in cubes. **Powdered (confectioners') sugar** is granulated sugar that has been processed to a fine powder.

MILK: Refers to cow's milk in the recipes in this book.

Buttermilk: Thick, smooth liquid made by culturing skim or part-skim milk with lactic acid bacteria.

Evaporated Milk: Whole milk with more than half of the water removed before the mixture is homogenized. Evaporated milk is a little thicker than whole milk and has a slightly "cooked" taste. Do not use it as a substitute for sweetened condensed milk in recipes.

Fat-Free (Skim) Milk: Contains virtually no fat.

One Percent Low-Fat Milk: Has 99 percent of milk fat removed.

Two Percent Reduced-Fat Milk: Has 98 percent of milk fat removed.

Sweetened Condensed Milk: Made when about half of the water is removed from whole milk and sweetener is added. Do not substitute it in recipes calling for evaporated milk.

Whole or Regular Milk: Has at least 3.5 percent milk fat.

ORGANIC: Foods are grown without the use of synthetic pesticides or chemical fertilizers. The USDA organic standards also prohibit the use of antibiotics, artificial (or synthetic) flavors, hormones, preservatives, synthetic colors, as well as ingredients that are irradiated or genetically engineered.

SPICES: Come from various parts of plants and trees: the bark, buds, fruits, roots, seeds and stems. Available grated, ground, powdered, in stick form or whole.

VINEGAR: Made from fermented liquids, such as wine, beer or cider, that have been converted by a bacterial activity to a weak solution of acetic acid.

Apple Cider Vinegar: From fermented apple cider and is milder than white vinegar.

Balsamic Vinegar: From Trebbiano grape juice and gets its dark color and pungent sweet flavor from aging in wooden barrels over a period of years.

Distilled White Vinegar: Made from grain-alcohol.

Herb Vinegars: Made by steeping herbs, such as basil, tarragon, and dill, in vinegar.

Rice Vinegar: Made from fermented rice.

Wine Vinegar: Made from red or white wine and is pleasantly pungent.

YEAST: Leavening used in all yeast doughs. The combination of warmth, food (sugar) and liquid causes yeast to release carbon dioxide bubbles that cause dough to rise. Yeast is very sensitive; too much heat will kill it, and cold will prevent it from growing. Always use yeast before its expiration date.

Bread Machine Yeast: A finely granulated strain of yeast that works exceptionally well in bread machines.

Compressed Fresh (Cake) Yeast: A small square of fresh, moist yeast found in the dairy refrigerator. Highly perishable, store in the refrigerator and use within two weeks or by the expiration date. One cake of yeast is equal to one envelope of dry yeast. This yeast isn't as popular as dry yeast so is more difficult to find.

Quick Active Dry Yeast: Dehydrated yeast that allows dough to rise in less time than regular yeast.

Regular Active Dry Yeast: Dehydrated yeast that is used in most yeast dough recipes. It is available in moisture-proof packets or jars. Each packet contains 2¼ teaspoons yeast.

Measuring Ingredients

It is very important to measure ingredients accurately for baking success. Not all ingredients are measured the same way or with the same type of measuring cups or measuring spoons. Here are some tips for using the correct measuring utensil and method when measuring ingredients.

Liquid Measuring Cups: Are usually glass or clear plastic. They have a spout for pouring and space above the top measuring line to avoid spills. Some plastic measuring cups have an angled rim inside so you read the measurement from above rather than eye level. They are available in one-, two-, four- and eight-cup sizes.

Dry Measuring Cups: To measure dry ingredients, such as sugar, and solid ingredients, such as butter. They usually are a set of cups that stack or "nest" inside one another. These cups are made to hold an exact amount when filled to the top. They are available as a set that contains ¼-, ⅓-, ½- and one-cup sizes.

Measuring Spoons: Are often sold as a set that includes ¼-, ½- and one-teaspoon sizes plus a one-tablespoon size. Some sets may have a ⅛-teaspoon size and a dash. These spoons are designed for measuring and should be used instead of spoons intended for eating. They are used for both liquid and dry ingredients.

Measuring Liquids: Use the smallest measuring cup size that can hold the amount needed. Place the cup on a level surface, then bend down to check the amount at eye level. To measure sticky liquids such as honey, lightly spray the cup with cooking spray so the liquid will be easier to remove.

Measuring Dry Ingredients: Gently fill a dry measuring cup to heaping, using a large spoon. Do not shake the cup or pack down the ingredients. While holding the cup over the storage container, level the cup off, using the straight edge of a knife, metal spatula or the handle of a wooden spoon.

Measuring Brown Sugar or Solid Fats: Fill a dry measuring cup using a spoon or rubber spatula. Pack down the ingredient, and level off, if necessary, so it is even with the top of the cup.

Measuring Chopped Nuts, Cookie Crumbs or Cereal: Fill a dry measuring cup lightly without packing down the ingredient, and level off so it is even with the top of the cup.

Measuring Butter or Margarine Sticks: Cut off the amount needed, following guideline marks on the wrapper, using a sharp knife. A whole ¼-pound stick equals ½ cup, half a stick is ¼ cup, and eighth of a stick is one tablespoon.

Measuring Salt, Baking Powder, Baking Soda, Spices and Herbs: Fill measuring spoon with salt, baking powder, baking soda or a ground spice and level off with the straight edge of a knife or small metal spatula. For fresh chopped or dried herbs, lightly fill the spoon to the top.

COMMON ABBREVIATIONS

Abbreviations used in this cookbook in the ingredient list are "oz" for ounce and "lb" for pound. The reason is many food labels use "oz" and "lb" rather than spelling out the word. Other recipe sources may use abbreviations, so here are some common ones you may see in recipes.

t	=	teaspoon
tsp	=	teaspoon
T	=	tablespoon
Tbsp	=	tablespoon
c	=	cup
oz	=	ounce
pt	=	pint
qt	=	quart
gal	=	gallon
lb	=	pound
in	=	inch
"	=	inch
pkg	=	package
doz	=	dozen
°	=	degree
F	=	Fahrenheit

MEASURING EQUIVALENTS

What's different, yet exactly the same? All these measurements! The recipes in this cookbook use the larger measurement, such as ¼ cup rather than 4 tablespoons, because it's quicker to measure and reduces the risk of making a mistake. The equivalency below will help you when measuring ingredients when you're baking.

Dash or pinch	=	less than ⅛ teaspoon		
1 tablespoon	=	3 teaspoons		
¼ cup	=	4 tablespoons		
⅓ cup	=	5 tablespoons + 1 teaspoon		
½ cup	=	8 tablespoons		
¾ cup	=	12 tablespoons		
1 cup	=	16 tablespoons	=	8 fluid ounces
2 cups	=	1 pint	=	16 fluid ounces
4 cups	=	1 quart	=	32 fluid ounces
4 quarts	=	1 gallon	=	128 fluid ounces
¼ pound	=	4 ounces		
½ pound	=	8 ounces		
1 pound	=	16 ounces		

Baking Equipment and Gadgets

Bare Essentials

So your kitchen has equipment with just a few gadgets, a couple of bowls and pots and pans. No problem, because you can still learn to bake with just the bare essentials and make several of the recipes in this cookbook. Here are some things you may want to have in your kitchen to get started.

PREPARATION AND MEASURING

Can Opener: Purchase one that fits comfortably in your hand and is easy to wash after each use.

Cutting Boards: Plastic cutting boards are available in a variety of sizes and colors. Wooden or thin, flexible silicone cutting boards and disposable cutting sheets are also good. Wash all cutting boards thoroughly with hot, soapy water after each use.

Knife, Chef's: It can be used for cutting large pieces of food or chopping. The wide blade with its curved cutting edge is perfect for the rocking motion used for chopping. Available in 8- to 10-inch blades.

Knife, Paring: A short blade used for peeling vegetables and fruits and cutting small pieces of food. Available in three- to four-inch blades.

Measuring Cups, Dry: Look for nests of metal or plastic cups, which usually increase in size from ¼ cup to one cup.

Measuring Cups, Liquid: These glass or plastic cups have a pour spout and space above the top measuring mark so the liquid doesn't spill. They are available in one-, two-, four- and eight-cup sizes.

Measuring Spoons: Look for sets of metal or plastic spoons that range in size from ¼ teaspoon to one tablespoon. Some sets contain ⅛ teaspoon and a ¾ teaspoon. Spoons are used to measure either dry or liquid ingredients.

Strainer, Wire Mesh: For draining fruits and vegetables after washing and draining liquid from canned and frozen fruits.

MIXING

Mixing Bowls: A set of three nested mixing bowls will give you a variety of sizes. Usually there is a one-quart, a 2½-quart and a 2½-quart bowl.

Spatula, Rubber or Silicone: Also called scrapers. For scraping the side of a mixing bowl, blender or food processor and for scraping out measuring cups, measuring spoons, mixing spoons and jars.

Spoons, Wooden or Plastic: For all-purpose mixing and stirring, it is best to use long-handled spoons for mixing. Wooden spoons are sturdy enough for stirring thick batters and doughs. Plastic spoons are better for mixing dry ingredients and thinner batters.

Wire Whisk: Use for mixing thin batters, sauces and beating eggs as well as for all-purpose mixing.

BAKING

Baking Pan, 13 × 9-inch: A rectangular metal pan for baking cakes, brownies, bars and sweet rolls. A 13 × 9-inch *baking dish* is made of heat-resistant glass.

Baking Pan, Eight- or Nine-inch: A square metal pan for baking cakes, bars, coffee cakes and some desserts. An eight- or nine-inch *baking dish* is made of heat-resistant glass.

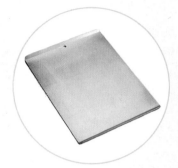

Cookie Sheet: Flat and rectangular baking sheet that may be open on one or more sides. The open sides allow good air circulation in the oven when baking cookies, biscuits, scones or shortcakes.

Cooling Rack: Place hot baked items on to cool and allows air to circulate around it.

Muffin Pan (Muffin Cups): One pan with 6 or 12 individual cups for baking muffins or cupcakes.

Pie Plate: A round heat-resistant glass pan with a flared side, designed for baking pies. A *pie pan* is made of metal and usually shiny.

Thermometer, Oven: Designed to read oven temperatures, which can often be inaccurately indicated by the oven dial. The spring-style thermometer is less expensive but not as reliable as a mercury oven thermometer.

Timer: If your stove doesn't have a timer, purchase a digital or dial one at a department or kitchen supply store.

Turner: Also referred to as a pancake turner, it is available in metal or for nonstick pans, heat-proof plastic. Use to remove cookies, biscuits and scones from a cookie sheet.

A Few More Essentials

Now that you have baked a few recipes and feel more confident, you may want to add to your basic kitchen baking equipment. Here are some additional basic items that you may want to purchase (or ask for as gifts) so you can increase your baking recipe repertoire. Also check out Baking Equipment and Gadget Wish List on page 254 for more ideas.

PREPARATION AND MEASURING

Egg Separator: For separating the egg white from the yolk.

Grater, Box: A box grater has different size openings on each side for shredding and grating and a slot for slicing. Use the larger holes for shredding and the small holes for grating.

Juicer: To squeeze fresh juice from lemons, limes and oranges.

Spatula, Small Metal: Use to level off ingredients when using dry ingredient measuring cups. Metal spatulas are also good for frosting cookies, bars and cakes.

MIXING

Thermometer, Instant-Read: Great for measuring the temperature of water when making yeast breads. There are two kinds of instant-read thermometers: dial or digital. Both work equally well so select the one you prefer.

Electric Mixer, Hand-Held: Used for mixing cake batter, cookie dough, and some desserts and for beating whipping cream and egg whites but not for thick mixtures like stiff cookie dough or yeast dough. Look for a comfortable shaped handle and weight. If it weighs too much, it will become heavy when holding for a length of time.

Rolling Pin: Used primarily to roll pastry and cookie dough but can also be used to crush crackers and cookies. A good choice is one made of hardwood with handles fitted with ball bearings. Wash it by hand and dry it thoroughly after every use.

BAKING

Cake Pan, Round: For making layer cakes, some coffee cakes and yeast rolls. They are available in nine- or eight-inch pans with nine-inch being the most common. You'll need two pans to bake layer cakes.

Loaf Pan: For making quick or yeast bread loaves and some cakes. They are available in either eight- or nine-inch size.

Knife, Serrated Bread: Has a serrated or scalloped edge and should have a blade that is at least seven to eight inches long. Used for slicing breads, coffee cakes and some cakes.

Pastry Brush: For greasing baking pans, brushing tops of unbaked pie crust and tops of baked yeast breads. A brush that has a movable metal shank is easier to clean. Also available in colorful silicone that is dishwasher safe.

DON'T FORGET YOUR POT HOLDERS!

Cloth pot holders and oven mitts should be thick enough to prevent burning your hands but easy to grasp and hold hot pans. They should have at least a double layer of heat-resistant batting and be machine washable. Oven mitts are good for removing pans from the oven because they protect your arms as well, but may not be as easy to use as pot holders so you may want to get a set of each. Be careful not to get your cloth pot holder or oven mitt damp before using it to pick up a hot pan; the water in the fabric conducts heat, and it can burn you. Silicone pot holders are colorful but aren't as easy to use because they aren't as flexible as cloth. However, they are excellent to place hot pans on and protect your countertops.

Know Your Baking Pans

The material and size of baking pans is important to baking success. Here are some guidelines when selecting baking pans.

Pan Types

SHINY PANS reflect heat, slowing the browning, and are recommended for baking cookies, bars, cakes and quick breads. Shiny bakeware, including aluminum, tin and stainless steel, will give you tender, light brown crusts and softer cookies that spread slightly more.

DARK AND DULL-FINISH PANS absorb more heat, so baked goods brown more quickly and evenly. Manufacturers of dark bakeware may recommend reducing the oven temperature by 25°F for some baked items to compensate for this. Dull-finish, including dull aluminum, tin and glass, is recommended for baking pies and yeast breads. Pie crusts will evenly brown on the bottom as well as on top. Breads brown evenly and have a crisper crust. Anodized aluminum pans are electrolytically coated to protect the surface, making it dull. These pans are good for baking yeast breads.

BLACK STEEL PANS give breads a crisp, dark crust and are often used for French bread and breadsticks to give them their distinctive crunch. Black steel popover pans are the best because the popovers will have a crisp, evenly browned crust.

SILICONE PANS, the newest in bakeware, are soft and flexible. They can withstand extreme heat and are safe for the dishwasher, microwave and freezer. Because the pans are flexible, they must be placed on a cookie sheet so they can be easily placed in and removed from the oven. The pans are hot when removed from the oven, so be sure to use hot pads when moving pans from the cookie sheet to the cooling rack. The pans must be sprayed with cooking spray before the batter or dough is added, or the baked food will stick. The baked foods will easily pop out after cooling by pushing on the bottom of the pan. They are available in many fun colors and shapes such as *round* cake pans, fluted tube cake pans, muffin pans, mini loaf pans and more.

INSULATED COOKIE SHEETS, also called cushioned or double layered, have two metal sheets with an insulated layer of air between so the heat is distributed evenly and hot spots are eliminated. This helps prevent uneven browning and baking. Many are available with a nonstick surface.

Pan Sizes

It is always best to use the size pan that is called for in the recipe. If a pan is too large, the baked item will be flat, low volume and overbaked. If a pan is too small, it may overflow and not be done in the center.

Here are some standard size pans:

8- or 9-inch square pan
8- or 9-inch round cake pan
8 × 4-inch loaf pan
9 × 5-inch loaf pan
9-inch glass pie plate
9- or 10-inch springform pan
9- or 10-inch tart pan

10-inch angel food (tube) cake pan
12-cup fluted tube cake pan
Cookie sheets
15 × 10 × 1-inch pan (or jelly roll pan)
Muffin cups, 2¾ × 1¼-inches

DON'T HAVE THAT SIZE PAN?

You're in the mood to bake, have the recipe in front of you and then discover you don't have the pan called for in the recipe. In a pinch, you can use a pan similar in size. Use the chart below to select the closest size pan.

Pan Substitute Chart

RECIPE CALLS FOR:	YOU HAVE:
One 13 × 9-inch pan	Two 9-inch round cake pans OR Two 8-inch round cake pans OR Two 8-inch square pans
One 9-inch round cake pan	One 8-inch square pan
Two 9-inch round cake pans	Three 3-inch round cake pans
One 8 × 4-inch loaf pan	Two 5½ × 3¼-inch loaf pans
One 9 × 5-inch loaf pan	Two 7½ × 3¾-inch loaf pans OR Three 5½ × 3¼-inch loaf pans
One 12-cup fluted tube	One 10-inch angel food (tube) cake pan OR Two 9 × 5-inch loaf pans

MEASURING BAKING PANS

Standard pan sizes are usually marked on the back of the pan, but if not, measure the pan to be sure it is the correct dimensions. With a ruler, measure the length and width across the top of the pan from the inside edge to the outside edge. To measure the volume of a fluted tube cake pan, fill the pan with water to the top using a measuring cup.

1 COOKIES and BARS

COOKIES AND BARS 101

Who doesn't love homemade cookies and bars? They're easy to make, portable and always a crowd pleaser. Read on to learn the basics for making cookies.

Types of Cookies

There are basically six types of cookies. And yes, bars and brownies are a type of cookie.

BARS: Dough is spread or pressed in a baking pan, then baked and cut into individual shapes (brownies).

DROP: Spoonfuls of dough are dropped on a cookie sheet (chocolate chip cookies).

MOLDED: Dough is formed into shapes either by using your hands (peanut butter cookies) or cutting with a knife (shortbread cookies).

PRESSED: Dough is placed in the tube of a cookie press (or cookie gun) and pressed out on a cookie sheet to make shapes (spritz cookies).

ROLLED: Stiff dough, usually chilled, is rolled out and cut into shapes using a cookie cutter or knife (sugar cookies).

REFRIGERATOR: Stiff dough is shaped into logs and refrigerated until firm and then cut into slices and baked (pinwheels).

Cookie Sheets and Baking Pans

There are many types of cookie sheets and having at least three or four cookie sheets to use is helpful. When one batch of cookies is finished baking, another is ready to go!

Choose sheets that are at least two inches narrower and shorter than the inside dimensions of your oven so heat can circulate around them. The sheet may be open on one to three sides. If the sheet has four sides, cookies may not brown as evenly.

When baking bars, use the exact size of pan called for in a recipe. Bars baked in pans that are too big become hard and overcooked, and those baked in pans that are too small can be doughy in the center and hard on the edges. Shiny metal pans are recommended for baking bars. They reflect the heat away from the bars, preventing the crust from getting too brown and hard.

Shiny smooth-surface or textured aluminum cookie sheets reflect heat, letting cookies bake evenly and brown properly. The recipes in this book were tested using shiny aluminum cookie sheets.

Insulated cookie sheets help prevent cookies from turning too dark on the bottom. Cookies may take longer to bake, the bottoms will be light colored and cookies may not brown as much overall. Cookies may be difficult to remove from cookie sheets because the cookie bottom is more tender.

Nonstick and dark surface cookie sheets may result in cookies smaller in diameter and more rounded because the bottoms bake before the cookie can spread. The bottoms will be more browned and may be hard. Check cookies at the minimum bake time so they don't get too brown or burn. Follow the manufacturer's directions; some recommend reducing the oven temperature by 25°F.

MIXING THE DOUGH

An electric mixer or spoon can be used for mixing the dough in most of the recipes in this book. The sugars, fats and liquids usually are beaten together first until well mixed. Flour and other dry ingredients are almost always stirred in by hand to avoid overmixing the dough, which can result in tougher cookies.

Storing Cookie Dough

To refrigerate unbaked cookie dough, cover it tightly and refrigerate up to 24 hours.

To freeze unbaked cookie dough, wrap it in waxed paper, plastic wrap or foil and place in resealable food-safe plastic freezer bags or freezer containers. Dough can also be formed into individual cookies before freezing. Label and freeze up to six months. Before baking, thaw frozen dough in the refrigerator at least eight hours. If the thawed dough is too stiff to work with, let it stand at room temperature until it's workable.

Softening Butter

Most cookie recipes call for room-temperature or softened butter or margarine. But how can you tell if it is soft enough? Butter that is too soft or is partially melted results in dough that is too soft, causing cookies to spread too much.

Let refrigerated butter soften at room temperature for 30 to 45 minutes. Perfectly softened butter should give gently to pressure and you should be able to leave a fingerprint and slight indentation on the butter, but it shouldn't be soft in appearance.

Perfectly softened butter

Butter is too soft

Butter is partially melted

Softening Butter in the Microwave

You can soften butter in the microwave but be very careful that you don't oversoften or it will start to melt on the edges.

Remove wrapper from the refrigerated butter and place the stick of butter on a microwavable plate. Or cut off the amount of butter needed and place in microwavable bowl or measuring cup. Microwave uncovered on High:

1 to 7 tablespoons: 10 to 20 seconds
1 stick (8 tablespoons): 15 to 30 seconds

SHAPING COOKIES

Baking cookies is easy and fun but sometimes making cookies all the same size so they bake evenly can be a challenge. Here are tips for shaping drop, molded and rolled cookie dough.

Measuring Drop Cookies

Should I use a tableware tablespoon or a measuring spoon tablespoon when the recipe tells me to "drop dough by rounded tablespoonfuls?" Use a tableware teaspoon or tablespoon when the recipe calls for "teaspoon or tablespoon" to measure the dough. The recipe should specify if you should use a measuring spoon instead of tableware. Push dough from the spoon onto the cookie sheet with another spoon or a rubber spatula.

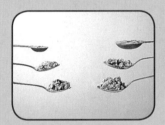

Top Row: *Level* measuring teaspoon and tablespoon. **Middle Row:** *Rounded* tableware teaspoon and tablespoon. **Bottom Row:** *Heaping* tableware teaspoon and tablespoon.

Scoop It!

Using a spring-handled cookie or ice-cream scoop is an easy way to make cookies the same size. Not all manufacturer's sizes are the same so measure the volume with water. Here are two size scoops that you may want:

#70 scoop = one level tablespoon
#16 scoop = ¼ cup

Molding Cookie Dough

An easy way to check if molded cookies, such as Peanut Butter or Snickerdoodles, will be the same size is to place a ruler on top of the bowl of dough. After shaping the dough into a ball, place it on the ruler to check that it is the size specified in the recipe.

Rolling Cookie Dough Evenly

When rolling cookie dough, use light pressure on the rolling pin, and roll evenly from center to edges, lifting the pin off at the edges.

To roll the dough evenly, you can purchase two square wooden dowels the thickness you want to roll the dough. Place the dough between the dowels and roll the pin over the dowels until dough is even.

Clean flat wooden or plastic rulers can be used instead of dowels. A ruler is about ⅛ inch thick. For ¼-inch-thick dough, stack two sets of ruler.

Place dough between rulers or dowels and roll the rolling pin over the rulers until dough is even.

BAKING COOKIES AND BARS

- Use completely cooled cookie sheets. Cookies will spread too much if put on a hot or warm cookie sheet. Let cookie sheet stand about 10 minutes to cool to room temperature. Or pop it in the freezer or refrigerator or run cool water on the back of the cookie sheet to cool.
- Make all cookies the same size so they bake evenly.
- Bake cookies and bars on the middle oven rack. For even baking, baking one sheet at a time is recommended. To bake two sheets at once, position oven racks as close to the middle as possible, and switch sheets halfway through baking so cookies bake more evenly.
- Check cookies and bars at the minimum bake time listed in the recipe to prevent overbaking them. Remove cookies from the cookie sheet to prevent them from continuing to bake and cool as directed.
- Remove cookies from a cookie sheet using a flat, thin turner. If cookies are left to cool on the cookie sheet too long, they become difficult to remove. Put the cookie sheet back in the oven for one to two minutes to warm the cookies, and then remove them from the sheet; they should come off easily.

- Cool cookies and bars on a cooling rack. The rack should be at least ½ inch above the counter top so air can circulate around the cookies.
- Cool bars and brownies in the pan on a cooling rack.

Bake a Test Cookie

A great way to make adjustments before baking a whole sheet of cookies is to bake one test cookie. If the cookie spreads too much, add one to two tablespoons of flour to the dough, or refrigerate the dough one to two hours before baking. If it's too dry, add one to two tablespoons of milk to the dough.

When Greasing Pans

Grease cookie sheets and baking pans with cooking spray or shortening when a recipe calls for it. Greasing with butter, margarine or oil isn't recommended because the area between the cookies will burn during baking.

Or instead of greasing, line cookie sheets with cooking parchment paper or a silicone baking mat.

Don't grease nonstick cookie sheets even if a recipe calls for greasing; the cookies may spread too much.

What Went Wrong?

Cookies

This Happened	This Is Why
Baked together	• cookies placed too close together • cookie sheet too warm
Very thin and flat	• cookie sheet too warm • butter or margarine too soft • too little flour • dough too soft and may need to chill
Dry and hard	• too much flour • oven temperature too hot • baked too long
Crisp but become soft	• stored tightly covered
Soft but become crisp or hard	• stored loosely covered

Bars

This Happened	This Is Why
Crumbly when cut	• not cooled completely
Dry and hard	• too much flour • incorrect pan size • oven temperature too hot • baked too long

Cookie Decorating Recipes

Decorator's Frosting

Stir 2 cups powdered sugar, ½ teaspoon vanilla and 2 tablespoons water or milk until smooth and spreadable. To tint frosting, stir in liquid food color, one drop at a time, until frosting is desired color. For intense, vivid color, use paste food color. (You would have to use too much liquid food color to get a vivid color, and the frosting will begin to separate and look curdled.)

Frosting Decorating Bag

Rather than drizzle the frosting from a spoon to make designs on frosted cookies, use a plastic bag to make a decorating bag. Spoon frosting into small food-safe resealable plastic bag and seal bag. Snip off a tiny piece of one corner of bag. Push the frosting down to the corner. Squeeze bag to make a design on frosted cookies after the frosting has dried and hardened.

Decorating Cookies

Cutout sugar cookies are delicious without decorating, but here are three easy ways to make them special.

Painted Cookies: Prepare Egg Yolk Paint (opposite page) or Food Color Paint (opposite page). Using a small clean brush, paint decorative designs on unbaked cutout cookies.

Marbled Cookies: Prepare Decorator's Frosting (above) and Food Color Paint (opposite page). Frost a baked cutout cookie, and while frosting is fresh and soft, spoon small drops of paint on frosting. Using a toothpick or small brush, swirl paint to create a marbleized pattern. Repeat with remaining cookies.

Flocked Cookies: Prepare Decorator's Frosting (above) and frost baked cutout cookies. Let stand until frosting is dried and hardened. Prepare another recipe of Decorator's Frosting. To drizzle, add enough water until frosting is thin enough to drizzle from the tip of a tableware spoon. Pipe or drizzle a design on a frosted cookie. Sprinkle colored sugar over design while frosting is fresh and soft. Shake off excess sugar. Repeat with remaining cookies.

Painted Cookie   Marbled Cookie   Flocked Cookie

Egg Yolk Paint

Stir together 1 egg yolk and ¼ teaspoon water. Tint with liquid food color to desired brightness. For several colors, divide egg mixture among small bowls and tint each one a different color. For food-safety reasons, use Egg Yolk Paint only on cookies that will be baked. Do not use on baked or frosted cookies.

Food Color Paint

Stir together small amounts of water and liquid food color. Paint on cookie dough before baking, or use to paint designs on frosted cutout cookies.

Storing Cookies and Bars

Store crisp cookies at room temperature in a loosely covered container. If crisp cookies become soft, put them on a cookie sheet in a 300°F oven for five minutes. Immediately remove cookies to a cooling rack and cool completely.

Store chewy and soft cookies at room temperature in resealable plastic food-storage bags or a tightly covered container. If soft cookies become dry and hard, put a slice of bread in the storage container and let stand for a day or two. The moisture from the bread will soften the cookies.

Don't store crisp and chewy or soft cookies together in the same container, or the crisp cookies will become soft.

Let frosted or decorated cookies set or harden before storing; store them between layers of waxed paper, plastic wrap or foil.

Store different flavors of cookies in separate containers, or they will pick up the flavors of the other cookies.

Most bars can be stored tightly covered, but check the recipe for sure; some may need to be loosely covered and others need to be refrigerated.

To freeze baked cookies and bars, tightly wrap and label; freeze unfrosted cookies up to 12 months and frosted cookies up to three months. Do not freeze meringue, custard-filled or cream-filled cookies. Thaw most cookies, covered, in the container at room temperature for one to two hours. For crisp cookies, remove from the container to thaw.

Chocolate Brownies

PREP TIME: 25 Minutes • **START TO FINISH:** 3 Hours 10 Minutes

16 brownies

Cooking spray to grease pan

5 oz unsweetened baking chocolate

⅔ cup butter or margarine

1¾ cups granulated sugar

2 teaspoons vanilla

3 large eggs

1 cup all-purpose flour

1 cup chopped walnuts, if desired

Chocolate Buttercream Frosting (page 65), if desired

1 Heat the oven to 350°F. Spray the bottom and sides of a 9-inch square pan with the cooking spray.

2 Cut the baking chocolate into pieces. In a 1-quart saucepan, melt the chocolate and butter over low heat, stirring constantly, just until the chocolate is melted. Remove from heat and cool 5 minutes.

3 In a medium bowl, beat the sugar, vanilla and eggs with an electric mixer on high speed 5 minutes. On low speed, beat in chocolate mixture, stopping occasionally to scrape batter from side and bottom of bowl with a rubber spatula. Beat in the flour, stopping occasionally to scrape bowl, just until mixed. Stir in the walnuts. Pour batter into the pan; use a rubber spatula to scrape batter from bowl, spread batter evenly in pan and smooth top of batter.

4 Bake 40 to 45 minutes or just until brownies begin to pull away from the sides of the pan. Be sure not to overbake brownies because the edges will get hard and dry. Place pan on a cooling rack. Let stand about 2 hours until completely cooled. Make Chocolate Buttercream Frosting; spread over brownies, using a metal spatula. For 16 brownies, cut into 4 rows by 4 rows.

High Altitude (3500–6500 ft): Bake 45 to 50 minutes.

1 Brownie: Calories 240; Total Fat 12g; Cholesterol 55mg; Sodium 55mg; Total Carbohydrate 31g (Dietary Fiber 1g); Protein 3g **% Daily Value:** Vitamin A 4%; Vitamin C 0%; Calcium 0%; Iron 10% **Carbohydrate Choices:** 2

Chocolate–Peanut Butter Brownies: Substitute ⅓ cup crunchy peanut butter for ⅓ cup of the butter. Omit walnuts. Before baking, arrange 16 one-inch chocolate-covered peanut butter cup candies, unwrapped, over top. Press into batter so tops of cups are even with top of batter.

Cutting Brownies

Use a plastic knife for cutting brownies or any bar with a chewy and dense texture. The brownies won't stick to the plastic knife.

Layered Coconut–Chocolate Chip Bars

PREP TIME: 10 Minutes • **START TO FINISH:** 2 Hours 40 Minutes

36 bars

Special Equipment: Rolling pin

½ cup butter or margarine
(1 stick)

20 to 24 graham cracker squares

1 cup chopped nuts

1 cup semisweet chocolate
chips (6 oz)

1½ cups flaked coconut

1 can (14 oz) sweetened
condensed milk (not
evaporated milk)

Crushing Graham Crackers

Place the crackers in a resealable plastic bag; close the bag tightly. Crush the crackers into fine crumbs using a rolling pin.

1 Heat the oven to 350°F. Place the butter in a medium microwavable bowl. Cover with a microwavable paper towel. Microwave on High 1 minute to 1 minute 15 seconds or until melted.

2 Meanwhile, place 10 of the cracker squares in a resealable food-storage plastic bag; seal the bag. Roll over crackers with a rolling pin or bottle, or press with bottom of small saucepan, to crush crackers into fine crumbs. Place crumbs in measuring cup. Crush the remaining crackers. You should have 1½ cups of crumbs.

3 Place crumbs in medium bowl; stir in the melted butter until well mixed. Using fingers, press crumb mixture firmly and evenly on the bottom of an ungreased or foil-lined 13 × 9-inch pan.

4 Sprinkle the nuts, chocolate chips and coconut over the crumb crust. Pour the condensed milk over the top.

5 Bake 20 to 25 minutes or until lightly browned. Place pan on a cooling rack. Let stand about 2 hours until completely cooled. For 36 bars, cut into 6 rows by 6 rows.

High Altitude (3500–6500 ft): No change.

1 Bar: Calories 140; Total Fat 9g; Cholesterol 10mg; Sodium 65mg; Total Carbohydrate 14g (Dietary Fiber 0g); Protein 2g **% Daily Value:** Vitamin A 2%; Vitamin C 0%; Calcium 4%; Iron 2% **Carbohydrate Choices:** 1

Toffee Bars

PREP TIME: 15 Minutes • **START TO FINISH:** 1 Hour 20 Minutes

32 bars

1 large egg

1 cup butter or margarine
    (2 sticks), room temperature

1 cup packed brown sugar

1 teaspoon vanilla

2 cups all-purpose flour

¼ teaspoon salt

⅔ cup milk chocolate chips

½ cup chopped nuts, if desired

1   Heat the oven to 350°F. Place an egg separator over a small bowl. Crack the egg over the egg separator to separate the yolk from the white. (Save the white for another recipe.) In a large bowl, place egg yolk.

2   Into the bowl with the egg yolk, stir the butter, brown sugar and vanilla with a wooden spoon until well mixed. Stir in the flour and salt until mixed. Using fingers, press the dough firmly and evenly on the bottom of an ungreased or foil-lined 13 × 9-inch pan. If dough is sticky, dip fingers in water or spray with cooking spray.

3   Bake 25 to 30 minutes or until very light brown (the crust will be soft).

4   Immediately sprinkle the chocolate chips over the hot crust. Let stand about 5 minutes or until chocolate has softened; spread chocolate evenly over bars, using a metal spatula. Sprinkle with the nuts.

5   Place pan on a cooling rack. Let stand 30 minutes before cutting. For 32 bars, cut into 8 rows by 4 rows while still warm.

High Altitude (3500–6500 ft): Bake 20 to 25 minutes.

1 Bar: Calories 130; Total Fat 7g; Cholesterol 20mg; Sodium 65mg; Total Carbohydrate 15g (Dietary Fiber 0g); Protein 1g **% Daily Value:** Vitamin A 4%; Vitamin C 0%; Calcium 0%; Iron 4% **Carbohydrate Choices:** 1

Line Pan with Foil

Turn pan upside down. Shape a piece of foil longer than pan around the pan. Carefully remove the foil and set aside.

Flip the pan over. Gently fit the shaped foil into the pan leaving the longer ends for handles. After cooling bars, lift by edges of foil to remove.

Lemon Bars

PREP TIME: 15 Minutes • **START TO FINISH:** 2 Hours

25 bars

1 cup all-purpose flour

½ cup butter or margarine (1 stick), room temperature

¼ cup powdered sugar

1 cup granulated sugar

2 teaspoons grated lemon peel, if desired

2 tablespoons lemon juice

½ teaspoon baking powder

¼ teaspoon salt

2 large eggs

4 to 6 drops yellow food color, if desired

1 tablespoon powdered sugar

1   Heat the oven to 350°F. In a small bowl, stir the flour, butter and ¼ cup powdered sugar with a wooden spoon until mixed. Using fingers, press the mixture firmly and evenly on the bottom and ½ inch up the sides of an ungreased 8-inch or 9-inch square pan. If dough is sticky, dip fingers in water or spray with cooking spray. Bake 20 minutes.

2   Meanwhile, in a medium bowl, beat the granulated sugar, lemon peel, lemon juice, baking powder, salt, eggs and food color with an electric mixer on high speed about 3 minutes or until light and fluffy. Carefully pour mixture over hot crust; use a rubber spatula to scrape mixture from bowl.

3   Bake 25 to 30 minutes or until no indentation remains when touched lightly in center. Place the pan on a cooling rack. Let stand about 1 hour until completely cooled. Sprinkle with 1 tablespoon powdered sugar, using a small wire strainer or shaker. For 25 bars, cut into 5 rows by 5 rows.

High Altitude (3500–6500 ft): Beat 2 tablespoons all-purpose flour into lemon-sugar mixture. Bake 30 to 35 minutes.

1 Bar: Calories 100; Total Fat 4g; Cholesterol 25mg; Sodium 65mg; Total Carbohydrate 13g (Dietary Fiber 0g); Protein 1g **% Daily Value:** Vitamin A 2%; Vitamin C 0%; Calcium 0%; Iron 0% **Carbohydrate Choices:** 1

Lemon-Coconut Bars: Stir ½ cup flaked coconut into egg mixture in step 2.

Grating Lemon Peel

Rub the lemon across the small rough holes of a grater. Grate only the yellow portion of the lemon peel because the white portion, or pith, is very bitter.

Best Chocolate Chip Cookies

PREP TIME: 1 Hour 25 Minutes • **START TO FINISH:** 1 Hour 40 Minutes

About 3½ dozen cookies

1½ cups butter or margarine
(3 sticks), room temperature

1¼ cups granulated sugar

1¼ cups packed brown sugar

1 tablespoon vanilla

2 large eggs

4 cups all-purpose flour

2 teaspoons baking soda

1 teaspoon salt

1 bag (24 oz) semisweet
chocolate chips (4 cups)

2 cups coarsely chopped nuts,
if desired

1   Heat the oven to 375°F. In a large bowl, beat the butter, both sugars, vanilla and eggs with an electric mixer on medium speed (or with a wooden spoon) until light and fluffy. Stir in the flour, baking soda and salt (the dough will be stiff). Stir in the chocolate chips and nuts.

2   For each cookie, scoop dough with a ¼-cup dry-ingredient measuring cup. Using the back of a knife or a metal spatula, level the dough even with the top of the cup. Push the dough onto an ungreased cookie sheet with a spoon or rubber spatula, placing cookies 2 inches apart. Flatten slightly with a fork.

3   Bake 12 to 15 minutes or until light brown (the centers will be soft). Cool 1 to 2 minutes on cookie sheets, then remove cookies to a cooling rack, using a turner. Cool cookie sheets 10 minutes between batches.

High Altitude (3500–6500 ft): No change.

1 Cookie: Calories 210; Total Fat 10g; Cholesterol 25mg; Sodium 150mg; Total Carbohydrate 28g (Dietary Fiber 1g); Protein 2g **% Daily Value:** Vitamin A 4%; Vitamin C 0%; Calcium 0%; Iron 6% **Carbohydrate Choices:** 2

Candy Cookies: Substitute 4 cups candy-coated chocolate candies for the chocolate chips.

Best Chocolate Chip Bars: Press dough in an ungreased 13 × 9-inch pan. Bake 15 to 20 minutes or until golden brown. Cool in pan on cooling rack. For 48 bars, cut into 8 rows by 6 rows.

Flattening Cookie Dough

Flatten mound of dough with a fork so it is round and about ¾ inch thick.

To: My friend

Ultimate Oatmeal Cookies

PREP TIME: 1 Hour • **START TO FINISH:** 1 Hour

About 3 dozen cookies

1¼ cups packed brown sugar

1 cup butter or margarine
  (2 sticks), room temperature

1 teaspoon baking soda

1 teaspoon ground cinnamon

1 teaspoon vanilla

½ teaspoon salt

2 large eggs

3 cups old-fashioned or
  quick-cooking oats*

1⅓ cups all-purpose flour

1 cup raisins, if desired

1 Heat the oven to 350°F. In a large bowl, stir the brown sugar, butter, baking soda, cinnamon, vanilla, salt and eggs with a wooden spoon until well mixed. Stir in the oats, flour and raisins until mixed.

2 For each cookie, scoop a rounded tablespoonful of dough, using a tableware spoon, and push it onto an ungreased cookie sheet with another spoon or rubber spatula, placing cookies 2 inches apart.

3 Bake 9 to 11 minutes or until light brown. Remove cookies from cookie sheets to a cooling rack, using a turner. Cool cookie sheets 10 minutes between batches.

*Oats can be toasted to add a nutty flavor to these cookies. To toast oats, spread on cookie sheet and bake at 375°F for 5 to 10 minutes, stirring occasionally, until light golden brown. Cool before adding to the cookie dough.

High Altitude (3500–6500 ft): Flatten cookies to about ½ inch before baking.

1 Cookie: Calories 120; Total Fat 6g; Cholesterol 25mg; Sodium 110mg; Total Carbohydrate 16g (Dietary Fiber 0g); Protein 2g **% Daily Value:** Vitamin A 4%; Vitamin C 0%; Calcium 0%; Iron 4% **Carbohydrate Choices:** 1

Ultimate Oatmeal Bars: Press dough in ungreased 8-inch square pan. Bake about 25 minutes or until light brown. Cool in pan on cooling rack. For 16 bars, cut into 4 rows by 4 rows.

Know Your Oats

Old-fashioned oats (left) or quick-cooking oats can be used in these cookies. The old-fashioned oats give a little more texture and flavor to the cookies because they are larger.

Chocolate Drop Cookies

PREP TIME: 1 Hour 25 Minutes • **START TO FINISH:** 1 Hour 25 Minutes
About 3 dozen cookies

COOKIES
Cooking spray to grease cookie sheets
2 oz unsweetened baking chocolate
1 cup granulated sugar
½ cup butter or margarine (1 stick), room temperature
⅓ cup buttermilk
1 teaspoon vanilla
1 large egg
1¾ cups all-purpose flour
½ teaspoon baking soda
½ teaspoon salt
1 cup chopped nuts

CHOCOLATE FROSTING
2 oz unsweetened baking chocolate
2 tablespoons butter or margarine
2 cups powdered sugar
3 tablespoons hot water

1   Heat the oven to 400°F. Spray cookie sheets with the cooking spray. Cut 2 oz baking chocolate into 4 pieces. In a 1-quart saucepan, heat the chocolate over very low heat until it begins to melt, then remove from heat and stir. Return to heat, stirring constantly, just until chocolate is melted.

2   In a large bowl, beat the granulated sugar, ½ cup butter, the buttermilk, vanilla, egg and melted chocolate with an electric mixer on medium speed (or with a wooden spoon) until well mixed. With a wooden spoon, stir in the flour, baking soda and salt until mixed. Stir in the nuts.

3   For each cookie, scoop a rounded tablespoonful of dough, using a tableware spoon, and push it onto a cookie sheet with another spoon or rubber spatula, placing cookies 2 inches apart.

4   Bake 8 to 10 minutes or until almost no indentation remains when touched in center. Immediately remove cookies from cookie sheets to a cooling rack, using a turner. Cool cookie sheets 10 minutes between batches. Let cookies stand about 30 minutes until completely cooled.

5   To make frosting, cut 2 oz baking chocolate into 4 pieces. In a 2-quart saucepan, heat the chocolate and 2 tablespoons butter over very low heat, stirring occasionally, until melted; remove from heat. Stir in the powdered sugar and hot water until smooth. (If frosting is too thick, add more water, 1 teaspoon at a time. If frosting is too thin, add more powdered sugar, 1 tablespoon at a time.) Spread frosting over cookies, using a metal spatula.

High Altitude (3500–6500 ft): No change.

1 Cookie: Calories 150; Total Fat 7g; Cholesterol 15mg; Sodium 80mg; Total Carbohydrate 18g (Dietary Fiber 0g); Protein 2g **% Daily Value:** Vitamin A 2%; Vitamin C 0%; Calcium 0%; Iron 6% **Carbohydrate Choices:** 1

Melting Chocolate

Chocolate will seize if melted over too high a heat or a very small amount of liquid is added. It will become thick, dull and grainy, which is called seizing.

To make seized chocolate smooth and creamy, beat in at least one tablespoon vegetable oil with a wire whisk. Heat over very low heat, stirring constantly.

Coconut Macaroons

PREP TIME: 1 Hour 55 Minutes • **START TO FINISH:** 2 Hours 25 Minutes

About 3½ dozen cookies

3 large eggs

¼ teaspoon cream of tartar

⅛ teaspoon salt

¾ cup granulated sugar

¼ teaspoon almond extract

2 cups flaked coconut

18 to 21 candied cherries, each cut into halves, if desired

1 About 30 minutes before making macaroons, place an egg separator over a small bowl. Crack each egg over the egg separator to separate the yolks from the whites. (Save egg yolks for another recipe.)

2 In a clean large bowl, place the egg whites, and let stand at room temperature up to 30 minutes.*

3 Heat the oven to 300°F. Line cookie sheets with a sheet of foil or cooking parchment paper.

4 Add the cream of tartar and salt to the egg whites. Beat with an electric mixer on high speed until foamy. Beat in the sugar, 1 tablespoon at a time; continue beating until stiff and glossy—do not underbeat. Pour into a medium bowl.

5 Sprinkle the almond extract and coconut over egg white mixture. With a rubber spatula, cut down vertically through the batter, then slide the spatula across the bottom of the bowl and up the side, turning the batter over. Rotate the bowl a quarter turn, and repeat this down-across-up motion. Continue folding just until ingredients are blended.

6 For each cookie, scoop a teaspoonful of dough, using a tableware spoon, and push it onto a lined cookie sheet with another spoon or rubber spatula, placing cookies 1 inch apart. Place 1 cherry piece on each cookie.

7 Bake 20 to 25 minutes or just until edges are light brown. Cool on cookie sheets 10 minutes, then remove cookies from foil to a cooling rack, using a turner. Cool cookie sheets 10 minutes between batches.

*Egg whites will have better volume when beaten at room temperature in a bowl that is clean and dry.

High Altitude (3500–6500 ft): No change.

1 Cookie: Calories 35; Total Fat 1.5g; Cholesterol 0mg; Sodium 20mg; Total Carbohydrate 5g (Dietary Fiber 0g); Protein 0g **% Daily Value:** Vitamin A 0%; Vitamin C 0%; Calcium 0%; Iron 0% **Carbohydrate Choices:** ½

Peppermint-Coconut Macaroons: Substitute peppermint extract for the almond extract.

Know Your Coconut

Two kinds of sweetened coconut are flaked or shredded. Flaked coconut is thin, flat pieces (left) and shredded is long, thin pieces and has more texture. In most recipes you can use either, depending on your personal preference.

Gingersnaps

PREP TIME: 1 Hour 15 Minutes • **START TO FINISH:** 2 Hours 15 Minutes
About 4 dozen cookies

1 cup packed brown sugar

¾ cup butter or margarine (1½ sticks), room temperature

¼ cup mild-flavor or full-flavor molasses

1 large egg

2¼ cups all-purpose flour

2 teaspoons baking soda

1 teaspoon ground cinnamon

1 teaspoon ground ginger

½ teaspoon ground cloves

¼ teaspoon salt

Cooking spray to grease cookie sheets

2 tablespoons granulated sugar

1 In a large bowl, beat the brown sugar, butter, molasses and egg with an electric mixer on medium speed (or with a wooden spoon) until well mixed. With a wooden spoon, stir in remaining ingredients except cooking spray and granulated sugar until mixed. Cover; refrigerate at least 1 hour.

2 Heat the oven to 375°F. Lightly spray cookie sheets with the cooking spray.

3 In a small bowl, place the granulated sugar. For each cookie, shape a rounded teaspoonful of dough, using a tableware spoon, into a ball, then dip the top of the ball into the sugar. Place balls, sugared sides up, about 3 inches apart on cookie sheets.

4 Bake 9 to 12 minutes or just until set. Remove cookies from cookie sheets to a cooling rack, using a turner. Cool cookie sheets 10 minutes between batches.

High Altitude (3500–6500 ft): Decrease baking soda to 1½ teaspoons.

1 Cookie: Calories 70; Total Fat 3g; Cholesterol 10mg; Sodium 90mg; Total Carbohydrate 11g (Dietary Fiber 0g); Protein 0g **% Daily Value:** Vitamin A 0%; Vitamin C 0%; Calcium 0%; Iron 2% **Carbohydrate Choices:** 1

Triple-Ginger Gingersnaps: Stir ¼ cup finely chopped crystallized ginger and 1 tablespoon grated gingerroot into the dough before shaping into balls.

Dip Cookie into Sugar

Dip the cookie dough ball into granulated sugar and roll it so the top is coated with sugar.

Peanut Butter Cookies

PREP TIME: 50 Minutes   •   **START TO FINISH:** 50 Minutes

About 2½ dozen cookies

½ cup granulated sugar

½ cup packed brown sugar

½ cup peanut butter

½ cup butter or margarine
  (1 stick), room temperature

1 large egg

1¼ cups all-purpose flour

¾ teaspoon baking soda

½ teaspoon baking powder

¼ teaspoon salt

2 tablespoons granulated sugar

1   Heat the oven to 375°F. In a large bowl, beat ½ cup granulated sugar, the brown sugar, peanut butter, butter and egg with an electric mixer on medium speed (or with a wooden spoon) until well mixed. With a wooden spoon, stir in the flour, baking soda, baking powder and salt until mixed.

2   In a small bowl, place 2 tablespoons granulated sugar. For each cookie, shape enough dough to make a 1¼-inch ball. (If dough is too soft, cover and refrigerate until firmer, about 30 minutes.) On ungreased cookie sheets, place balls about 3 inches apart. Press a fork into dough in bowl so sugar will stick to the fork. Dip a fork into the sugar, then press on balls in a crisscross pattern until about ¾ inch thick.

3   Bake 9 to 10 minutes or until light brown. Cool on cookie sheets 5 minutes, then remove cookies from cookie sheets to a cooling rack, using a turner. Cool cookie sheets 10 minutes between batches.

High Altitude (3500–6500 ft): Decrease baking soda to ½ teaspoon.

1 Cookie: Calories 110; Total Fat 5g; Cholesterol 15mg; Sodium 105mg; Total Carbohydrate 13g (Dietary Fiber 0g); Protein 2g **% Daily Value:** Vitamin A 2%; Vitamin C 0%; Calcium 0%; Iron 2% **Carbohydrate Choices:** 1

Flatten Cookie with Fork

Dip a fork into granulated sugar and press it on the cookie dough ball. Press the fork across the fork mark to make a crisscross pattern.

Snickerdoodles

PREP TIME: 50 Minutes   •   **START TO FINISH:** 50 Minutes

About 4 dozen cookies

1½ cups granulated sugar

**1 cup butter or margarine
(2 sticks), room temperature**

2 large eggs

2¾ cups all-purpose flour

2 teaspoons cream of tartar

1 teaspoon baking soda

¼ teaspoon salt

¼ cup granulated sugar

1 tablespoon ground cinnamon

1   Heat the oven to 400°F. In a large bowl, beat 1½ cups sugar, the butter and eggs with an electric mixer on medium speed (or with a wooden spoon) until well mixed. With a wooden spoon, stir in the flour, cream of tartar, baking soda and salt until mixed.

2   In a small bowl, stir ¼ cup sugar and the cinnamon until mixed. For each cookie, shape enough dough to make a 1¼-inch ball. (If dough is too soft, cover and refrigerate until firmer, about 30 minutes.) Roll balls in cinnamon-sugar mixture. On ungreased cookie sheets, place the balls 2 inches apart.

3   Bake 8 to 10 minutes or until set. Immediately remove cookies from cookie sheets to a cooling rack, using a turner. Cool cookie sheets 10 minutes between batches.

High Altitude (3500–6500 ft): Before baking, flatten dough balls to ½-inch thickness with glass dipped in remaining sugar-cinnamon mixture.

1 Cookie: Calories 90; Total Fat 4g; Cholesterol 20mg; Sodium 70mg; Total Carbohydrate 13g (Dietary Fiber 0g); Protein 1g **% Daily Value:** Vitamin A 2%; Vitamin C 0%; Calcium 0%; Iron 2% **Carbohydrate Choices:** 1

Holiday Snickerdoodles: Omit the ¼ cup granulated sugar. In a small bowl, mix 2 tablespoons red colored sugar and 1½ teaspoons ground cinnamon. In another small bowl, mix 2 tablespoons green colored sugar and 1½ teaspoons ground cinnamon. Roll half of the dough balls in the red sugar mixture and the remaining half in the green sugar mixture.

Shaping Cookie Dough

For even baking, make sure the balls of dough are the same shape and size. Place a ruler across the back of the bowl to measure each ball of dough.

Shortbread Cookies

PREP TIME: 45 Minutes • **START TO FINISH:** 45 Minutes

2 dozen cookies

Special Equipment: Rolling pin

¾ **cup butter or margarine (1½ sticks), room temperature**

¼ **cup granulated sugar**

1¾ **cups all-purpose flour**

½ **teaspoon vanilla or almond extract**

Cutting Cookie Dough

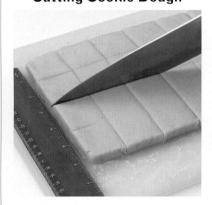

To cut even-sized shortbread cookies, use a ruler and mark the long and short sides of the dough in 1½-inch intervals. Cut into squares using a sharp knife or pizza cutter.

1 Heat the oven to 350°F. In a large bowl, beat the butter and sugar with an electric mixer on medium speed (or with a wooden spoon) until well mixed. With a wooden spoon, stir in the flour and almond extract until mixed. (If the dough is crumbly, mix in additional 1 to 2 tablespoons room-temperature butter or margarine.)

2 Lightly sprinkle flour over a cutting board or countertop. On the floured surface, roll dough with a rolling pin into 9 × 6-inch rectangle, ½ inch thick. (If dough is too soft, cover and refrigerate until firmer, about 30 minutes.) Cut into 1½-inch squares with a knife, or cut with 1½-inch cookie cutters. On ungreased cookie sheets, place squares or shapes about 1 inch apart.

3 Bake 12 to 14 minutes or until set. Remove cookies from cookie sheets to a cooling rack, using a turner. Cool cookie sheets 10 minutes between batches.

High Altitude (3500–6500 ft): No change.

1 Cookie: Calories 90; Total Fat 6g; Cholesterol 15mg; Sodium 40mg; Total Carbohydrate 9g (Dietary Fiber 0g); Protein 1g **% Daily Value:** Vitamin A 4%; Vitamin C 0%; Calcium 0%; Iron 2% **Carbohydrate Choices:** ½

Brown Sugar Shortbread Cookies: Substitute ¼ cup packed brown sugar for the granulated sugar and vanilla for the almond extract.

Sugar Cookies

PREP TIME: 1 Hour 35 Minutes • **START TO FINISH:** 3 Hours 35 Minutes
About 5 dozen cookies

Special Equipment: Rolling pin

1½ cups powdered sugar

1 cup butter or margarine
(2 sticks), room temperature

1 teaspoon vanilla

½ teaspoon almond extract

1 large egg

2½ cups all-purpose flour

1 teaspoon baking soda

1 teaspoon cream of tartar

Cooking spray to grease cookie
sheets

Coarse or colored sugars,
if desired

Decorator's Frosting (page 28),
if desired

Small candies or decors,
if desired

Cutting Sugar Cookies

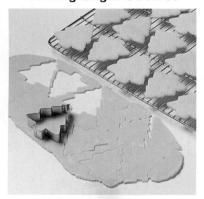

**Alternate the cookie cutter
direction** to help reduce the
amount of dough that will be
rerolled. Also, alternate the baked
cookies on the cooling rack to
save space.

1   In a large bowl, beat 1½ cups powdered sugar, the butter,
1 teaspoon vanilla, the almond extract and egg with an electric
mixer on medium speed (or with a wooden spoon) until well
mixed. With a wooden spoon, stir in the flour, baking soda and
cream of tartar until mixed. Cover; refrigerate at least 2 hours.

2   Heat the oven to 375°F. Lightly spray cookie sheets with the
cooking spray. Lightly sprinkle flour over a cutting board or
countertop. Divide dough in half. On the floured surface, roll
one half at a time with a rolling pin until ¼ inch thick.

3   Cut dough into desired shapes with 2½-inch cookie cutters.
On the cookie sheets, place cutouts about 2 inches apart. After
cutting as many cookies as possible, lightly press the scraps of
dough together; reroll the dough and cut additional cookies. If
cookies will not be frosted, sprinkle cutouts with sugar.

4   Bake 7 to 8 minutes or until edges are light brown. Remove
cookies from cookie sheets to a cooling rack, using a turner.
Cool cookie sheets 10 minutes between batches. Let cookies stand
about 30 minutes until completely cooled.

5   Make Decorator's Frosting; spread over cookies, using a small
metal spatula. Decorate as desired with sugars and candies.

High Altitude (3500–6500 ft): No change

1 Cookie: Calories 70; Total Fat 3g; Cholesterol 10mg; Sodium 45mg; Total Carbohydrate 9g
(Dietary Fiber 0g); Protein 0g **% Daily Value:** Vitamin A 0%; Vitamin C 0%; Calcium 0%;
Iron 0% **Carbohydrate Choices:** ½

Gingerbread Cookies

PREP TIME: 1 Hour 40 Minutes • **START TO FINISH:** 3 Hours 40 Minutes

About 5 dozen 2½-inch cookies

Special Equipment: Rolling pin

½ cup packed brown sugar

½ cup butter or margarine (1 stick), room temperature

½ cup mild-flavor or full-flavor molasses

⅓ cup cold water

3½ cups all-purpose flour

2 teaspoons baking soda

2 teaspoons ground ginger

½ teaspoon ground allspice

½ teaspoon ground cinnamon

¼ teaspoon ground cloves

¼ teaspoon salt

Cooking spray to grease cookie sheets

Decorator's Frosting (page 28), if desired

Colored sugars, if desired

Small candies, if desired

1   In a large bowl, beat the brown sugar, butter, molasses and water with an electric mixer on medium speed (or with a wooden spoon) until well mixed. With a wooden spoon, stir in remaining ingredients except cooking spray until mixed. Cover; refrigerate at least 2 hours.

2   Heat the oven to 350°F. Lightly spray cookie sheets with the cooking spray. Lightly sprinkle flour over a cutting board or countertop. Divide dough in half. On floured surface, roll dough with a rolling pin until ¼ inch thick.

3   Cut dough with floured gingerbread boy or girl cookie cutter or other shaped cookie cutter. On the cookie sheets, place cutouts about 2 inches apart. After cutting as many cookies as possible, lightly press the scraps of dough together; reroll the dough and cut additional cookies.

4   Bake 10 to 12 minutes or until no indentation remains when touched. Immediately remove cookies from cookie sheets to a cooling rack, using a turner. Cool cookie sheets 10 minutes between batches. Let cookies stand about 30 minutes until completely cooled.

5   Make Decorator's Frosting. Add food coloring if desired. Place frosting in a small resealable food-storage plastic bag and seal it. Push the frosting down in one corner. With a scissor, snip off the corner to make a small hole. Squeeze the bag to pipe the frosting and make desired design. Or spread frosting over cookies with a small metal spatula. Decorate as desired with colored sugars and candies.

High Altitude (3500–6500 ft): Bake 8 to 10 minutes.

1 Cookie: Calories 60; Total Fat 1.5g; Cholesterol 0mg; Sodium 65mg; Total Carbohydrate 10g (Dietary Fiber 0g); Protein 0g **% Daily Value:** Vitamin A 0%; Vitamin C 0%; Calcium 0%; Iron 2% **Carbohydrate Choices:** ½

Rolling Dough Between Paper

Roll dough between two sheets of waxed paper or cooking parchment rather than on a floured surface. Carefully peel off the top sheet of waxed paper before cutting the cookie shapes.

2 CAKES

CAKES 101

Baking and sharing a homemade cake can be so rewarding. With a little practice you'll gain the confidence you need to get great results every time.

Types of Cakes

All cakes fall into one of two categories: butter cakes or foam cakes.

Butter cakes (or shortening cakes) are made with butter, margarine or shortening, flour, eggs, a liquid and baking powder or baking soda. A butter cake should have a fine-grained, even texture with a tender and slightly moist crumb. When baked, the top should be slightly rounded and smooth.

Butter cakes are versatile and can be baked in a rectangular or square pan, round pans for layer cakes, muffin pans for cupcakes or a tube pan such as angel food cake pan or fluted pan.

Foam cakes, like angel food, depend on beaten egg whites for their light and airy texture. For more information, see pages 218–219.

Cake Pans

Use the size of pan called for in a recipe. To check a pan's size, measure across the top from inside edge to inside edge. If the pan is too large, the cake will be pale, flat and dry. If a pan is too small, the cake will form a peak or overflow the pan.

Use shiny pans, if you have them, because they reflect heat and produce tender, light brown crusts.

Dark pans or pans with dark nonstick coating absorb heat more easily than shiny pans, so cakes may brown more quickly. Manufacturers may suggest reducing the oven temperature by 25°F.

Fill cake pans no more than half full. To determine the volume of novelty pans (heart or star shape, for example), fill the pan with water, then measure the water; use half that amount of batter. Cupcakes can be made with any extra batter.

Muffin pans are used for baking cupcakes. Shiny pans work best because they reflect the heat and the cupcakes don't overbake and become dry. Muffin pans are available in 6-cup and 12-cup sizes. Most butter cake recipes make 2 dozen cupcakes so it is best to have two 12-cup pans.

MIXING CAKE BATTER

Before mixing the batter, have all the ingredients at room temperature for best results. The cake will have better volume if the eggs are at room temperature. Eggs can stand at room temperature up to 30 minutes before using. Room-temperature butter (see page 25) is easier to mix with other ingredients and disperse evenly throughout the batter.

Use either an electric hand-held mixer or a standard stand mixer for mixing the batter. Cake recipes in this cookbook were tested with an electric hand-held mixer. If you don't have an electric mixer, you can mix the batter using a wooden spoon or whisk. It will take longer until all the ingredients are blended together and the batter is smooth but it will work just fine.

Making Cupcakes

Most butter cakes that are made with 2¼ to 2½ cups all-purpose flour will make about 24 cupcakes.

Place a paper baking cup in each of 24 regular-size muffin cups. Spoon the batter into the cups, filling each ⅔ full. Bake 20 to 25 minutes or until a toothpick inserted in the center comes out clean. Remove cupcakes from pan to cooling racks. Cool completely, about 30 minutes. Frost with desired frosting.

If you have just one 12-cup muffin pan or a 6-cup muffin pan, cover and refrigerate remaining batter while baking the first batch of cupcakes. Cool the pan about 15 minutes, and then bake the rest of the batter, adding 1 to 2 minutes to the bake time.

Line Round Pan with Paper

To be extra sure your layer cakes pop out of the pan easily, you can line the round pans with waxed paper or cooking parchment paper. Place the pan upright on the piece of paper and trace around it with the tip of a paring knife. Using kitchen scissors, cut along the tracing lines. Spray the inside bottom of pan lightly with baking spray with flour. Place the paper in the bottom of the pan then spray paper and sides of pan with more baking spray. After baking, remove the cake from the pan and carefully peel off the paper.

BAKING CAKES

- Place oven rack in the middle position.
- Place pans on the center of the rack. Arrange round cake pans so they don't touch, leaving at least one inch of space between pans and sides of the oven. When making a recipe that uses three round pans, refrigerate batter in third pan if all pans will not fit in the oven at one time; bake third pan separately.

- Spray pans with cooking spray or baking spray or grease and flour pans as recommended in each recipe.
- Cool cakes that will not be removed from the pan, like 13 × 9-inch cakes, in the pan on a cooling rack until completely cool. Cool cakes that will be removed from the pan, like round, fluted or tube pan cakes, in their pan(s) on wire racks for 5 to 10 minutes, then remove the cake and cool completely on wire racks.

Removing Round Cake from Pan

It is important to remove the cake layers from the pans correctly so they don't tear or break. First insert a dinner knife between the cake and the pan and slide it around the side to loosen the edge.

Cool cake in pan as directed in recipe. To prevent cooling-rack marks on top of cake layer, place a clean kitchen towel over the rack.

Place rack on top of layer. Invert as a unit and remove pan.

Place original cooling rack on layer; turn over both racks as a unit to top of cake is up.

What Went Wrong?

Butter Cakes

This Happened	This Is Why
Pale	• too little sugar • baking time too short
Does not rise properly	• too much liquid • too much fat • pan too large • oven too cool
Peaked or cracked on top	• too much flour • oven too hot
Rim around edge	• pan sprayed with too much cooking or baking spray
Coarse grained	• too much butter or shortening • underbeaten
Crumbly	• too much butter or shortening • too much sugar • underbeaten • too little egg (use large eggs)
Dry	• too much baking powder • baking time too long
Heavy, too moist	• too much liquid • too much shortening • too little flour
Batter overflows	• too much batter in pan • pan too small • too much leavening
Sticks to pan	• pan not greased enough • cake left in pan too long before being removed

Storing Cakes

To store unfrosted cakes, cool cakes completely, at least one hour, before storing. If covered when warm, they become sticky and difficult to frost. Store loosely covered so the surface stays dry.

Store cakes frosted with a creamy-type frosting under a cake safe (or large inverted bowl), or cover loosely with foil, plastic wrap or waxed paper.

Store cakes frosted with whipped cream toppings or cream fillings in the refrigerator.

Whether frosted or unfrosted, cakes with very moist ingredients, like applesauce, shredded carrots and mashed bananas, should be refrigerated during humid weather or in humid climates. If stored at room temperature, mold can grow quickly.

Freezing Cakes

To freeze unfrosted cakes, cool cakes completely, at least one hour. Place cakes in cardboard bakery boxes to prevent crushing, then cover with foil, plastic wrap or large freezer bags. Properly packaged, unfrosted cakes can be kept frozen three to four months.

Frosted and glazed cakes freeze well, but the frosting or glaze may stick to the wrapping. To prevent sticking, freeze cake uncovered one hour, then insert toothpicks around the top and side of cake, and wrap. Frozen frosted cakes keep two to three months.

Freeze cakes in single pieces or smaller portions to thaw quickly.

Decorating gel, hard candies and colored sugars do not freeze well because they tend to run during thawing. It's best to decorate after cake as thawed.

THE FROSTING ON THE CAKE!

Frosting or glazing a homemade cake not only gives it a finished touch but adds a bit of flavor and texture. Frosting also seals in moisture and helps keep the cake fresher longer. While a frosted cake is impressive to look at, frosting or glazing isn't hard to do: the secret is to be sure the cake is completely cooled and the frosting or glaze is the right consistency.

Making Frosting and Glaze

Use butter and margarine in stick form rather than tub or whipped varieties, which contain more water and/or air and less fat, so frostings made with them turn out too soft.

If powdered sugar has lumps, sift it through a wire strainer to avoid grainy frosting.

Frosting should be soft enough to spread and hold its shape. If frosting is too stiff, it will pull and tear the cake surface, adding crumbs to the frosting. If frosting is too thin, add more powdered sugar, a couple of tablespoons at a time; if too thick, add a few drops of water or milk.

Glazes should be thin enough to pour from the tip of a tableware spoon onto the cake. The glaze should spread easily over the top of the cake, and some glaze should run down the side of the cake.

Use a flexible metal spatula for frosting a layer cake or spreading a glaze on top of a cake. An offset metal spatula (page 256) is good for frosting cakes that are stored and served in the baking pan.

To Frost or Not to Frost

If you choose not to frost your cake, you can dust it with powdered sugar to add a bit of sweetness and a special touch.

Sprinkle powdered sugar evenly over the top of the cake, using a wire strainer or shaker.

For a more interesting look, place a doily, stencil or simple cutout shape on the cake before dusting with powdered sugar. Carefully remove the pattern.

Frosting a Layer Cake

You may want to place four strips of waxed paper around the edge of the cake plate before placing the layer on the plate. The waxed paper will help keep the plate from getting messy as you frost, and the strips can easily be removed from under the frosted cake.

Brush any loose crumbs from cooled cake layer. Place first layer, rounded side down, on plate. Spread about ⅓ cup creamy frosting (½ cup fluffy frosting) over the top of first layer to within about ½ inch of edge.

Place second cake layer, rounded side up, on frosted first layer. Coat side of cake with a very thin layer of frosting to seal in crumbs. Frost side of cake in swirls, making a rim about ¼ inch high above the top of the cake. Spread remaining frosting on top, just to the built-up rim.

Glazing Cakes

Cakes baked in a tube or fluted tube pan are usually glazed rather than frosted.

Pour or drizzle glaze over top of flat cake; spread with metal spatula or back of spoon, letting some glaze drizzle down side.

Spoon glaze over top of fluted cake, letting some glaze drizzle down side and center.

Cutting Frosted Cakes

Use a sharp, thin knife to cut butter cakes and a long serrated knife for angel food cakes.

If the frosting sticks, dip the knife in hot water and wipe clean with a damp paper towel after cutting each piece.

To store remaining cake, cover cut area with plastic wrap to prevent drying.

Frosting and Glaze Recipes

Vanilla Buttercream Frosting

Frosts a 13 × 9-inch cake generously, or fills and frosts an 8- or 9-inch two-layer cake.

3 cups powdered sugar
⅓ cup butter or margarine, room temperature
1½ teaspoons vanilla
1 to 2 tablespoons milk

In a medium bowl, mix the powdered sugar and butter with a spoon or electric mixer on low speed until well mixed. Stir in vanilla and 1 tablespoon of the milk. Gradually beat in just enough remaining milk to make frosting smooth and spreadable.

Chocolate Buttercream Frosting: Add ⅓ cup baking cocoa with the powdered sugar. Increase vanilla to 2 teaspoons and milk to 3 to 4 tablespoons.

Peanut Butter Frosting: Substitute peanut butter for the butter. Increase milk to ¼ cup, adding more if necessary, a few drops at a time.

Cream Cheese Frosting

Frosts a 13 × 9-inch cake generously, or fills and frosts an 8- or 9-inch two-layer cake.

1 package (8 oz) cream cheese, room temperature
¼ cup butter or margarine (½ stick), room temperature
1 tablespoon milk
1 teaspoon vanilla
4 cups powdered sugar

In a medium bowl, beat the cream cheese, butter, milk and vanilla with an electric mixer on low speed until smooth. On low speed, gradually beat in powdered sugar, 1 cup at a time, until mixture is smooth and spreadable. Store frosted cake or any remaining frosting covered in the refrigerator.

Caramel Frosting

Frosts a 13 × 9-inch cake, or fills and frosts an 8- or 9-inch two-layer cake.

½ cup butter or margarine (1 stick)
1 cup packed brown sugar
¼ cup milk
2 cups powdered sugar

In a 2-quart saucepan, melt the butter over medium heat. Stir in the brown sugar. Heat to boiling, stirring constantly; reduce heat to low. Boil and stir 2 minutes. Stir in the milk. Heat to boiling; remove from heat. Cool to lukewarm, about 30 minutes. Gradually stir in powdered sugar. Place saucepan of frosting in bowl of cold water. Beat with spoon until mixture is smooth and spreadable. If frosting becomes too stiff, stir in additional milk, 1 teaspoon at a time, or heat over low heat, stirring constantly.

Vanilla Glaze

Glazes one 12-cup bundt cake, 10-inch angel food cake or top of an 8- or 9-inch layer cake.

2 tablespoons butter or margarine
2 cups powdered sugar
1 teaspoon vanilla
2 to 4 tablespoons hot water

In 1½-quart saucepan, melt butter over low heat; remove from heat. Stir in powdered sugar and vanilla. Stir in hot water, 1 tablespoon at a time, until smooth and thin enough to drizzle.

Lemon Glaze: Stir ½ teaspoon grated lemon peel into melted butter. Substitute lemon juice for the vanilla and hot water.

Orange Glaze: Stir ½ teaspoon grated orange peel into melted butter. Substitute orange juice for the vanilla and hot water.

Chocolate Glaze

Glazes one 12-cup bundt cake, 10-inch angel food cake or top of an 8- or 9-inch layer cake.

¾ cup semisweet chocolate chips
3 tablespoons butter or margarine
3 tablespoons corn syrup
2 to 3 teaspoons hot water

In 1-quart saucepan, heat chocolate chips, butter and corn syrup over low heat, stirring frequently, until chocolate chips are melted. Cool about 10 minutes. Stir in hot water, 1 teaspoon at a time, until consistency of thick syrup.

Chocolate Chip Snack Cake

PREP TIME: 10 Minutes • **START TO FINISH:** 1 Hour 5 Minutes

9 servings

1⅔ cups all-purpose flour

1 cup packed brown sugar or
  granulated sugar

¼ cup unsweetened baking
  cocoa

1 teaspoon baking soda

½ teaspoon salt

1 cup water

⅓ cup vegetable oil

1 teaspoon white vinegar

½ teaspoon vanilla

⅓ cup miniature chocolate chips

3 tablespoons granulated sugar

1   Heat the oven to 350°F.

2   In an ungreased 8-inch square pan, stir the flour, brown sugar, cocoa, baking soda and salt with a fork until well mixed. Stir in the water, oil, vinegar and vanilla until well mixed. Using a rubber spatula, spread batter evenly in pan and smooth top of batter. Sprinkle with the chocolate chips and granulated sugar.

3   Bake 35 to 40 minutes or until a toothpick inserted in the center comes out clean. To serve cake while warm, cool in pan on cooling rack 15 minutes; to serve it cool, let stand about 2 hours.

High Altitude (3500–6500 ft): Increase flour to 1¾ cups; decrease baking soda to ½ teaspoon. Bake 40 to 45 minutes.

1 Serving: Calories 260; Total Fat 9g; Cholesterol 0mg; Sodium 280mg; Total Carbohydrate 43g (Dietary Fiber 1g); Protein 3g **% Daily Value:** Vitamin A 0%; Vitamin C 0%; Calcium 2%; Iron 10% **Carbohydrate Choices:** 3

Chocolate Snack Cake: Omit the miniature chocolate chips and 3 tablespoons granulated sugar. After baking, sprinkle the top with powdered sugar, using a small wire strainer or shaker, before serving.

Stir Batter in Pan

Stir the ingredients with a fork in a circular motion, including in the corners, until well blended.

Yellow Cake

PREP TIME: 25 Minutes • **START TO FINISH:** 2 Hours 5 Minutes

15 servings for 13 × 9-inch cake; 12 servings for layer cake

Baking spray with flour to grease pan

2¼ cups all-purpose flour

1¼ cups granulated sugar

½ cup butter or margarine (1 stick), room temperature

1¼ cups milk

3 teaspoons baking powder

1 teaspoon salt

1 teaspoon vanilla

3 large eggs

Chocolate Buttercream Frosting (page 65)

or Peanut Butter Frosting (page 65)

1   Heat the oven to 350°F. Spray the bottom and sides of either one 13 × 9-inch pan or two 8-inch or 9-inch round cake pans with the baking spray with flour.

2   In a large bowl, beat all ingredients except frosting with an electric mixer on low speed 30 seconds, stopping frequently to scrape batter from side and bottom of bowl with a rubber spatula. Beat on high speed 3 minutes, stopping occasionally to scrape bowl. Pour batter into 13 × 9-inch pan or round pans; use a rubber spatula to scrape batter from bowl, spread batter evenly in pan and smooth top of batter. (If batter in round pans is not divided evenly, spoon batter from one pan to the other.)

3   Bake 13 × 9-inch pan 30 to 35 minutes, 8-inch round pans 30 to 35 minutes or 9-inch round pans 25 to 30 minutes, or until a toothpick inserted in the center comes out clean.

4   Cool 13 × 9-inch cake in pan completely on cooling rack, about 1 hour. Cool round cakes in pans 10 minutes, then remove onto cooling racks to finish cooling completely. (See Removing Round Cake from Pan, page 62.)

5   Make desired frosting. For 13 × 9-inch cake, spread frosting over the top, using a metal spatula. For layer cake, place one layer, rounded side down, on a cake plate; using a metal spatula, spread ⅓ cup of the frosting over the top. Add second layer, rounded side up. Frost top and sides. (See Frosting a Layer Cake, page 64.)

High Altitude (3500–6500 ft): Do not use 8-inch pans. Decrease baking powder to 2½ teaspoons. Recipe will make 30 cupcakes.

1 Serving: Calories 370; Total Fat 12g; Cholesterol 70mg; Sodium 370mg; Total Carbohydrate 61g (Dietary Fiber 1g); Protein 4g **% Daily Value:** Vitamin A 8%; Vitamin C 0%; Calcium 10%; Iron 8% **Carbohydrate Choices:** 4

Lemon–Poppy Seed Cake: Omit the vanilla. Add 1 tablespoon grated lemon peel and 2 tablespoons poppy seed with the other ingredients.

Yellow Cupcakes: See Making Cupcakes on page 61.

Testing Cake Doneness

Insert a toothpick near the center of the cake after the minimum baking time. If the pick comes out clean, the cake is done.

Chocolate Cake

PREP TIME: 20 Minutes • **START TO FINISH:** 2 Hours 5 Minutes

15 servings for 13 × 9-inch cake; 12 servings for layer cake

Baking spray with flour to grease pan

2¼ cups all-purpose flour

1⅔ cups granulated sugar

¾ cup butter or margarine (1½ sticks), room temperature

⅔ cup unsweetened baking cocoa

1¼ cups water

1¼ teaspoons baking soda

1 teaspoon salt

1 teaspoon vanilla

¼ teaspoon baking powder

2 large eggs

Chocolate Buttercream Frosting (page 65)

or Vanilla Buttercream Frosting (page 65)

1 Heat the oven to 350°F. Spray the bottom and sides of either one 13 × 9-inch pan or two 9-inch round cake pans with the baking spray with flour.

2 In a large bowl, beat all ingredients except frosting with an electric mixer on low speed 30 seconds, stopping frequently to scrape batter from side and bottom of bowl with a rubber spatula. Beat on high speed 3 minutes, stopping occasionally to scrape bowl. Pour batter into 13 × 9-inch pan or round pans; use a rubber spatula to scrape batter from bowl, spread batter evenly in pan and smooth top of batter. (If batter in round pans is not divided evenly, spoon batter from one pan to the other.)

3 Bake 13 × 9-inch pan 40 to 45 minutes, 9-inch round pans 30 to 35 minutes, or until a toothpick inserted in the center comes out clean.

4 Cool 13 × 9-inch cake in pan completely on cooling rack, about 1 hour. Cool round cakes in pans 10 minutes, then remove onto cooling racks to finish cooling completely. (See Removing Round Cake from Pan, page 62.)

5 Make desired frosting. For 13 × 9-inch cake, spread frosting over the top, using a metal spatula. For layer cake, place one layer, rounded side down, on a cake plate; using a metal spatula, spread ⅓ cup of the frosting over the top. Add second layer, rounded side up. Frost top and sides. (See Frosting a Layer Cake, page 64.)

High Altitude (3500–6500 ft): For cake, no change. For cupcakes, heat oven to 375°F.

1 Serving: Calories 410; Total Fat 15g; Cholesterol 65mg; Sodium 310mg; Total Carbohydrate 64g (Dietary Fiber 2g); Protein 4g **% Daily Value:** Vitamin A 10%; Vitamin C 0%; Calcium 4%; Iron 10% **Carbohydrate Choices:** 4

Chocolate Cupcakes: See Making Cupcakes on page 61.

Baking Cocoa vs. Cocoa Mix

Baking cocoa is dried chocolate liquor, with the cocoa butter removed, and ground into an un-sweetened powder (left). Cocoa drink mixes have powdered milk and sugar added and should not be used for baking cocoa.

Marble Cake

PREP TIME: 15 Minutes • **START TO FINISH:** 2 Hours 10 Minutes

15 servings for 13 × 9-inch cake; 12 servings for layer cake

Baking spray with flour to grease pan

5 large eggs

2¼ cups all-purpose flour

1⅔ cups granulated sugar

⅔ cup shortening

1¼ cups milk

3½ teaspoons baking powder

1 teaspoon salt

1 teaspoon vanilla or almond extract

3 tablespoons unsweetened baking cocoa

⅛ teaspoon baking soda

Chocolate Buttercream Frosting (page 65)

or Vanilla Buttercream Frosting (page 65)

1 Heat the oven to 350°F. Spray the bottom and sides of either one 13 × 9-inch pan or two 9-inch round cake pans with the baking spray with flour.

2 Place an egg separator over a small bowl. Crack open each egg over the separator to separate the yolks from the whites. (Save yolks for another recipe.)

3 In a large bowl, beat the flour, sugar, shortening, milk, baking powder, salt and vanilla with an electric mixer on low speed 30 seconds, stopping frequently to scrape batter from side and bottom of bowl with a rubber spatula. Beat on high speed 2 minutes, stopping occasionally to scrape bowl.

4 Add egg whites; beat on high speed 2 minutes, stopping occasionally to scrape bowl. Spoon enough batter into a 2-cup liquid measuring cup to measure 1¾ cups; stir in the cocoa and baking soda.

5 Pour white batter into 13 × 9-inch pan or round pans; use a rubber spatula to scrape batter from bowl, spread batter evenly in pan and smooth top of batter. (If batter in round pans is not divided evenly, spoon batter from one pan to the other.) Drop chocolate batter by tablespoons randomly onto white batter. To make a marbled design, pull a knife through the batters in S-shaped curves in one continuous motion. Turn pan one-fourth turn and repeat marbling.

6 Bake 13 × 9-inch pan 40 to 45 minutes, round pans 30 to 35 minutes, or until toothpick inserted in center comes out clean.

7 Cool 13 × 9-inch cake in pan completely on cooling rack, about 1 hour. Cool round cakes in pans 10 minutes, then remove

Marbling Cake Batter

Drop chocolate batter onto white batter. Pull a knife through batter in a continuous S-shaped curve.

Turn pan one-fourth turn and repeat marbling.

onto cooling racks to finish cooling completely. (See Removing Round Cake from Pan, page 62.)

8 Make desired frosting. For 13 × 9-inch cake, spread frosting over the top, using a metal spatula. For layer cake, place one layer, rounded side down, on a cake plate; using a metal spatula, spread about ⅓ cup of the frosting over the top. Add second layer, rounded side up. Frost top and sides. (See Frosting a Layer Cake, page 64.)

High Altitude (3500–6500 ft): Heat oven to 375°F. Decrease sugar to 1½ cups and baking powder to 2¼ teaspoons. Increase milk to 1⅓ cups. Bake 13 × 9-inch pan 35 to 40 minutes; bake round pans 25 to 30 minutes.

1 Serving: Calories 530; Total Fat 20g; Cholesterol 105mg; Sodium 430mg; Total Carbohydrate 80g (Dietary Fiber 2g); Protein 7g **% Daily Value:** Vitamin A 6%; Vitamin C 0%; Calcium 15%; Iron 10% **Carbohydrate Choices:** 5

White Cake: Omit the unsweetened baking cocoa and baking soda. After beating in the egg whites, pour the batter into the pan(s). Bake, cool and frost as directed in the recipe.

Tres Leches Cake

PREP TIME: 30 Minutes • **START TO FINISH:** 4 Hours 15 Minutes
15 servings

CAKE
Cooking spray to grease pan
2¼ cups all-purpose flour
1¼ cups granulated sugar
**½ cup butter or margarine
(1 stick), room temperature**
1¼ cups milk
3 teaspoons baking powder
1 teaspoon salt
1 teaspoon vanilla
3 large eggs

TRES LECHES MIXTURE
1 cup whipping cream
1 cup whole milk
**1 can (14 oz) sweetened condensed
milk (not evaporated)**
⅓ cup rum*

TOPPING
1 cup whipping cream
2 tablespoons rum*
½ teaspoon vanilla
½ cup chopped pecans

Piercing Cake with Fork

Pierce the top of hot cake with fork before pouring the milk mixture evenly over the top.

1 Heat the oven to 350°F. Spray just the bottom of a 13 × 9-inch pan with the cooking spray.

2 In a large bowl, beat cake ingredients with an electric mixer on low speed 30 seconds, stopping frequently to scrape batter from side and bottom of bowl with a rubber spatula. Beat on high speed 3 minutes, stopping occasionally to scrape bowl. Pour batter into the pan; use a rubber spatula to scrape batter from bowl, spread batter evenly in pan and smooth top of batter.

3 Bake 30 to 35 minutes or until a toothpick inserted in the center comes out clean. Let stand 5 minutes.

4 Pierce top of hot cake every ½ inch with a long-tined fork or long skewer, wiping fork occasionally to reduce sticking.

5 In a large bowl, stir 1 cup whipping cream, the whole milk, condensed milk and ⅓ cup rum until well mixed. Carefully pour milk mixture evenly over top of hot cake. Cover with plastic wrap; refrigerate about 3 hours or until cake is chilled and most of the milk mixture has been absorbed into cake.

6 About 30 minutes before topping cake, place a medium bowl and the beaters of electric mixer in refrigerator to chill. These will be used to beat the whipping cream, which beats better in a cold bowl.

7 Pour 1 cup whipping cream into the chilled bowl, and add 2 tablespoons rum and ½ teaspoon vanilla. Insert the chilled beaters in the electric mixer. Beat on high speed until whipped cream forms soft peaks when beaters are lifted. Frost cake with whipped cream mixture. Sprinkle with pecans. Store cake covered in the refrigerator.

*One tablespoon rum extract plus enough water to measure ⅓ cup can be substituted for the ⅓ cup rum extract. One teaspoon rum extract can be substituted for the 2 tablespoons rum.

High Altitude (3500–6500 ft): Decrease baking powder to 2½ teaspoons.

1 Serving: Calories 470; Total Fat 23g; Cholesterol 105mg; Sodium 390mg; Total Carbohydrate 52g (Dietary Fiber 0g); Protein 8g **% Daily Value:** Vitamin A 15%; Vitamin C 0%; Calcium 20%; Iron 8% **Carbohydrate Choices:** 3½

Sour Cream–Spice Cake

PREP TIME: 20 Minutes • **START TO FINISH:** 2 Hours 5 Minutes

15 servings for 13 × 9-inch cake; 12 servings for layer cake

Baking spray with flour to
   grease pan

2¼ cups all-purpose flour

1½ cups packed brown sugar

1 cup sour cream

1 cup raisins

½ cup chopped walnuts

½ cup butter or margarine
   (1 stick), room temperature

½ cup water

2 teaspoons ground cinnamon

1¼ teaspoons baking soda

1 teaspoon baking powder

¾ teaspoon ground cloves

½ teaspoon salt

½ teaspoon ground nutmeg

2 large eggs

Caramel Frosting (page 65)

or Vanilla Buttercream Frosting
   (page 65)

Chopped nuts, if desired

1 Heat the oven to 350°F. Spray the bottom and sides of either one 13 × 9-inch pan or two 8-inch or 9-inch round cake pans with the baking spray with flour.

2 In a large bowl, beat all ingredients except frosting with an electric mixer on low speed 30 seconds, stopping frequently to scrape batter from side and bottom of bowl with a rubber spatula. Beat on high speed 3 minutes, stopping occasionally to scrape bowl. Pour batter into 13 × 9-inch pan or round pans; use a rubber spatula to scrape batter from bowl, spread batter evenly in pan and smooth top of batter. (If batter in round pans is not divided evenly, spoon batter from one pan to the other.)

3 Bake 13 × 9-inch pan 40 to 45 minutes, round pans 30 to 35 minutes, or until a toothpick inserted in the center comes out clean.

4 Cool 13 × 9-inch cake in pan completely on cooling rack, about 1 hour. Cool round cakes in pans 10 minutes, then remove onto cooling racks to finish cooling completely. (See Removing Round Cake from Pan, page 62.)

5 Make desired frosting. For 13 × 9-inch cake, spread frosting over the top, using a metal spatula. For layer cake, place one layer, rounded side down, on a cake plate; using a metal spatula, spread ⅓ cup of the frosting over the top. Add second layer, rounded side up. Frost top and sides. (See Frosting a Layer Cake, page 64.) Sprinkle with nuts.

High Altitude (3500–6500 ft): Heat oven to 375°F.

1 Serving: Calories 450; Total Fat 17g; Cholesterol 65mg; Sodium 310mg; Total Carbohydrate 69g (Dietary Fiber 1g); Protein 4g **% Daily Value:** Vitamin A 10%; Vitamin C 0%; Calcium 8%; Iron 10% **Carbohydrate Choices:** 4½

Checking Baking Powder

Check if baking powder still packs a punch by stirring one teaspoon baking powder into ⅓ cup hot water. If it actively bubbles, it's fine to use.

Applesauce Cake

PREP TIME: 15 Minutes • **START TO FINISH:** 2 Hours 5 Minutes

15 servings for 13 × 9-inch cake; 12 servings for layer cake

Baking spray with flour to grease pan

2½ cups all-purpose flour

1½ cups unsweetened applesauce

1¼ cups granulated sugar

½ cup butter or margarine (1 stick), room temperature

½ cup water

1½ teaspoons baking soda

1½ teaspoons salt

¾ teaspoon ground cinnamon

½ teaspoon ground cloves

½ teaspoon ground allspice

¼ teaspoon baking powder

2 large eggs

1 cup raisins

½ cup chopped walnuts

Vanilla Buttercream Frosting (page 65)

or Caramel Frosting (page 65)

Walnut pieces, if desired

1 Heat the oven to 350°F. Spray the bottom and sides of either one 13 × 9-inch pan or two 8-inch or 9-inch round cake pans with the baking spray with flour.

2 In a large bowl, beat all ingredients except raisins, walnuts and frosting with an electric mixer on low speed 30 seconds, stopping frequently to scrape batter from side and bottom of bowl with a rubber spatula. Beat on high speed 3 minutes, stopping occasionally to scrape bowl. With a rubber spatula, stir in the raisins and walnuts. Pour batter into 13 × 9-inch pan or round pans; use a rubber spatula to scrape batter from bowl, spread batter evenly in pan and smooth top of batter. (If batter in round pans is not divided evenly, spoon batter from one pan to the other.)

3 Bake 13 × 9-inch pan 45 to 50 minutes, round pans 40 to 45 minutes, or until a toothpick inserted in the center comes out clean.

4 Cool 13 × 9-inch cake in pan completely on cooling rack, about 1 hour. Cool round cakes in pans 10 minutes, then remove onto cooling racks to finish cooling completely. (See Removing Round Cake from Pan, page 62.)

5 Make desired frosting. For 13 × 9-inch cake, spread frosting over the top, using a metal spatula. For layer cake, place one layer, rounded side down, on a cake plate; using a metal spatula, spread ⅓ cup of the frosting over the top. Add second layer, rounded side up. Frost top and sides. (See Frosting a Layer Cake, page 64.) Garnish with walnuts.

High Altitude (3500–6500 ft): No change.

1 Serving: Calories 460; Total Fat 16g; Cholesterol 60mg; Sodium 480mg; Total Carbohydrate 74g (Dietary Fiber 2g); Protein 4g **% Daily Value:** Vitamin A 8%; Vitamin C 0%; Calcium 4%; Iron 10% **Carbohydrate Choices:** 5

Whole Wheat–Applesauce Cake: Use 1¼ cups whole wheat flour and 1¼ cups all-purpose flour instead of 2½ cups all-purpose flour.

Measuring Applesauce

Measure applesauce in a liquid measuring cup for best results. Too much applesauce and the cake may have a sink on top; too little applesauce the cake may be dry.

Banana Cake

PREP TIME: 15 Minutes • **START TO FINISH:** 2 Hours 5 Minutes

15 servings for 13 × 9-inch cake; 12 servings for layer cake

Baking spray with flour to grease pan

3 very ripe medium bananas, peeled

2½ cups all-purpose flour

1¼ cups granulated sugar

½ cup butter or margarine (1 stick), room temperature

½ cup buttermilk

1½ teaspoons baking soda

1 teaspoon salt

1 teaspoon baking powder

2 large eggs

⅔ cup chopped nuts

Chocolate Buttercream Frosting (page 65)

or Caramel Frosting (page 65)

Mashing Bananas

Mash ripe bananas using a potato masher or fork until moist and some small pieces of banana remain.

1 Heat the oven to 350°F. Spray the bottom and sides of either one 13 × 9-inch pan or two 8-inch or 9-inch round cake pans with the baking spray with flour.

2 In a medium bowl, place the bananas. Mash with a potato masher or fork to measure 1½ cups.

3 In a large bowl, beat the mashed bananas and remaining ingredients except nuts and frosting with an electric mixer on low speed 30 seconds, stopping frequently to scrape batter from side and bottom of bowl with a rubber spatula. Beat on high speed 3 minutes, stopping occasionally to scrape bowl. With a rubber spatula, stir in the nuts. Pour batter into 13 × 9-inch pan or round pans; use a rubber spatula to scrape batter from bowl, spread batter evenly in pan and smooth top of batter. (If batter in round pans is not divided evenly, spoon batter from one pan to the other.)

4 Bake 13 × 9-inch pan 45 to 50 minutes, round pans 40 to 45 minutes, or until a toothpick inserted in the center comes out clean.

5 Cool 13 × 9-inch cake in pan completely on cooling rack, about 1 hour. Cool round cakes in pans 10 minutes, then remove onto cooling racks to finish cooling completely. (See Removing Round Cake from Pan, page 62.)

6 Make desired frosting. For 13 × 9-inch cake, spread frosting over the top, using a metal spatula. For layer cake, place one layer, rounded side down, on a cake plate; using a metal spatula, spread ⅓ cup of the frosting over the top. Add second layer, rounded side up. Frost top and sides. (See Frosting a Layer Cake, page 64.)

High Altitude (3500–6500 ft): Do not use 8-inch pans.

1 Serving: Calories 410; Total Fat 15g; Cholesterol 55mg; Sodium 410mg; Total Carbohydrate 64g (Dietary Fiber 2g); Protein 5g **% Daily Value:** Vitamin A 8%; Vitamin C 0%; Calcium 4%; Iron 8% **Carbohydrate Choices:** 4

Carrot Cake

PREP TIME: 15 Minutes • **START TO FINISH:** 2 Hours

15 servings for 13 × 9-inch cake; 12 servings for layer cake

Baking spray with flour to
    grease pan

6 medium carrots

1½ cups granulated sugar

1 cup vegetable oil

3 large eggs

2 cups all-purpose flour

1½ teaspoons ground cinnamon

1 teaspoon baking soda

1 teaspoon vanilla

½ teaspoon salt

¼ teaspoon ground nutmeg

1 cup coarsely chopped nuts

Cream Cheese Frosting
    (page 65)

or Vanilla Buttercream Frosting
    (page 65)

Shredding Carrots

Shred the carrot by rubbing it across the larger holes of a box grater or across a flat plane grater with large holes.

1 Heat the oven to 350°F. Spray the bottom and sides of either one 13 × 9-inch pan or two 8-inch or 9-inch round cake pans with the baking spray with flour.

2 Peel the carrots with a vegetable peeler. Shred the carrots by rubbing them across the larger holes of a box grater (do not grate) to measure 3 cups; set aside.

3 In a large bowl, beat the sugar, oil and eggs with an electric mixer on low speed about 30 seconds or until well mixed. Add remaining ingredients except carrots, nuts and frosting. Beat on low speed 1 minute, stopping occasionally to scrape batter from side and bottom of bowl with a rubber spatula. With the rubber spatula, stir in the carrots and nuts. Pour batter into 13 × 9-inch pan or round pans; use a rubber spatula to scrape batter from bowl, spread batter evenly in pan and smooth top of batter. (If batter in round pans is not divided evenly, spoon batter from one pan to the other.)

4 Bake 13 × 9-inch pan 40 to 45 minutes, round pans 30 to 35 minutes, or until a toothpick inserted in the center comes out clean.

5 Cool 13 × 9-inch cake in pan completely on cooling rack, about 1 hour. Cool round cakes in pans 10 minutes, then remove onto cooling racks to finish cooling completely. (See Removing Round Cake from Pan, page 62.)

6 Make desired frosting. For 13 × 9-inch cake, spread frosting over the top, using a metal spatula. For layer cake, place one layer, rounded side down, on a cake plate; using a metal spatula, spread ⅓ cup of the frosting over the top. Add second layer, rounded side up. Frost top and sides. (See Frosting a Layer Cake, page 64.) Store cake covered in the refrigerator.

High Altitude (3500–6500 ft): No change.

1 Serving: Calories 560; Total Fat 29g; Cholesterol 65mg; Sodium 260mg; Total Carbohydrate 69g (Dietary Fiber 2g); Protein 6g **% Daily Value:** Vitamin A 90%; Vitamin C 0%; Calcium 4%; Iron 8% **Carbohydrate Choices:** 4½

Fresh Apple Cake: Peel and chop 3 medium tart apples to measure 3 cups. Substitute apples for the carrots.

Pineapple-Carrot Cake: Add 1 can (8 ounces) crushed pineapple, drained, and ½ cup flaked or shredded coconut with the carrots.

Zucchini Cake: Shred about 1½ medium unpeeled zucchini by rubbing them across the larger holes of a shredder to measure 3 cups. Substitute zucchini for the carrots.

Red Velvet Cupcakes

PREP TIME: 40 Minutes • **START TO FINISH:** 1 Hour 35 Minutes

24 cupcakes

CUPCAKES

24 paper baking cups

2¼ cups all-purpose flour

¼ cup unsweetened baking cocoa

1 teaspoon salt

½ cup butter or margarine (1 stick), room temperature

1½ cups granulated sugar

2 large eggs

1 bottle (1 oz) red food color (about 2 tablespoons)

1½ teaspoons vanilla

1 cup buttermilk*

1 teaspoon baking soda

1 tablespoon white vinegar

MARSHMALLOW BUTTERCREAM FROSTING

1 jar (7 to 7½ oz) marshmallow creme

1 cup butter or margarine (2 sticks), room temperature

2 cups powdered sugar

Filling Cupcake Cups

Spoon batter into paper cups using a tableware spoon, filling each ⅔ full.

1   Heat the oven to 350°F. Place a paper baking cup in each of 24 regular-size muffin cups.

2   In a small bowl, mix the flour, cocoa and salt; set aside. In a large bowl, beat ½ cup butter and the granulated sugar with an electric mixer on medium speed until mixed. Add the eggs; beat 1 to 2 minutes or until light and fluffy. Using a rubber spatula, stir in the food color and vanilla.

3   On low speed, beat in ½ of the flour mixture just until mixed, then beat in ½ of the buttermilk until mixed. Repeat beating in flour mixture alternately with the buttermilk just until mixed. Beat in the baking soda and vinegar until well mixed. Spoon the batter into the cups, filling each ⅔ full. (See Making Cupcakes, page 61.)

4   Bake 20 to 22 minutes or until a toothpick inserted in the center of a cupcake comes out clean. Remove cupcakes from pan to cooling racks. Cool completely, about 30 minutes.

5   Remove lid and foil seal from jar of marshmallow creme. Microwave marshmallow creme on High 15 to 20 seconds to soften. In a large bowl, beat marshmallow creme and 1 cup butter with electric mixer on medium speed until smooth. Beat in the powdered sugar until smooth. Spoon 1 heaping tablespoon frosting onto each cupcake, swirling frosting with back of spoon.

High Altitude (3500–6500 ft): Increase eggs to 3. Use 30 muffin cups.

1 Cupcake: Calories 280; Total Fat 12g; Cholesterol 50mg; Sodium 260mg; Total Carbohydrate 39g (Dietary Fiber 0g); Protein 2g **% Daily Value:** Vitamin A 8%; Vitamin C 0%; Calcium 2%; Iron 4% **Carbohydrate Choices:** 2½

*To substitute for buttermilk, stir 1 tablespoon white vinegar or lemon juice into 1 cup milk.

Red Velvet Layer Cake: Spray the bottom and sides of two 8-inch or 9-inch round cake pans with baking spray with flour. Make batter as directed in steps 2 and 3 except pour batter into pans. Bake 30 to 35 minutes, or until a toothpick inserted in the center comes out clean. Cool 15 minutes and then remove from pans. Cool completely; frost as desired.

Golden Pound Cake

PREP TIME: 15 Minutes • **START TO FINISH:** 4 Hours 10 Minutes

16 servings

Special Equipment: 12-cup fluted tube cake pan or 10 × 4-inch angel food (tube) cake pan

---

Baking spray with flour to grease pan

3 cups all-purpose flour

1 teaspoon baking powder

¼ teaspoon salt

2¾ cups granulated sugar

1¼ cups butter or margarine (2½ sticks), room temperature

1 teaspoon vanilla or almond extract

5 large eggs

1 cup evaporated milk (from 12-oz can) or regular milk

Chocolate Glaze (page 65) or Vanilla Glaze (page 65)

1 Heat the oven to 325°F. Spray a 12-cup fluted tube cake pan or 10 × 4-inch angel food (tube) cake pan with the baking spray with flour.

2 In a medium bowl, mix the flour, baking powder and salt; set aside.

3 In a large bowl, beat the sugar, butter, vanilla and eggs with an electric mixer on low speed 30 seconds, stopping frequently to scrape batter from side and bottom of bowl with a rubber spatula. Beat on high speed 5 minutes, stopping occasionally to scrape bowl. On low speed, beat in ½ of the flour mixture just until mixed, then beat in ½ of the milk until mixed. Repeat beating in flour mixture alternately with the milk until mixed. Pour batter into the pan, turning the pan a couple of times to evenly distribute the batter. Use a rubber spatula to scrape batter from bowl, spread batter evenly in pan and smooth top of batter.

4 Bake 1 hour 25 minutes to 1 hour 35 minutes or until a tooth-pick inserted halfway between side and center of pan comes out clean.

5 Cool cake in pan on cooling rack 20 minutes. To remove cake from pan, place a cooling rack upside down on pan; holding rack and pan with pot holders, turn rack and pan over together, then remove pan. Cool completely, about 2 hours.

6 Make desired glaze. Spoon glaze from the tip of a spoon over top of the cake, allowing some glaze to drizzle down the sides.

High Altitude (3500–6500 ft): Decrease sugar to 2½ cups and butter to 1 cup. Do not beat batter on high speed 5 minutes.

1 Serving: Calories 470; Total Fat 22g; Cholesterol 115mg; Sodium 220mg; Total Carbohydrate 62g (Dietary Fiber 1g); Protein 6g **% Daily Value:** Vitamin A 15%; Vitamin C 0%; Calcium 8%; Iron 8% **Carbohydrate Choices:** 4

Lemon Pound Cake: Substitute 1 teaspoon lemon extract for the vanilla, and fold 2 to 3 teaspoons grated lemon peel into batter.

Triple-Ginger Pound Cake: Add 1 tablespoon grated gingerroot, 2 teaspoons ground ginger and ½ cup finely chopped crystallized ginger with the flour mixture. Spread with Lemon Glaze (page 65), if desired.

Removing Cake from Pan

Place a cooling rack upside down on pan. Holding rack and pan with pot holders turn rack and pan over together, then remove pan.

Brown Sugar Bundt Cake with Caramel Sauce

PREP TIME: 25 Minutes • **START TO FINISH:** 4 Hours

20 servings

Special Equipment: 12-cup fluted tube cake pan

CAKE
Baking spray with flour to grease pan

1½ cups packed light brown sugar

1 cup granulated sugar

1½ cups butter or margarine (3 sticks), room temperature

½ cup milk

1 teaspoon vanilla

5 large eggs

3 cups all-purpose flour

1 teaspoon baking powder

¼ teaspoon salt

CARAMEL SAUCE
1 cup butter (2 sticks)*

½ cup packed light brown sugar

2 tablespoons milk

1 tablespoon light corn syrup

1 teaspoon vanilla

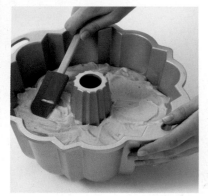

Spreading Batter in Pan

Spoon the batter into the pan and, using a rubber spatula, spread the batter evenly to the edge and center.

1 Heat the oven to 325°F. Spray a 12-cup fluted tube cake pan with the baking spray with flour.

2 In a large bowl, beat 1½ cups brown sugar, the granulated sugar and 1½ cups butter with an electric mixer on low speed until well mixed. Add ½ cup milk, 1 teaspoon vanilla and eggs. Beat on medium speed 2 minutes.

3 On medium speed, beat in the flour, baking powder and salt until mixture is smooth and well mixed. Pour batter into the pan, turning the pan a couple of times to evenly distribute the batter. Use a rubber spatula to scrape batter from bowl, spread batter evenly in pan and smooth top of batter.

4 Bake 1 hour 5 minutes to 1 hour 15 minutes or until toothpick inserted halfway between side and center of pan comes out clean.

5 Cool in pan on cooling rack 20 minutes. To remove cake from pan, place a cooling rack upside down on pan; holding rack and pan with pot holders, turn rack and pan over together, then remove pan. Cool completely, about 2 hours.

6 In a 2-quart saucepan, heat all of the sauce ingredients except the vanilla to boiling over medium heat, stirring constantly. Boil and stir 2 minutes. Remove from heat; cool 10 minutes. Stir in 1 teaspoon vanilla. Serve warm sauce with cake.

*We recommend using only butter for the Caramel Sauce because it gives the sauce a rich, buttery flavor.

High Altitude (3500–6500 ft): Heat oven to 350°F. Decrease granulated sugar to ½ cup and butter in cake to 1 cup; increase milk in cake to ¾ cup. Bake 55 to 65 minutes.

1 Serving: Calories 430; Total Fat 25g; Cholesterol 115mg; Sodium 250mg; Total Carbohydrate 47g (Dietary Fiber 0g); Protein 4g **% Daily Value:** Vitamin A 15%; Vitamin C 0%; Calcium 6%; Iron 8% **Carbohydrate Choices:** 3

Decadent Chocolate Cake
with Raspberry Sauce

PREP TIME: 40 Minutes • **START TO FINISH:** 2 Hours 35 Minutes
12 servings

Special Equipment: 8 × 2½-inch springform pan

CAKE
Baking spray with flour to grease pan

4 eggs

1 cup semisweet chocolate chips (6 oz)

½ cup butter or margarine (1 stick)

½ cup all-purpose flour

½ cup granulated sugar

RASPBERRY SAUCE
1 box (10 oz) frozen raspberries, thawed

¼ cup granulated sugar

2 tablespoons cornstarch

1 to 2 tablespoons orange- or raspberry-flavored liqueur, if desired

GLAZE
½ cup semisweet chocolate chips

2 tablespoons butter or margarine

2 tablespoons light corn syrup

GARNISH, IF DESIRED
Sweetened Whipped Cream (page 193)

Fresh raspberries

1 Heat the oven to 325°F. Spray the bottom and side of an 8 × 2½-inch springform pan or 9-inch round cake pan with the baking spray.

2 Place an egg separator over a small bowl. Crack open 1 egg, letting the yolk fall into the center of the separator and the egg white slip through the slots into the bowl. Place yolk in another small bowl, then separate remaining eggs. Set aside.

3 In a 2-quart saucepan, melt 1 cup chocolate chips and ½ cup butter over low heat, stirring occasionally. Remove from heat; cool 5 minutes. Stir in the flour until smooth. Stir in the egg yolks until well mixed; set aside.

4 Pour the egg whites into a large bowl; beat with an electric mixer on high speed until foamy. Beat in ½ cup sugar, 1 tablespoon at a time, until soft peaks form. Gently stir chocolate mixture into egg whites. Pour batter into the pan.

5 Bake springform pan 35 to 40 minutes, round cake pan 30 to 35 minutes, or until a toothpick inserted in the center comes out clean (top will appear dry and cracked). Cool in pan on cooling rack 10 minutes. Before releasing and removing the side of the springform pan, carefully run a metal spatula between the cake and inside of the pan; release and remove side of pan, leaving cake on bottom of pan for serving. If using 9-inch round pan, invert onto cooling rack, then invert right side up on second cooling rack. (See Removing Round Cake from Pan, page 62.) Cool completely, about 1 hour.

6 Place a strainer in a 2-cup glass measuring cup or small bowl. Pour thawed raspberries into strainer, reserving juice in measuring cup. Add enough water to reserved raspberry juice to measure 1 cup. In a 1-quart saucepan, mix ¼ cup sugar and the cornstarch. Stir in juice and thawed raspberries. Heat to boiling over medium heat, stirring constantly. Boil and stir 1 minute; strain through strainer or colander to remove seeds. Stir in liqueur; set aside.

7 Place cake on a serving plate. In a 1-quart saucepan, heat ½ cup chocolate chips, 2 tablespoons butter and the corn syrup over medium heat, stirring occasionally, until chips are melted. Spread over top of cake, allowing some to drizzle down the side.

8 Make Sweetened Whipped Cream. Serve cake with raspberry sauce, whipped cream and fresh raspberries.

High Altitude (3500–6500 ft): Bake springform pan 50 to 55 minutes; bake round cake pan 35 to 40 minutes.

1 Serving: Calories 350; Total Fat 19g; Cholesterol 100mg; Sodium 95mg; Total Carbohydrate 40g (Dietary Fiber 2g); Protein 4g **% Daily Value:** Vitamin A 10%; Vitamin C 4%; Calcium 2%; Iron 8% **Carbohydrate Choices:** 2½

Straining Raspberry Sauce

Strain sauce through a strainer placed over a bowl to remove the raspberry seeds.

3 PIES and TARTS

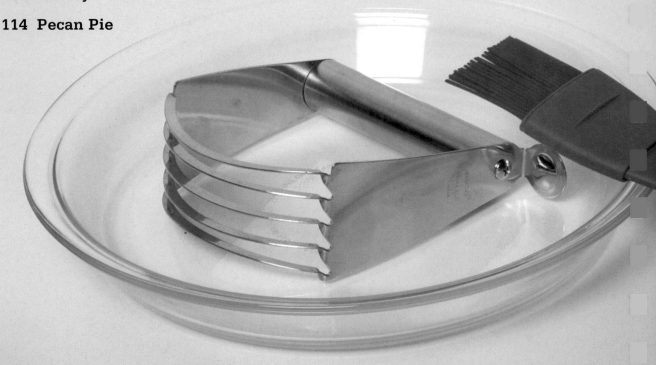

PIES AND TARTS 101

Pie is always a favorite dessert, whether it's a warm fruit-filled pie or a chilled refreshing custard-type pie. Pies don't require any special ingredients and are easy to make. With a little practice making pastry, you will be baking blue-ribbon pies.

Types of Pies

There are three basic categories of pies: fruit pies, custard pies and cream pies.

Fruit Pies usually are baked pies that have a bottom and top crust with a fruit-mixture filling. Some fruit pies or tarts have a baked bottom crust that is filled with fresh fruits and refrigerated. A favorite fruit pie is apple pie.

Custard Pies have a custard-type filling that is baked in a single crust pie. The crust can be partially baked before adding the custard filling to help prevent the crust from becoming soggy. Pumpkin and pecan pie are two popular types of custard pies.

Cream Pies have a baked single crust that is filled with a cooked pudding-type filling.

These pies can be topped with whipped cream or meringue. Banana cream pie and lemon meringue are favorite cream pies.

Tarts are similar to pies with a pastry crust and a filling, but they have no top crust. They are made in a tart pan, which has a straight side rather than a slop side like a pie plate.

Pie and Tart Pans

For tender, flaky crusts, choose heat-resistant glass pie plates or dull-finish (anodized) aluminum pie pans. Shiny pie pans are not recommended because they reflect heat, causing a soggy bottom crust.

The most standard size pie plate is nine inches in diameter and at least 1½ inches deep. It will hold about 3½ cups filling.

Nonstick pie pans can cause an unfilled one-crust pie pastry to shrink excessively during baking. To hold the pastry in place,

fold it over the edge of the pie plate and press firmly.

Tart pans have a fluted straight edge and are available with either an attached or removable bottom. They come in shiny, dark and nonstick finishes. All three are acceptable and produce evenly brown curst. However, a dark (black) pan may brown too quickly and require reducing the oven temperature by 25°F.

WORKING WITH PASTRY

The secret to an ideal pie is a tender, flaky crust. To achieve this, measure the ingredients accurately, mix the ingredients just enough to hold together and avoid over handling the dough.

Making and Handling Pastry

1 Cut shortening into flour and salt, using a pastry blender or tossing with a fork, until particles are the size of small peas.

2 Sprinkle with cold water and toss with fork until all the flour is moistened and pastry almost leaves side of bowl.

3 Roll from center to outside in all directions, using less pressure on edges to prevent edge from getting too thin. Roll two inches larger than pie plate.

4 Lift and turn pastry occasionally to help prevent sticking to surface. If edge of pastry splits, patch it with a small piece of pastry by gently pressing it over the split.

5 Fold pastry into fourths and place in pie plate with point in center. Unfold and ease into plate, avoiding stretching, which causes it to shrink when baked.

6 Or instead of folding the pastry into fourths, roll it loosely around the rolling pin and transfer to pie plate. Unroll pastry and ease into plate.

Making Pat-in-Pan Crust

Shape pastry into a ball and place in pie plate. Press pastry, using finger tips, in bottom and up side of pie plate.

WORKING WITH PASTRY (CONTINUED)

Placing the pastry in the pan correctly and fluting the edge (making a decorative pattern around the crust) are essential steps when making a pie.

Making Two-Crust Pie

Cut slits, using a sharp knife, in top pastry. Carefully center pastry on top of filling, with overhang over edge of plate, and unfold.

Fold and roll overhanging pastry under edge of bottom pastry. Press together to seal.

Form a stand-up rim of even thickness around edge of pie plate, continuing to press edges together. This seals pastry and makes fluting easier.

Fluting Pastry Edges

Fork Edge: Flatten pastry evenly on rim of pie plate. Firmly press tines of fork around edge. To prevent sticking, occasionally dip fork into flour.

Pinch Edge: Place index finger on inside of pastry rim and thumb and index finger (or knuckles) on outside. Pinch pastry into V shape along edge. Pinch again to sharpen points.

Rope Edge: Place side of thumb on pastry rim at an angle. Pinch pastry by pressing the knuckle of your index finger down into pastry toward thumb.

Baking Unfilled Crust

Sometimes you want to bake a pie crust before filling it, like for cream pies where the filling isn't baked. Here are two steps to help prevent the unfilled crust from shrinking and puffing up during baking.

1 Keep the crust anchored to the pan during baking by pressing it firmly against the sides and bottom of the pan. Be careful not to stretch the crust or it will shrink during baking.

2 Prick the unbaked pastry all over with a fork to let steam escape during baking. (Don't prick the crust of one-crust pies like pecan where the filling is baked because the filling will seep under the crust during baking.)

Glazed Baked Pie

In a small bowl, stir together ½ cup powdered sugar, 2 to 3 teaspoons milk, orange juice or lemon juice and, if desired, 2 teaspoons grated orange peel or lemon peel. Brush or drizzle over warm baked two-crust pie, not letting glaze run over the edge of the pie.

Top Crust Treatments

Here are three easy ways to make your two-crust pie look special. If the crust starts to brown too quickly, put a sheet of foil loosely on top of the pie to slow the browning.

Shiny crust: Brush crust with whipping cream or whole milk

Sugary crust: Brush crust lightly with water; sprinkle with granulated or coarse sugar or white coarse.

Glazed crust: Brush crust with a beaten egg or egg yolk mixed with a little water.

BAKING PIES

Pies are baked at higher temperatures than cakes (375°F to 425°F) so that the rich pastry dries and becomes flaky and golden brown and the filling cooks all the way through.

Pastry and crumb crusts have enough fat in them that pie plates and pans usually don't need to be greased.

Place the pie in the center of the preheated oven. If baking two pies side by side, place them so they do not touch each other or the sides of the oven.

If baking two pies on separate oven racks, stagger the placement so one pie is not directly over the other one.

When a one-crust pie is filled after baking, prick the unbaked pastry in the pie plate all over with a fork. This allows the steam to escape and helps prevent the crust from puffing up during baking. You can carefully line the crust with a piece of foil and fill the foil with uncooked rice or beans to help prevent the crust from shrinking. About halfway through the bake time, carefully remove the foil so the crust becomes brown and crisp.

When a one-crust pie is filled before baking, like pumpkin or pecan pie, don't prick the crust because the filling will seep under the crust during baking.

To prevent pie crust edges and top crust from getting too brown, cover them with strips of foil or a circle of foil (see Covering Edge with Foil, below).

Custard pies are done when a tableware knife inserted in the center of the pie comes out clean. Check doneness at the minimum bake time because overbaking may cause the filling to break down and become watery.

A two-crust pie should have a golden brown, blistered top crust and a crisp, brown undercrust. It should cut easily and the pieces should hold their shape when served.

Cover Edge with Foil

Cover the edge of pie crust with foil after the first 15 minutes of baking or as directed in the recipe. From a twelve-inch-square piece of foil, cut out a seven-inch circle from the center, and gently fold the foil "ring" around the edge of the crust. Be careful—the pie will be hot.

Storing Pies and Tarts

Baked fruit pies or tarts can be stored at room temperature.

Cream pies and tarts should be stored covered in the refrigerator.

Baked custard-type pies and tarts should be cooled on a cooling rack 30 minutes. Cover loosely and refrigerate until chilled. Store covered in the refrigerator.

What Went Wrong?

This Happened	This Is Why
Crust is pale	• baked in shiny pan instead color of in dull pan • underbaked
Bottom crust is soggy	• baked in shiny pan instead of a glass or dull pan • oven temperature too low
Crust is tough	• too much water • too much flour • dough was mixed and handled too much
Crust too tender; falls apart	• too little water • too much fat
Crust dry and mealy, not flaky	• fat was cut in too finely • too little water

Freezing Pies and Tarts

Cream pies and pies with meringue toppings can't be frozen because they break down and become watery.

Custard pies, such as pumpkin or pecan pies, must be baked before freezing. Cool baked pies completely and place pies in the freezer uncovered. When completely frozen, wrap tightly in foil or place in resealable plastic freezer bags. Freeze pies up to four months.

Fruit pies can be frozen unbaked or baked. Cool baked pies completely before freezing. Place pies in the freezer uncovered. When completely frozen, wrap tightly in foil or in a resealable plastic freezer bags. Freeze baked pies up to four months and unbaked pies up to three months. To serve unbaked pies: Unwrap and bake frozen pie at 475°F for 15 minutes; reduce oven temperature to 375°F and bake for 45 minutes longer or until center is bubbly. To serve baked pies: Unwrap and bake frozen pie at 325°F for 45 minutes or until thawed and warm.

To freeze unbaked one-crust pie crusts, place crusts in the freezer until completely frozen. Once frozen, wrap in foil or place in resealable plastic freezer bags and freeze up to two months. Don't thaw unbaked crusts; bake them right after taking them out of the freezer.

To freeze one-crust baked pie crusts, place in the freezer until completely frozen. Once frozen, wrap crusts in foil or place in resealable plastic freezer bags and freeze up to four months. To thaw baked pie crusts, unwrap and let stand at room temperature or heat in the oven at 350°F for about six minutes.

Pastry for Pies and Tarts

One-Crust Pie

1 cup all-purpose flour
½ teaspoon salt
⅓ cup plus 1 tablespoon shortening*
2 to 3 tablespoons cold water

Two-Crust Pie

2 cups all-purpose flour
1 teaspoon salt
⅔ cup plus 2 tablespoons shortening*
4 to 6 tablespoons cold water

1   In a medium bowl, mix the flour and salt. Cut in the shortening, using a pastry blender (or tossing with a fork), until particles are the size of small peas. Sprinkle with cold water, 1 tablespoon at a time, tossing with a fork until all flour is moistened and pastry almost leaves the side of the bowl (1 to 2 teaspoons more water can be added if necessary).

2   Lightly sprinkle flour over a cutting board or countertop. Gather the pastry into a ball. On the floured surface, shape pastry into a flattened round. (For Two-Crust Pie, divide pastry in half and shape into 2 rounds.) Wrap flattened round(s) of pastry in plastic wrap and refrigerate about 45 minutes or until pastry is firm and cold, yet pliable. This allows the shortening to become slightly firm, which helps make the baked pastry more flaky. If refrigerated longer, let pastry soften slightly before rolling.

3   On a lightly floured surface, roll pastry round with a floured rolling pin into a circle that is 2 inches larger than an upside-down 9-inch glass pie plate. Fold pastry into quarters or roll pastry loosely around a rolling pin and transfer to pie plate. Unfold or unroll pastry and ease into plate. (See Making and Handling Pastry, page 95.)

*You can substitute butter for half of the shortening. For One-Crust Pie, use 3 tablespoons each butter and shortening; for Two-Crust Pie, use ⅓ cup plus 1 tablespoon each butter and shortening.

4   To finish preparing the pie, use one of the following methods:

One-Crust Pie: After placing pastry in pie plate, trim overhanging edge of pastry 1 inch from rim of pie plate. Fold and roll pastry under edge to make even with plate; flute (see Fluting Pastry Edges, page 96). Fill and bake as directed in pie recipe.

Prebaked Pie Crust (Pie Shell): Heat oven to 475°F. After placing pastry in pie plate, trim overhanging edge of pastry 1 inch from rim of pie plate. Fold and roll pastry under edge to make even with plate; flute (see Fluting Pastry Edges, page 96). Prick bottom and side of pastry thoroughly with fork. Bake 8 to 10 minutes or until light brown. Cool completely on a cooling rack, about 30 minutes.

Two-Crust Pie: After placing bottom crust in pie plate, spoon desired filling into pastry-lined pie plate. Trim overhanging edge of bottom pastry ½ inch from rim of plate. Roll other round of pastry. Fold top pastry into quarters and cut slits so steam can escape (see Cutting Slits in Top Pastry, page 108). Place pastry over filling and unfold. Trim overhanging edge of top pastry 1 inch from rim of plate. Fold and roll top edge under lower edge, pressing on rim to seal (see Making Two-Crust Pie, page 96); flute (see Fluting Pastry Edges, page 96). Bake as directed in pie recipe.

Pat-in-Pan Pastry

1⅓ cups all-purpose flour
½ teaspoon salt
⅓ cup vegetable oil
2 tablespoons cold water

1   In a medium bowl, stir the flour, salt and oil until all flour is moistened. Sprinkle with cold water, 1 tablespoon at a time, tossing with fork until all water is absorbed.

2   Gather the pastry into a ball. Press in the bottom and up the side of pie plate; flute (see Fluting Pastry Edges, page 96).

Unbaked Pie Crust: Fill and bake as directed in the pie recipe.

Prebaked Pie Crust: Heat the oven to 475°F. Prick the bottom and side of the pastry thoroughly with a fork. Bake 10 to 12 minutes or until light brown. Cool completely on a cooling rack, about 30 minutes. Fill as directed in the pie recipe.

Crumb Crust

Heat the oven to 350°F. Place the butter in a small microwavable bowl; cover with a microwavable paper towel. Microwave on High 30 to 50 seconds or until melted. Mix the crumbs, melted butter and sugar until well mixed. Reserve 3 tablespoons crumb mixture for garnishing top of pie before serving, if desired.

Using fingers or base of a dry measuring cup, press remaining mixture firmly against the bottom and side of pie plate. Bake about 10 minutes or until light brown. Cool on cooling rack. Fill the crust as directed in pie recipe.

CRUST	CRUMBS	BUTTER	SUGAR
Graham Cracker	1½ cups (about 24 squares, finely crushed)	⅓ cup	3 tablespoons
Chocolate Cookie	1½ cups (about 30 cookies, finely crushed)	¼ cup	Omit
Vanilla Cookie	1½ cups (about 38 cookies, finely crushed)	¼ cup	Omit

Key Lime Pie

PREP TIME: 20 Minutes • **START TO FINISH:** 2 Hours 50 Minutes

8 servings

Graham Cracker Crumb Crust (page 101)

4 large eggs

1 can (14 oz) sweetened condensed milk (not evaporated)

½ cup fresh or bottled Key lime juice or regular lime juice

1 or 2 drops green food color, if desired

¾ cup whipping cream

2 tablespoons granulated sugar

1 teaspoon vanilla

1 Make the Graham Cracker Crumb Crust as directed except do not bake it.

2 Heat the oven to 375°F. Place an egg separator over a small bowl. Crack open each egg over the egg separator to separate the yolks from the whites. (Save egg whites for another recipe.)

3 In a medium bowl, beat the egg yolks, milk, lime juice and food color with an electric mixer on medium speed about 1 minute or until well blended. Pour mixture into the unbaked crust.

4 Bake 14 to 16 minutes or until the center of the filling is set. Cool on a cooling rack 15 minutes. Cover; refrigerate until chilled, at least 2 hours but no longer than 3 days.

5 About 30 minutes before serving pie, place a medium bowl and the beaters of electric mixer in refrigerator to chill. These will be used to beat the whipping cream, which beats better in a cold bowl.

6 Pour the whipping cream into the chilled bowl, and add the sugar and vanilla. Insert the chilled beaters in the electric mixer. Beat on high speed until whipped cream forms soft peaks when beaters are lifted. Spread whipped cream over pie. Store pie covered in refrigerator.

High Altitude (3500–6500 ft): Bake 15 to 17 minutes.

1 Serving: Calories 450; Total Fat 23g; Cholesterol 165mg; Sodium 250mg; Total Carbohydrate 53g (Dietary Fiber 0g); Protein 7g **% Daily Value:** Vitamin A 15%; Vitamin C 4%; Calcium 20%; Iron 4% **Carbohydrate Choices:** 3½

Know Your Limes

Key limes (right) are smaller, rounder and more yellow in color than regular Persian limes. They are often sold in mesh bags in the produce section. Bottled Key lime juice is available at many supermarkets.

"Jamocha" Ice Cream Pie

PREP TIME: 20 Minutes • **START TO FINISH:** 4 Hours 20 Minutes

8 servings

COFFEE PAT-IN-PAN PIE CRUST*

1 cup all-purpose flour

½ cup butter or margarine (1 stick), room temperature

2 teaspoons instant coffee granules or crystals

FILLING

2 pints (4 cups) coffee ice cream

¾ cup hot fudge topping

Chocolate-covered coffee beans or coffee-flavored chocolate candies, if desired

1 Heat the oven to 400°F. In a medium bowl, mix crust ingredients with a wooden spoon until a dough forms. Using fingers, press the dough firmly and evenly against the bottom and side of a 9-inch glass pie plate. Bake 12 to 15 minutes or until light brown. Cool completely on cooling rack, about 45 minutes.

2 Meanwhile, place 1 pint of ice cream in the refrigerator about 30 minutes until slightly softened.

3 Spread the softened ice cream in the cooled pie crust, using the back of a tableware tablespoon. Cover; freeze about 1 hour or until firm.

4 Meanwhile, place the other pint of ice cream in the refrigerator about 30 minutes until slightly softened.

5 Spread the hot fudge topping over ice cream in pie crust. Carefully spread remaining pint of softened ice cream over topping. Cover; freeze at least 2 hours until ice cream is firm, but for no longer than 2 weeks.

6 To serve, let pie stand at room temperature about 10 minutes before cutting. Garnish with chocolate-covered coffee beans.

*The Chocolate Cookie Crumb Crust (page 101) can be used instead of the coffee-flavored crust.

High Altitude (3500–6500 ft): For pie crust, add up to 1 tablespoon water to dough if necessary.

1 Serving: Calories 420; Total Fat 22g; Cholesterol 55mg; Sodium 240mg; Total Carbohydrate 50g (Dietary Fiber 2g); Protein 6g **% Daily Value:** Vitamin A 15%; Vitamin C 0%; Calcium 10%; Iron 10% **Carbohydrate Choices:** 3

Triple Chocolate Ice Cream Pie: Prepare Chocolate Cookie Crumb Crust (page 101) for the Coffee Pat-in-Pan Pie Crust. Substitute chocolate ice cream for the coffee ice cream.

Spreading Ice Cream

Spread the softened ice cream evenly in the pie crust using the back of a tableware tablespoon.

Apple Crostata

PREP TIME: 40 Minutes • **START TO FINISH:** 3 Hours

8 servings

Pastry for One-Crust Pie
(page 100)

4 medium tart apples (such as
Granny Smith, Jonathan,
McIntosh or Rome)

¼ cup granulated sugar

3 tablespoons all-purpose flour

1 tablespoon granulated sugar

½ teaspoon ground cinnamon

½ cup caramel topping,
if desired

Fold Pastry over Apples

Fold edge of pastry over apples,
making pleats so pastry fits
around the apples.

1 Make pastry as directed for One-Crust Pie through step 2.

2 Lightly sprinkle flour over a cutting board or countertop. Using a floured rolling pin, roll pastry into a 13-inch round. Fold pastry into fourths. Place pastry on an ungreased large cookie sheet and unfold. Cover with plastic wrap to keep moist while making filling.

3 Heat the oven to 425°F. Peel the apples. Cut each apple into quarters; remove core. Cut the apple quarters into ¼-inch slices to measure 4 cups.

4 In a large bowl, mix ¼ cup granulated sugar and the flour. Stir in the apple slices. Mound the apple mixture on center of the pastry to within 3 inches of the edge.

5 Fold the edge of the pastry over the apples, making pleats so pastry lays flat on apples. In a small bowl, mix 1 tablespoon granulated sugar and the cinnamon. Sprinkle mixture evenly over the apples and pastry.

6 Bake 30 to 35 minutes or until crust is light golden brown. To prevent excessive browning, cover center of pie with 5-inch square of foil during last 10 to 15 minutes of baking. Cool on cookie sheet on cooling rack 1 hour, or serve warm. Serve crostata with caramel topping.

High Altitude (3500–6500 ft): No change.

1 Serving: Calories 220; Total Fat 10g; Cholesterol 0mg; Sodium 150mg; Total Carbohydrate 30g (Dietary Fiber 1g); Protein 2g **% Daily Value:** Vitamin A 0%; Vitamin C 2%; Calcium 0%; Iron 6% **Carbohydrate Choices:** 2

Fresh Apple Pie

PREP TIME: 30 Minutes • **START TO FINISH:** 4 Hours 5 Minutes

8 servings

Pastry for Two-Crust Pie (page 100)

6 medium tart apples (such as Granny Smith, Jonathan, McIntosh or Rome)

½ cup granulated sugar

¼ cup all-purpose flour

¾ teaspoon ground cinnamon

¼ teaspoon ground nutmeg

Dash of salt

2 tablespoons cold butter or margarine, if desired

2 teaspoons water

1 tablespoon granulated sugar

1   Make pastry as directed for Two-Crust Pie.

2   Heat the oven to 425°F. Peel the apples. Cut each apple into quarters; remove core. Cut the apple quarters into ¼-inch slices to measure 6 cups.

3   In a large bowl, mix ½ cup sugar, the flour, cinnamon, nutmeg and salt. Stir in the apples. Spoon mixture into pastry-lined pie plate. Cut the butter into small pieces; sprinkle over apples.

4   Cover apple mixture with top pastry that has slits cut in it; seal (see Making Two-Crust Pie, page 96) and flute (see Fluting Pastry Edges, page 96). Brush top pastry with 2 teaspoons water, using a pastry brush; sprinkle with 1 tablespoon sugar. Cover edge of pastry with a 2- to 3-inch-wide strip of foil to prevent excessive browning.

5   Bake 30 minutes; remove foil. Bake 10 to 20 minutes longer or until crust is golden brown and juice begins to bubble through slits in crust. Cool on a cooling rack at least 2 hours.

High Altitude (3500–6500 ft): No change.

1 Serving: Calories 420; Total Fat 21g; Cholesterol 0mg; Sodium 310mg; Total Carbohydrate 53g (Dietary Fiber 2g); Protein 4g **% Daily Value:** Vitamin A 0%; Vitamin C 4%; Calcium 0%; Iron 10% **Carbohydrate Choices:** 3½

Cutting Slits in Top Pastry

Fold pastry into quarters. With a paring knife, make several cuts on the folded edges. The slits allow the steam to escape during baking.

Blueberry Pie

PREP TIME: 30 Minutes • **START TO FINISH:** 4 Hours

8 servings

Pastry for Two-Crust Pie (page 100)

6 cups fresh blueberries

¾ cup granulated sugar

½ cup all-purpose flour

½ teaspoon ground cinnamon, if desired

1 tablespoon lemon juice

1 tablespoon cold butter or margarine

1 Make pastry as directed for Two-Crust Pie.

2 Place the blueberries in a strainer, and rinse with cool water; dry on paper towels. Remove any stems and discard any crushed berries.

3 Heat the oven to 425°F. In a large bowl, mix the sugar, flour and cinnamon. Stir in the blueberries. Spoon blueberry mixture into pastry-lined pie plate. Sprinkle any remaining sugar mixture over blueberry mixture. Sprinkle with lemon juice. Cut the butter into small pieces; sprinkle over blueberries.

4 Cover blueberry mixture with top pastry that has slits cut in it; seal (see Making Two-Crust Pie, page 96) and flute (see Fluting Pastry Edges, page 96). Cover edge of pastry with a 2- to 3-inch-wide strip of foil to prevent excessive browning.

5 Bake 30 minutes; remove foil. Bake 5 to 15 minutes longer or until crust is golden brown and juice begins to bubble through slits in crust. Cool on a cooling rack at least 2 hours.

High Altitude (3500–6500 ft): Bake 30 minutes; remove foil. Bake 15 to 25 minutes longer.

1 Serving: Calories 480; Total Fat 22g; Cholesterol 0mg; Sodium 310mg; Total Carbohydrate 64g (Dietary Fiber 4g); Protein 5g **% Daily Value:** Vitamin A 2%; Vitamin C 10%; Calcium 0%; Iron 10% **Carbohydrate Choices:** 4

Quick Blueberry Pie: Substitute 6 cups drained canned blueberries or unsweetened frozen (thawed and drained) blueberries for the fresh blueberries.

Raspberry Pie: Increase sugar to 1 cup. Substitute fresh raspberries for the blueberries and omit the lemon juice.

Blackberry Pie: Increase sugar to 1 cup. Substitute fresh blackberries for the blueberries and omit the lemon juice.

Boysenberry Pie: Increase sugar to 1 cup. Substitute fresh boysenberries for the blueberries and omit the lemon juice.

Dotting with Butter

Cut the butter into small pieces; sprinkle over blueberries.

Cherry Pie

PREP TIME: 40 Minutes • **START TO FINISH:** 4 Hours 10 Minutes

8 servings

Pastry for Two-Crust Pie (page 100)

6 cups fresh sour cherries (such as Early Richmond and Montmorency)

1⅓ cups granulated sugar

½ cup all-purpose flour

2 tablespoons cold butter or margarine

1   Make pastry as directed for Two-Crust Pie.

2   Heat the oven to 425°F. Place the cherries in a strainer, and rinse with cool water; dry on paper towels. To remove pits from cherries, push the end of a plastic drinking straw into the stem end of each cherry to push the pit out the other side, or use a cherry pitter.

3   In a large bowl, mix the sugar and flour. Stir in the cherries. Spoon cherry mixture into pastry-lined pie plate. Cut the butter into small pieces; sprinkle over cherries.

4   Cover cherry mixture with top pastry that has slits cut in it; seal (see Making Two-Crust Pie, page 96) and flute (see Fluting Pastry Edges, page 96). Cover edge of pastry with a 2- to 3-inch-wide strip of foil to prevent excessive browning.

5   Bake 30 minutes; remove foil. Bake 5 to 15 minutes longer or until crust is golden brown and juice begins to bubble through slits in crust. Cool on a cooling rack at least 2 hours.

High Altitude (3500–6500 ft): Place cookie sheet on oven rack below pie to catch any drippings. Bake 40 to 50 minutes. Cover edge of crust with foil for first 40 minutes; uncover for last 10 minutes.

1 Serving: Calories 560; Total Fat 24g; Cholesterol 10mg; Sodium 320mg; Total Carbohydrate 80g (Dietary Fiber 3g); Protein 5g **% Daily Value:** Vitamin A 4%; Vitamin C 6%; Calcium 2%; Iron 10% **Carbohydrate Choices:** 5

Quick Cherry Pie: Substitute 6 cups frozen unsweetened pitted red tart cherries, thawed and drained, or 3 cans (14.5 ounces each) pitted red tart cherries, drained, for the fresh cherries.

Removing Pits from Cherries

Push a plastic drinking straw into the stem end to push the pit out the other side.

Pecan Pie

PREP TIME: 20 Minutes • **START TO FINISH:** 3 Hours 55 Minutes

8 servings

Pastry for One-Crust Pie (page 100)

⅓ cup butter or margarine

⅔ cup granulated sugar

1 cup corn syrup

½ teaspoon salt

3 large eggs

1 cup pecan halves or broken pecans

1 Make pastry as directed for One-Crust Pie.

2 Heat the oven to 375°F. In a 1-quart saucepan, heat the butter over low heat until melted. In a medium bowl, beat the butter and remaining ingredients except pecans with a wire whisk until well blended. Stir in the pecans. Pour mixture into pastry-lined pie plate.

3 Cover edge of pastry with a 2- to 3-inch-wide strip of foil to prevent excessive browning.

4 Bake 30 minutes; remove foil. Bake 10 to 20 minutes longer or until the center of the filling is set. Cool on a cooling rack 30 minutes. Cover loosely and store in refrigerator. Store remaining pie covered in refrigerator.

High Altitude (3500–6500 ft): No change.

1 Serving: Calories 530; Total Fat 29g; Cholesterol 100mg; Sodium 400mg; Total Carbohydrate 63g (Dietary Fiber 1g); Protein 5g **% Daily Value:** Vitamin A 8%; Vitamin C 0%; Calcium 2%; Iron 8% **Carbohydrate Choices:** 4

Chocolate-Pecan Pie: Melt 2 ounces unsweetened baking chocolate with the butter.

Kentucky Pecan Pie: Add 2 tablespoons bourbon with the corn syrup, if desired. Stir in 1 cup (6 ounces) semisweet chocolate chips with the pecans.

Do-Ahead Pecan Pie: Cool pie completely after baking. Freeze uncovered at least 3 hours. Wrap tightly and freeze up to 1 month. Before serving, unwrap pie and let stand at room temperature until completely thawed; or unwrap and thaw at room temperature 1 hour, then heat in oven at 375°F for 35 to 40 minutes until warm.

Measuring Corn Syrup

Spray the measuring cup lightly with cooking spray and the corn syrup will slide right out.

Pumpkin Pie

PREP TIME: 20 Minutes • **START TO FINISH:** 2 Hours 50 Minutes

8 servings

Pastry for One-Crust Pie (page 100) or Pat-in-Pan Pastry (page 101)

2 large eggs

½ cup granulated sugar

1 teaspoon ground cinnamon

½ teaspoon salt

½ teaspoon ground ginger

⅛ teaspoon ground cloves

1 can (15 oz) pumpkin (not pumpkin pie mix)*

1 can (12 oz) evaporated milk (not sweetened condensed)

Sweetened Whipped Cream (page 193), if desired

Testing Pie Doneness

Insert a tableware knife in the center of the pie. If it comes out clean and no filling is clinging to the knife, the pie is done.

---

1 Make pastry as directed for One-Crust Pie, or make Pat-in-Pan Pastry.

2 Heat the oven to 425°F. After fluting edge of pastry in pie plate, carefully line pastry with a double thickness of foil, gently pressing foil to bottom and side of pastry. Let foil extend over edge to prevent excessive browning. Bake 10 minutes; carefully remove foil and bake 2 to 4 minutes longer or until pastry just begins to brown and has become set. If crust bubbles, gently push bubbles down with back of spoon.

3 In a medium bowl, beat the eggs slightly with a wire whisk. Beat in remaining ingredients except whipped cream.

4 Cover edge of pie crust with a 2- to 3-inch-wide strip of foil to prevent excessive browning. To keep from spilling the pie filling when placing pie in oven, first pull out oven rack, then place pie plate on rack and pour filling into hot pie crust. Carefully push rack back into oven.

5 Bake 15 minutes. Reduce oven temperature to 350°F. Bake about 45 minutes longer, removing foil after 30 minutes, until a tableware knife inserted in the center comes out clean. Cool on a cooling rack 30 minutes. Cover loosely and store in refrigerator.

6 Make Sweetened Whipped Cream; serve with pie. Store remaining pie covered in refrigerator.

High Altitude (3500–6500 ft): No change.

1 Serving: Calories 300; Total Fat 15g; Cholesterol 65mg; Sodium 360mg; Total Carbohydrate 33g (Dietary Fiber 2g); Protein 7g **% Daily Value:** Vitamin A 170%; Vitamin C 2%; Calcium 15%; Iron 10% **Carbohydrate Choices:** 2

*Be sure to use canned pumpkin, not pumpkin pie mix. The mix has sugar and spices in it, so if you have purchased the pumpkin pie mix, follow the directions on that label. Or if you like, use 1½ cups mashed cooked fresh pumpkin.

Praline Pumpkin Pie: Make pie as directed except decrease second bake time to 35 minutes. Mix ⅓ cup packed brown sugar, ⅓ cup chopped pecans and 1 tablespoon butter or margarine, room temperature. Sprinkle over pie. Bake about 10 minutes longer or until a knife inserted in center comes out clean.

Sweet Potato Pie: Substitute 1 can (17 ounces) vacuum-packed sweet potatoes for the pumpkin. Mash the sweet potatoes with a potato masher.

Fresh Strawberry Pie

PREP TIME: 25 Minutes • **START TO FINISH:** 4 Hours 30 Minutes

8 servings

Pastry for One-Crust Pie (page 100)

1½ quarts (3 pints) fresh strawberries

1 cup granulated sugar

3 tablespoons cornstarch

½ cup water

1 package (3 oz) cream cheese, room temperature

1 Make pastry as directed for Prebaked Pie Crust; bake and cool as directed.

2 Rinse the strawberries with cool water, and dry on paper towels. Cut out the hull, or "cap," of each strawberry with the point of a paring knife. In a small bowl, mash enough of the strawberries with a fork to measure 1 cup. Reserve remaining whole strawberries.

3 In a 2-quart saucepan, mix the sugar and cornstarch. Gradually stir in ½ cup water and mashed strawberries. Cook over medium heat, stirring constantly, until mixture thickens and boils. Boil and stir 1 minute; remove from heat and cool.

4 In a small bowl, beat the cream cheese with a spoon until smooth. Spread cream cheese in the pie crust. Top with remaining whole strawberries. Pour cooked strawberry mixture over the top.

5 Refrigerate about 3 hours or until set. Store remaining pie covered in refrigerator.

High Altitude (3500–6500 ft): No change.

1 Serving: Calories 330; Total Fat 14g; Cholesterol 10mg; Sodium 180mg; Total Carbohydrate 48g (Dietary Fiber 2g); Protein 3g **% Daily Value:** Vitamin A 4%; Vitamin C 110%; Calcium 2%; Iron 8% **Carbohydrate Choices:** 3

Hulling Strawberries

Cut out the hull, or cap, with the point of a paring knife. Insert knife at an angle into the strawberry under the leaves next to the stem. Keeping the knife at an angle, cut around the stem. Remove the stem and leaves.

Classic French Silk Pie

PREP TIME: 30 Minutes • **START TO FINISH:** 3 Hours 30 Minutes

10 servings

Pastry for One-Crust Pie (page 100)

3 oz unsweetened baking chocolate

1 cup granulated sugar

¾ cup butter (1½ sticks), room temperature*

1½ teaspoons vanilla

¾ cup fat-free egg product or 3 pasteurized eggs**

¾ cup whipping cream

2 tablespoons granulated sugar

1 teaspoon vanilla

Baking cocoa, if desired

1   Make pastry as directed for Prebaked Pie Crust; bake and cool as directed.

2   Cut baking chocolate into 6 pieces. In a 1-quart saucepan, heat the chocolate over very low heat until it begins to melt, then remove from heat and stir. Return to heat, stirring constantly, just until chocolate is melted.

3   In a medium bowl, beat 1 cup sugar and the butter with an electric mixer on medium speed until light and fluffy. Beat in 1½ teaspoons vanilla and melted chocolate. On high speed, gradually beat in egg product until light and fluffy (about 3 minutes). Pour mixture into pie crust. Refrigerate until set, at least 2 hours but no longer than 24 hours.

4   About 30 minutes before serving pie, place a medium bowl and the beaters of electric mixer in refrigerator to chill. These will be used to beat the whipping cream, which beats better in a cold bowl.

5   Pour the whipping cream into the chilled bowl, and add 2 tablespoons sugar and 1 teaspoon vanilla. Insert the chilled beaters in the electric mixer. Beat on high speed until whipped cream forms soft peaks when beaters are lifted. Spread whipped cream over pie. Sprinkle with cocoa, using a strainer or shaker. Store remaining pie covered in refrigerator.

*We recommend using only butter because the filling will curdle instead of being smooth and creamy when made with margarine.

**Using a fat-free egg product substitute or pasteurized eggs eliminates the risk of salmonella that can be contracted from raw eggs. Both can be found in the dairy case.

High Altitude (3500–6500 ft): No change.

1 Serving: Calories 450; Total Fat 32g; Cholesterol 55mg; Sodium 260mg; Total Carbohydrate 36g (Dietary Fiber 2g); Protein 5g **% Daily Value:** Vitamin A 15%; Vitamin C 0%; Calcium 4%; Iron 15% **Carbohydrate Choices:** 2½

Mocha French Silk Pie: Beat in 1½ teaspoons instant coffee granules or crystals with the chocolate.

Adding Eggs

Gradually add egg product to chocolate mixture and beat on high speed until light and fluffy.

Banana Cream Pie

PREP TIME: 30 Minutes • **START TO FINISH:** 3 Hours

8 servings

Pastry for One-Crust Pie (page 100) or Pat-in-Pan Pastry (page 101)

4 large eggs

⅔ cup granulated sugar

¼ cup cornstarch

½ teaspoon salt

3 cups milk

2 tablespoons butter or margarine, room temperature

2 teaspoons vanilla

2 firm ripe large bananas

1 cup Sweetened Whipped Cream (page 193)

1 Make pastry as directed for Prebaked Pie Crust; bake and cool as directed. Or make Pat-in-Pan Pastry and bake as directed for Prebaked Pie Crust.

2 Place an egg separator over a small bowl. Crack open each egg over the egg separator to separate the yolks from the whites. (Save egg whites for another recipe.) Place yolks in a medium bowl. Beat the yolks with a fork; set aside.

3 In a 2-quart saucepan, mix ⅔ cup sugar, the cornstarch and salt. Gradually stir in the milk. Cook over medium heat, stirring constantly, until mixture thickens and boils. Boil and stir 1 minute.

4 Immediately stir at least half of the hot mixture gradually into the yolks, then stir the egg mixture back into hot mixture in saucepan. Boil and stir 1 minute; remove from heat. Stir in the butter and 2 teaspoons vanilla. Cool at room temperature 30 minutes.

5 Peel each banana, and slice into pie crust. Pour warm filling over bananas. Press plastic wrap on surface of filling to prevent a tough layer from forming on top. Refrigerate at least 2 hours until set but no longer than 24 hours. Make Sweetened Whipped Cream. Remove plastic wrap from top of pie. Spread whipped cream over top of pie. Store remaining pie covered in refrigerator.

High Altitude (3500–6500 ft): No change.

1 Serving: Calories 410; Total Fat 22g; Cholesterol 135mg; Sodium 360mg; Total Carbohydrate 47g (Dietary Fiber 1g); Protein 7g **% Daily Value:** Vitamin A 10%; Vitamin C 6%; Calcium 15%; Iron 6% **Carbohydrate Choices:** 3

Chocolate Cream Pie: Increase sugar in filling to 1½ cups and cornstarch to ⅓ cup; omit butter and bananas. Stir in 2 ounces unsweetened baking chocolate, cut up, after stirring in milk in step 3.

Chocolate-Banana Cream Pie: Make Chocolate Cream Pie filling. Cool filling slightly. Slice 2 large bananas into pie crust; pour warm filling over bananas. Continue as directed in step 5. Garnish finished pie with banana slices if desired.

Coconut Cream Pie: Omit bananas. Stir in ¾ cup flaked coconut with the butter and vanilla. After topping pie with whipped cream, sprinkle with additional ¼ cup flaked coconut.

Covering Cream Filling

Pour warm filling into pie crust. Press a piece of plastic wrap directly on the filling to prevent a tough layer from forming.

Three-Berry Tart

PREP TIME: 30 Minutes • **START TO FINISH:** 3 Hours

10 servings

Special Equipment: Rolling pin; 9-inch tart pan with removable bottom

CINNAMON CRUST
20 to 24 graham cracker squares

⅓ cup butter or margarine

1 teaspoon ground cinnamon

3 tablespoons granulated sugar

FILLING
1 package (8 oz) cream cheese, room temperature

½ cup granulated sugar

2 tablespoons lemon juice

1 cup whipping cream

½ pint (1 cup) fresh blueberries*

½ pint (1 cup) fresh blackberries

½ pint (1 cup) fresh raspberries

¼ cup strawberry jam

1 tablespoon orange juice

Removing Tart from Pan

Place the pan on a wide, short can and pull down the side of the pan to remove it. If you don't have a can, hold the tart in both hands and push the bottom up and let the side of the pan slip onto your arm.

1 Heat the oven to 350°F. Place half of the cracker squares in a resealable food-storage plastic bag; seal the bag. Roll over crackers with a rolling pin or bottle, or press with bottom of small saucepan, to crush crackers into fine crumbs; place crumbs in a measuring cup. Crush the remaining crackers and add to measuring cup. You should have 1½ cups of crumbs.

2 Place the butter in a small microwavable bowl; cover with a microwavable paper towel. Microwave on High 30 to 50 seconds or until melted.

3 Mix the cracker crumbs, melted butter, cinnamon and 3 tablespoons sugar. Using fingers, press mixture in bottom and up side of an ungreased 9-inch tart pan with removable bottom. Bake 8 to 12 minutes or until golden brown. Cool completely on a cooling rack, about 20 minutes.

4 In a large bowl, beat the cream cheese, ½ cup sugar and the lemon juice with an electric mixer on low speed until blended. Add whipping cream; beat on high speed 3 to 5 minutes or until light and fluffy. Spread mixture in tart shell, using a rubber spatula. Refrigerate at least 2 hours.

5 If necessary, use a thin-bladed knife to loosen the side of the pan from any places where it sticks to the crust. Remove the tart from the side of the pan by placing the pan on a wide, short can and pulling down the side of the pan to remove it.

6 Place the berries in a strainer, and rinse with cool water; dry on paper towels. Arrange the berries on chilled filling. In a small microwavable bowl, microwave the jam uncovered on High about 20 seconds or until warm. Stir in the orange juice with a fork; mix well. Brush strawberry glaze over berries, using a pastry brush.

*Three cups of all blueberries, blackberries or raspberries can be used instead of the three different berries.

High Altitude (3500–6500 ft): Heat oven to 375°F.

1 Serving: Calories 380; Total Fat 23g; Cholesterol 70mg; Sodium 220mg; Total Carbohydrate 39g (Dietary Fiber 2g); Protein 3g **% Daily Value:** Vitamin A 15%; Vitamin C 15%; Calcium 6%; Iron 6% **Carbohydrate Choices:** 2½

Rhubarb Cream Tart

PREP TIME: 30 Minutes • **START TO FINISH:** 3 Hours 30 Minutes

8 servings

Special Equipment: 9 × 3-inch springform pan

CRUST AND TOPPING

About 2 teaspoons butter or margarine, room temperature, to grease pan

1½ cups all-purpose flour

¾ cup packed brown sugar

½ cup cold butter or margarine (1 stick)

FILLING

1 lb fresh rhubarb

⅓ cup hazelnuts (filberts) or pecan halves

2 large eggs

¾ cup granulated sugar

2 tablespoons all-purpose flour

¼ teaspoon salt

½ cup half-and-half

Pressing Crust into Pan

Using fingers or the bottom of measuring cup, press the crumb mixture firmly and evenly on the bottom and side of springform pan.

1   Heat the oven to 350°F. Spread 2 teaspoons butter over the bottom and sides of a 9 × 3-inch springform pan or 9-inch square pan, using a paper towel or piece of waxed paper.

2   In a medium bowl, mix 1½ cups flour and the brown sugar. Cut ½ cup butter into small pieces; add to flour mixture. Cut in butter, using pastry blender or fork, until mixture is crumbly. Reserve ½ cup mixture for topping. Using fingers or the bottom of a measuring cup, press remaining mixture firmly and evenly on the bottom and 1¼ inches up the side of the springform pan or bottom only of square pan. Bake 10 to 13 minutes or until light golden brown and set.

3   Remove the leaves from the rhubarb and discard them. Wash the rhubarb stalks. Cut enough of the stalks into ¼-inch slices to measure 2 cups. Finely chop the nuts to measure ¼ cup.

4   In a small bowl, beat the eggs with an electric mixer on high speed about 1 minute or until lemon colored. Beat in the granulated sugar, 2 tablespoons flour, the salt and half-and-half until well blended.

5   Sprinkle the rhubarb over warm crust. Pour egg mixture over rhubarb. Add hazelnuts to reserved crumbly mixture; sprinkle over top.

6   Bake 40 to 45 minutes or until set and a knife inserted in the center comes out clean. Cool at least 2 hours on a cooling rack before serving.

7   Before releasing and removing the side of the pan, carefully run a metal spatula between the tart and inside of the pan. Release and remove side of pan, leaving tart on pan bottom for serving. Store tart covered in refrigerator.

High Altitude (3500–6500 ft): No change.

1 Serving: Calories 420; Total Fat 18g; Cholesterol 90mg; Sodium 190mg; Total Carbohydrate 60g (Dietary Fiber 1g); Protein 6g **% Daily Value:** Vitamin A 10%; Vitamin C 0%; Calcium 10%; Iron 10% **Carbohydrate Choices:** 4

4 QUICK BREADS

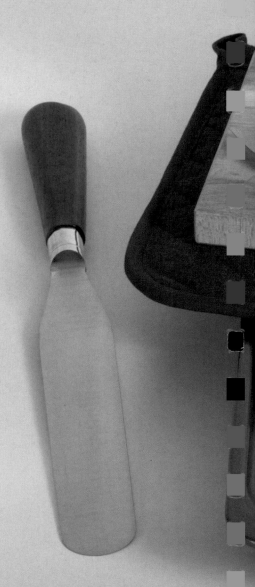

QUICK BREADS 101

Quick breads are quicker and easier to make than yeast breads because they are leavened with baking powder or baking soda rather than yeast and don't require kneading or rising. Be sure your baking powder and baking soda are fresh by checking the container for the expiration date.

Types of Quick Breads

Here are some common types of quick breads:

Loaves: quick breads baked in a loaf pan, usually with fruit, nuts or vegetables mixed in. The ideal loaf has a golden brown rounded top with a lengthwise crack. The crust should be thin and tender. The interior should be moist with small, even holes, with fruit and/or nuts evenly distributed throughout.

Coffee Cakes: quick bread batter that is baked in a round, square, rectangular or tube pan. They are most often sweet and contain fruit, nuts or spices. Some coffee cakes have a streusel topping to add flavor and texture.

Muffins: individual cake-like quick breads baked in muffin pans, often with fruits and nuts mixed in. Making muffins takes a gentle hand. Stir the batter just enough to moisten the flour; batter will have some small lumps. The ideal muffin has a golden brown, slightly rounded bumpy top and tender crumb. The interior should be moist and even-textured.

Baking Powder Biscuits: individual-size quick breads where the dough is rolled and cut into circles or dropped from a spoon and baked. The secret to flaky, tender biscuits is to thoroughly blend the shortening and dry ingredients and handle the dough correctly. The ideal biscuit is light golden brown, with a high, smooth level top, a tender texture and a flaky, slightly moist interior.

A Perfect Slice

Cool loaves completely, about two hours, before slicing so they don't crumble. For easiest slicing, store loaves tightly covered for 24 hours before cutting. Cut with a serrated or sharp, thin-bladed knife, using a light sawing motion.

Quick Bread Pans

The type of pan you use for baking quick breads is important.

For golden brown, tender breads, use shiny pans and cookie sheets because they reflect the heat.

When making muffins and loaves, usually only the bottoms of the pans are greased so that the batter doesn't form a lip (overhanging or hard, dry edges) during baking.

Dark or dark nonstick pans absorb more heat so baked goods may brown more quickly. Manufacturers may suggest reducing the oven temperature by 25°F, and some recommend not greasing or using cooking spray. If you're using insulated pans, you may need to increase the baking time slightly.

MIXING QUICK BREADS

Chop or shred fruits, vegetables or nuts before you start making the batter. If you mix the batter and then stop to chop, the leavening will start working and the batter may get too stiff. Mix quick breads by hand using a spoon because it's easy to overmix the batter with an electric mixer. Mix according to each recipe's directions because if mixed too much, quick breads become tough and heavy with long holes or tunnels. Most batters are mixed until the ingredients are just moistened and will be lumpy.

Make Baking Powder Biscuits

Cut shortening into flour mixture until the mixture looks like fine crumbs.

Stir in milk until dough leaves sides of bowl (dough will be soft and sticky).

Roll or pat the dough on a lightly floured surface into a ½-inch-thick round.

What Went Wrong?

Loaf

This Happened	This Is Why
Didn't rise	• too much mixing • check expiration date on leavening
Tough	• too much mixing • not enough fat
Tunnels	• too much mixing
Rims around the edges	• sides of pan were greased
Compact	• too much flour • too little leavening

Muffins

This Happened	This Is Why
Pale	• oven too cool
Peaked with smooth tops	• too much mixing
Tough and heavy	• too much flour • too much mixing
Long holes or tunnels	• too much mixing
Dry	• too much flour • baked too long
Sticks to pan	• pan not properly greased
Dark crust but center not done	• oven too hot

Baking Powder Biscuits

This Happened	This Is Why
Didn't rise	• too little baking powder • too much mixing • oven too hot
Dark bottom crust	• oven rack placed too low in oven • oven too hot
Tough texture	• too little shortening • too much mixing or handling • too much flour
Not flaky	• too little shortening • too much mixing • not kneaded enough

Banana Bread

PREP TIME: 15 Minutes • **START TO FINISH:** 3 Hours 25 Minutes

2 loaves (24 slices each)

Cooking spray to grease pans

3 very ripe medium bananas

1¼ cups granulated sugar

**½ cup butter or margarine
    (1 stick), room temperature**

2 large eggs

½ cup buttermilk

1 teaspoon vanilla

2½ cups all-purpose flour

1 teaspoon baking soda

1 teaspoon salt

1 cup chopped nuts, if desired

1   Move the oven rack to a low position so that the tops of the pans will be in the center of the oven. Heat the oven to 350°F. Spray just the bottoms of two 8 × 4-inch loaf pans with the cooking spray.

2   Peel the bananas and place in a medium bowl. Mash with a potato masher or fork to measure 1½ cups.

3   In a large bowl, stir the sugar and butter until well mixed. Stir in the eggs until well mixed. Stir in the mashed bananas, buttermilk and vanilla; beat with spoon until smooth. Stir in the flour, baking soda and salt just until moistened. Stir in the nuts. Divide batter evenly between the pans; use a rubber spatula to scrape batter from bowl. Spread batter evenly in pans and smooth top of batter. (If batter is not divided evenly, spoon batter from one pan to the other.)

4   Bake about 1 hour or until a toothpick inserted in the center comes out clean. Cool 10 minutes in pans on a cooling rack.

5   Loosen the sides of the bread from each pan, using a metal spatula or table knife. Carefully tip each pan on its side on a cooling rack, then tap gently to remove bread from pan. Place the bread, top side up, on the cooling rack. Cool completely, about 2 hours, before slicing; cut with a serrated knife. Wrap tightly and store at room temperature up to 4 days, or refrigerate up to 10 days.

High Altitude (3500–6500 ft): Bake 8-inch loaves about 1 hour 5 minutes, 9-inch loaf about 1 hour 20 minutes.

1 Slice: Calories 70; Total Fat 2.5g; Cholesterol 15mg; Sodium 95mg; Total Carbohydrate 12g (Dietary Fiber 0g); Protein 1g **% Daily Value:** Vitamin A 0%; Vitamin C 0%; Calcium 0%; Iron 0% **Carbohydrate Choices:** 1

Blueberry-Banana Bread: Omit nuts. Stir 1 cup fresh or frozen (not thawed) blueberries into the batter.

Selecting Ripe Bananas

Banana skin should be turning brown with black spots, and the banana should be very soft to the touch.

Pumpkin Bread

PREP TIME: 15 Minutes • **START TO FINISH:** 3 Hours 15 Minutes

2 loaves (24 slices each)

Cooking spray to grease pans

1 can (15 oz) pumpkin (not pumpkin pie mix)

1⅔ cups granulated sugar

⅔ cup vegetable oil

2 teaspoons vanilla

4 large eggs

3 cups all-purpose or whole wheat flour

2 teaspoons baking soda

1 teaspoon salt

1 teaspoon ground cinnamon

½ teaspoon ground cloves

½ teaspoon baking powder

½ cup coarsely chopped nuts

½ cup raisins, if desired

1 Move the oven rack to a low position so that the tops of the pans will be in the center of the oven. Heat the oven to 350°F. Spray just the bottoms of two 8 × 4-inch loaf pans with the cooking spray.

2 In a large bowl, stir the pumpkin, sugar, oil, vanilla and eggs with a wooden spoon until well mixed. Stir in remaining ingredients except nuts and raisins. Stir in the nuts and raisins. Divide batter evenly between the pans; use a rubber spatula to scrape batter from bowl. Spread batter evenly in pan and smooth top of batter. (If batter is not divided evenly, spoon batter from one pan to the other.)

3 Bake 50 to 60 minutes or until a toothpick inserted in the center comes out clean. Cool 10 minutes in pans on a cooling rack.

4 Loosen the sides of the bread from each pan, using a metal spatula or table knife. Carefully tip each pan on its side on a cooling rack, then tap gently to remove bread from pan. Place the bread, top side up, on the cooling rack. Cool completely, about 2 hours, before slicing; cut with a serrated knife. Wrap tightly and store at room temperature up to 4 days, or refrigerate up to 10 days.

High Altitude (3500–6500 ft): Heat oven to 375°F.

1 Slice: Calories 100; Total Fat 4.5g; Cholesterol 20mg; Sodium 115mg; Total Carbohydrate 14g (Dietary Fiber 0g); Protein 2g **% Daily Value:** Vitamin A 30%; Vitamin C 0%; Calcium 0%; Iron 4% **Carbohydrate Choices:** 1

Zucchini Bread: Use 3 cups shredded unpeeled zucchini (2 to 3 medium) for the pumpkin.

Oven Rack Position

Move the oven rack to a low position so the top of a loaf pan is in the center of the oven.

Cranberry Bread

PREP TIME: 15 Minutes • **START TO FINISH:** 3 Hours 15 Minutes
2 loaves (24 slices each)

Cooking spray to grease pans

3 cups fresh or frozen (thawed) cranberries

1⅔ cups granulated sugar

⅔ cup vegetable oil

½ cup milk

2 teaspoons grated orange or lemon peel

2 teaspoons vanilla

4 large eggs

3 cups all-purpose or whole wheat flour

2 teaspoons baking soda

1 teaspoon salt

½ teaspoon baking powder

½ cup coarsely chopped nuts

1 Move the oven rack to a low position so that the tops of the pans will be in the center of the oven. Heat the oven to 350°F. Spray just the bottoms of two 8 × 4-inch loaf pans with the cooking spray.

2 In a large bowl, stir the cranberries, sugar, oil, milk, orange peel, vanilla and eggs with a wooden spoon until well mixed. Stir in remaining ingredients. Divide batter evenly between the pans; use a rubber spatula to scrape batter from bowl. Spread batter evenly in pan and smooth top of batter. (If batter is not divided evenly, spoon batter from one pan to the other.)

3 Bake 1 hour to 1 hour 5 minutes or until a toothpick inserted in the center comes out clean. Cool 10 minutes in pans on a cooling rack.

4 Loosen the sides of the bread from each pan, using a metal spatula or table knife. Carefully tip each pan on its side on a cooling rack, then tap gently to remove bread from pan. Place the bread, top side up, on the cooling rack. Cool completely, about 2 hours, before slicing; cut with a serrated knife. Wrap tightly and store at room temperature up to 4 days, or refrigerate up to 10 days.

High Altitude (3500–6500 ft): Heat oven to 375°F. Decrease sugar to 1⅓ cups and vegetable oil to ⅓ cup. Increase milk to 1 cup. Bake about 50 minutes.

1 Slice: Calories 100; Total Fat 4.5g; Cholesterol 20mg; Sodium 115mg; Total Carbohydrate 14g (Dietary Fiber 0g); Protein 2g **% Daily Value:** Vitamin A 0%; Vitamin C 0%; Calcium 0%; Iron 2% **Carbohydrate Choices:** 1

Removing Bread from Pan

Tip the pan on its side on a cooling rack and gently tap the pan to remove the bread.

Cornbread

PREP TIME: 10 Minutes • **START TO FINISH:** 35 Minutes

12 servings

Cooking spray to grease pan

¼ cup butter or margarine (½ stick)

1 cup milk

1 large egg

1¼ cups yellow, white or blue cornmeal

1 cup all-purpose flour

½ cup granulated sugar

1 tablespoon baking powder

½ teaspoon salt

1 Heat the oven to 400°F. Spray the bottom and sides of an 8-inch square pan or 9-inch round cake pan with the cooking spray.

2 In a 1-quart saucepan, heat the butter over low heat until melted.

3 In a large bowl, beat the melted butter, milk and egg with a fork or wire whisk until well mixed. Add the cornmeal, flour, sugar, baking powder and salt all at once; stir just until the flour is moistened (batter will be lumpy). Pour batter into the pan; use a rubber spatula to scrape batter from bowl. Spread batter evenly in pan and smooth top of batter.

4 Bake 20 to 25 minutes or until golden brown and a toothpick inserted in the center comes out clean. Serve warm.

High Altitude (3500–6500 ft): Heat oven to 425°F. Decrease sugar to ¼ cup and baking powder to 2 teaspoons.

1 Serving: Calories 180; Total Fat 5g; Cholesterol 30mg; Sodium 260mg; Total Carbohydrate 29g (Dietary Fiber 0g); Protein 4g **% Daily Value:** Vitamin A 4%; Vitamin C 0%; Calcium 10%; Iron 8% **Carbohydrate Choices:** 2

Corn Muffins: Place a paper baking cup in each of 12 regular-size muffin cups, or spray just the bottoms of the cups with cooking spray. Fill each cup about ¾ full with batter. Bake as directed in step 4. Remove muffins from the pan to a cooling rack.

Cornbread Doneness Test

A toothpick inserted in the center will have uncooked batter clinging to it if the cornbread is not fully baked.

Irish Soda Bread

PREP TIME: 10 Minutes • **START TO FINISH:** 1 Hour 25 Minutes

1 loaf (8 slices)

Cooking spray to grease cookie sheet

2½ cups all-purpose flour

2 tablespoons granulated sugar

1 teaspoon baking soda

1 teaspoon baking powder

½ teaspoon salt

3 tablespoons butter or margarine, room temperature

⅓ cup raisins

About 1 cup buttermilk

1 tablespoon butter or margarine, room temperature

1   Heat the oven to 375°F. Spray a cookie sheet with the cooking spray.

2   In a large bowl, mix the flour, sugar, baking soda, baking powder and salt. Cut in 3 tablespoons butter, using a pastry blender or fork, until mixture looks like fine crumbs. Stir in raisins and just enough buttermilk until mixture forms a soft dough and leaves the side of the bowl.

3   Lightly sprinkle flour over a cutting board or countertop. Place dough on floured surface; gently roll in the flour to coat. To knead dough, fold dough toward you. With the heels of your hands, push dough away from you with a short rocking motion. Move dough a quarter turn and repeat for 1 to 2 minutes. Dough will feel springy and smooth.

4   Shape dough into a round loaf, about 6½ inches in diameter. Place on the cookie sheet. Using a serrated knife, cut an X shape about ½ inch deep on top of the loaf.

5   Bake 35 to 45 minutes or until golden brown. Remove loaf from cookie sheet to a cooling rack. Brush 1 tablespoon butter over loaf, using a pastry brush. Cool completely, about 30 minutes, before slicing; cut with a serrated knife.

High Altitude (3500–6500 ft): No change.

1 Slice: Calories 240; Total Fat 7g; Cholesterol 15mg; Sodium 440mg; Total Carbohydrate 39g (Dietary Fiber 1g); Protein 5g **% Daily Value:** Vitamin A 4%; Vitamin C 0%; Calcium 8%; Iron 10% **Carbohydrate Choices:** 2½

Cutting X on Loaf

Cut an X-shape on top of the loaf, about ½ inch deep, using a serrated knife.

Cherry Swirl Coffee Cake

PREP TIME: 20 Minutes • **START TO FINISH:** 1 Hour 5 Minutes

30 bars or 18 squares

COFFEE CAKE

Cooking spray to grease pan

1½ cups granulated sugar

1 cup butter or margarine (2 sticks), room temperature

1½ teaspoons baking powder

1 teaspoon vanilla

1 teaspoon almond extract

4 large eggs

3 cups all-purpose flour

1 can (21 oz) cherry pie filling

GLAZE

1 cup powdered sugar

1 to 2 tablespoons milk

1 Heat the oven to 350°F. Generously spray the bottom and sides of one 15 × 10 × 1-inch pan or two 9-inch square pans with the cooking spray.

2 In a large bowl, beat the granulated sugar, butter, baking powder, vanilla, almond extract and eggs with an electric mixer on low speed 30 seconds, stopping frequently to scrape batter from side and bottom of bowl with a rubber spatula. Beat on high speed 3 minutes, stopping occasionally to scrape bowl. Stir in the flour (batter will be thick).

3 Spread ⅔ of the batter in the 15-inch pan, or spread ⅓ of the batter in each square pan; use a rubber spatula to scrape batter from bowl. Spread batter evenly in pan and smooth top of batter. Spread the pie filling over the batter (filling may not cover the batter completely). Using a tableware tablespoon, drop the remaining batter in mounds about 2 inches apart on the pie filling.

4 Bake about 45 minutes or until a toothpick inserted near the center comes out clean.

5 Meanwhile, in a small bowl, mix the glaze ingredients with a spoon until mixture is smooth and thin enough to drizzle. Over the warm coffee cake, drizzle glaze from the tip of a tableware teaspoon, moving the spoon back and forth to make thin lines of glaze. For bars, cut cake in 15-inch pan into 6 rows by 5 rows; or for squares, cut cake in each square pan into 3 rows by 3 rows.

High Altitude (3500–6500 ft): Heat oven to 375°F. Decrease granulated sugar to 1¼ cups. Bake about 40 minutes.

1 Bar: Calories 190; Total Fat 7g; Cholesterol 45mg; Sodium 75mg; Total Carbohydrate 29g (Dietary Fiber 0g); Protein 2g **% Daily Value:** Vitamin A 4%; Vitamin C 0%; Calcium 2%; Iron 4% **Carbohydrate Choices:** 2

Apricot Swirl Coffee Cake: Use 1 can (21 oz) apricot pie filling for the cherry pie filling.

Blueberry Swirl Coffee Cake: Use 1 can (21 oz) blueberry pie filling for the cherry pie filling.

Dropping Batter on Coffee Cake

Drop the remaining batter from a tableware tablespoon in mounds about two inches apart on the pie filling.

Fresh Raspberry Coffee Cake

PREP TIME: 20 Minutes • **START TO FINISH:** 1 Hour 10 Minutes

9 servings

COFFEE CAKE
Baking spray with flour to grease pan

½ cup butter or margarine (1 stick)

¾ cup milk

1 teaspoon vanilla

1 large egg

2 cups all-purpose flour

½ cup granulated sugar

2 teaspoons baking powder

½ teaspoon salt

1 cup fresh raspberries

GLAZE
½ cup powdered sugar

1 tablespoon butter or margarine, room temperature

2 to 3 teaspoons water

¼ teaspoon almond extract

1 Heat the oven to 400°F. Spray a 9-inch or 8-inch square pan with the baking spray.

2 In a 1-quart saucepan, heat the butter over low heat until melted.

3 In a medium bowl, beat melted butter, the milk, vanilla and egg with a spoon until well mixed. Stir in the flour, granulated sugar, baking powder and salt just until the flour is moistened. Gently stir in the raspberries. Pour batter in the pan; use a rubber spatula to scrape batter from bowl. Spread batter evenly in pan and smooth top of batter.

4 Bake 25 to 30 minutes or until the top is golden brown and a toothpick inserted in the center comes out clean. Cool 20 minutes on a cooling rack.

5 Meanwhile, in a small bowl, mix the glaze ingredients with a spoon until mixture is smooth and thin enough to drizzle. Over the warm coffee cake, drizzle glaze from the tip of a tableware teaspoon, moving the spoon back and forth to make thin lines of glaze.

High Altitude (3500–6500 ft): Do not use 8-inch pan.

1 Serving: Calories 300; Total Fat 13g; Cholesterol 55mg; Sodium 340mg; Total Carbohydrate 42g (Dietary Fiber 1g); Protein 5g **% Daily Value:** Vitamin A 8%; Vitamin C 4%; Calcium 10%; Iron 8% **Carbohydrate Choices:** 3

Fresh Blackberry Coffee Cake: Use 1 cup fresh blackberries for the raspberries.

Fresh Blueberry Coffee Cake: Use 1 cup fresh blueberries for the raspberries.

Drizzling Glaze on Coffee Cake

Drizzle the glaze from the tip of a tableware teaspoon by moving the spoon back and forth to make lines of glaze.

Sour Cream Coffee Cake

PREP TIME: 30 Minutes • **START TO FINISH:** 2 Hours
16 servings

Cooking spray to grease pan

BROWN SUGAR FILLING
½ cup packed brown sugar
½ cup finely chopped nuts
1½ teaspoons ground cinnamon

COFFEE CAKE
3 cups all-purpose or whole
   wheat flour
1½ teaspoons baking powder
1½ teaspoons baking soda
¾ teaspoon salt
1½ cups granulated sugar
¾ cup butter or margarine
   (1½ sticks), room temperature
1½ teaspoons vanilla
3 large eggs
1½ cups sour cream

GLAZE
½ cup powdered sugar
¼ teaspoon vanilla
2 to 3 teaspoons milk

1 Heat the oven to 350°F. Spray the bottom and sides of a 10 × 4-inch angel food (tube) cake pan, 12-cup fluted tube cake pan or two 9 × 5-inch loaf pans with the cooking spray.

2 In a small bowl, stir the filling ingredients until well mixed; set aside. In a large bowl, stir the flour, baking powder, baking soda and salt until well mixed; set aside.

3 In another large bowl, beat the granulated sugar, butter, 1½ teaspoons vanilla and eggs with an electric mixer on medium speed 2 minutes, stopping occasionally to scrape batter from side and bottom of bowl with a rubber spatula. On low speed, beat in ½ of the flour mixture just until mixed, then beat in ½ of the sour cream until mixed. Repeat beating in flour mixture alternately with the sour cream until mixed.

4 For angel food or fluted tube cake pan, spread ⅓ of the batter (about 2 cups) in pan, then sprinkle with ⅓ of the filling; repeat twice. For loaf pans, spread ¼ of the batter (about 1½ cups) in each pan, then sprinkle each with ¼ of the filling; repeat once.

5 Bake angel food or fluted tube cake pan about 1 hour, loaf pans about 45 minutes, or until a toothpick inserted halfway between side and center of pan comes out clean.

6 Cool 10 minutes in pan(s) on a cooling rack. To remove cake from a tube pan, place a cooling rack upside down on pan; holding rack and pan with pot holders, turn rack and pan over together, then remove pan. To remove cakes from loaf pans, loosen the sides of bread from each pan, using a knife. Carefully tip each pan on its side on a cooling rack, then tap gently to remove bread from pan. Place the bread, top side up, on the cooling rack. Cool cake(s) 20 minutes.

7 Meanwhile, in a small bowl, mix the glaze ingredients with a spoon until mixture is smooth and thin enough to drizzle. Over the coffee cake, drizzle glaze from the tip of a tableware teaspoon, moving the spoon back forth to make thin lines of glaze. Serve coffee cake warm or cooled.

High Altitude (3500–6500 ft): Decrease baking powder and baking soda to ¾ teaspoon each, butter to ½ cup and sour cream to 1¼ cups.

1 Serving: Calories 360; Total Fat 17g; Cholesterol 75mg; Sodium 360mg; Total Carbohydrate 49g (Dietary Fiber 1g); Protein 5g **% Daily Value:** Vitamin A 10%; Vitamin C 0%; Calcium 6%; Iron 8% **Carbohydrate Choices:** 3

Layering Coffee Cake

Spread 2 cups batter in the pan and sprinkle with ⅓ of the filling. Repeat with remaining batter and filling.

Almond–Poppy Seed Muffins

PREP TIME: 15 Minutes • **START TO FINISH:** 35 Minutes

12 muffins

MUFFINS

12 paper baking cups or cooking spray to grease pan

½ **cup granulated sugar**

⅓ **cup vegetable oil**

1 large egg

½ **teaspoon almond extract**

½ **cup sour cream**

¼ **cup milk**

1⅓ **cups all-purpose flour**

½ **teaspoon baking powder**

½ **teaspoon salt**

¼ **teaspoon baking soda**

2 tablespoons poppy seed

TOPPING

3 teaspoons granulated sugar

2 tablespoons sliced almonds

1 Heat the oven to 375°F. Place a paper baking cup in each of 12 regular-size muffin cups, or spray the cups with cooking spray.

2 In a large bowl, stir ½ cup sugar, the oil, egg and almond extract until blended. Beat in the sour cream and milk with a spoon until mixed. Stir in the flour, baking powder, salt, baking soda and poppy seed just until flour is moistened (batter will be lumpy). Spoon the batter into the cups, dividing batter evenly.

3 Sprinkle 3 teaspoons sugar and the almonds over batter in cups.

4 Bake 14 to 17 minutes or until a toothpick inserted in the center comes out clean. If muffins were baked in paper baking cups, immediately remove from pan to a cooling rack. If muffins were baked in a sprayed pan, leave in pan for about 5 minutes, then remove from pan to a cooling rack. Serve warm or cooled.

High Altitude (3500–6500 ft): Bake 16 to 19 minutes.

1 Muffin: Calories 180; Total Fat 10g; Cholesterol 25mg; Sodium 160mg; Total Carbohydrate 21g (Dietary Fiber 0g); Protein 3g **% Daily Value:** Vitamin A 0%; Vitamin C 0%; Calcium 6%; Iron 6% **Carbohydrate Choices:** 1½

Removing Muffins from Pan

Run a knife blade between the muffin and pan. Carefully flip the muffin up and place on the cooling rack.

Bran Muffins

PREP TIME: 15 Minutes • **START TO FINISH:** 50 Minutes

12 muffins

12 paper baking cups or cooking spray to grease pan

1¼ cups Fiber One® cereal or 2 cups bran cereal flakes

1⅓ cups milk

½ cup raisins, if desired

½ teaspoon vanilla

¼ cup vegetable oil

1 large egg

1¼ cups all-purpose flour

½ cup packed brown sugar

3 teaspoons baking powder

¼ teaspoon salt

¼ teaspoon ground cinnamon, if desired

1   Heat the oven to 400°F. Place a paper baking cup in each of 12 regular-size muffin cups, or spray just the bottoms of the cups with cooking spray.

2   Place cereal in a resealable food-storage plastic bag; seal the bag. Roll over cereal with a rolling pin or bottle, or press with bottom of small saucepan, to crush cereal into fine crumbs.

3   In a medium bowl, stir the crushed cereal, milk, raisins and vanilla until well mixed. Let stand about 5 minutes or until cereal has softened. Beat in the oil and egg with a fork.

4   In another medium bowl, stir the flour, brown sugar, baking powder, salt and cinnamon until well mixed. Stir flour mixture into cereal mixture just until flour is moistened (batter will be lumpy). Spoon the batter into the cups, dividing batter evenly.

5   Bake 20 to 25 minutes or until a toothpick inserted in the center comes out clean. If muffins were baked in paper baking cups, immediately remove from pan to a cooling rack. If muffins were baked in a sprayed pan, leave in pan about 5 minutes, then remove from pan to a cooling rack. Serve warm if desired.

High Altitude (3500–6500 ft): Decrease baking powder to 2 teaspoons. Bake 23 to 28 minutes.

1 Muffin: Calories 170; Total Fat 6g; Cholesterol 20mg; Sodium 210mg; Total Carbohydrate 26g (Dietary Fiber 3g); Protein 3g **% Daily Value:** Vitamin A 4%; Vitamin C 0%; Calcium 15%; Iron 10% **Carbohydrate Choices:** 2

Date-Bran Muffins: Stir in 1 cup chopped dates with the flour mixture in step 4.

Softening Cereal

Let the crushed cereal mixture stand about five minutes or until the cereal is softened and most of the milk is absorbed.

Streusel-Topped Blueberry Muffins

PREP TIME: 20 Minutes • **START TO FINISH:** 50 Minutes

12 muffins

12 paper baking cups or cooking spray to grease pan

STREUSEL TOPPING
¼ cup all-purpose flour
¼ cup packed brown sugar
¼ teaspoon ground cinnamon
2 tablespoons cold butter or margarine

MUFFINS
¾ cup milk
¼ cup vegetable oil
1 large egg
2 cups all-purpose flour
½ cup granulated sugar
2 teaspoons baking powder
½ teaspoon salt
1 cup fresh, canned (drained) or frozen blueberries

1 Heat the oven to 400°F. Place a paper baking cup in each of 12 regular-size muffin cups, or spray just the bottoms of the cups with the cooking spray.

2 In a medium bowl, stir ¼ cup flour, the brown sugar and cinnamon until mixed. Cut in the butter, using a pastry blender or fork, until mixture is crumbly; set aside.

3 In a large bowl, beat the milk, oil and egg with a fork or wire whisk until blended. Add 2 cups flour, the granulated sugar, baking powder and salt all at once; stir just until flour is moistened (batter will be lumpy). Gently stir in the blueberries. Spoon the batter into the cups, dividing batter evenly. Sprinkle each with about 1 tablespoon streusel.

4 Bake 20 to 25 minutes or until golden brown. If muffins were baked in paper baking cups, immediately remove from pan to a cooling rack. If muffins were baked in a sprayed pan, leave in pan about 5 minutes, then remove from pan to a cooling rack. Serve warm or cooled.

Making Blueberry Muffins

Carefully stir blueberries into the batter to help prevent them from breaking and turning the batter blue.

Using a spring-handled ice cream scoop is an easy way to fill muffin cups.

High Altitude (3500–6500 ft): Decrease baking powder to 1½ teaspoons.

1 Muffin: Calories 220; Total Fat 7g; Cholesterol 25mg; Sodium 210mg; Total Carbohydrate 33g (Dietary Fiber 1g); Protein 4g **% Daily Value:** Vitamin A 2%; Vitamin C 0%; Calcium 8%; Iron 8% **Carbohydrate Choices:** 2

Scones

PREP TIME: 15 Minutes • **START TO FINISH:** 35 Minutes

8 scones

1¾ cups all-purpose flour

3 tablespoons granulated sugar

2½ teaspoons baking powder

½ teaspoon salt

⅓ cup cold butter or margarine

1 large egg

½ teaspoon vanilla

4 to 6 tablespoons whipping cream

Additional 1 tablespoon whipping cream

2 teaspoons white decorator sugar crystals or granulated sugar

1 Heat the oven to 400°F. In a large bowl, stir the flour, 3 tablespoons sugar, the baking powder and salt until mixed. Cut in the butter, using a pastry blender or fork, until mixture looks like fine crumbs.

2 In a small bowl, beat the egg with a fork until yolk and white are mixed. Using the fork, stir the egg, vanilla and just enough of the 4 to 6 tablespoons whipping cream into the flour mixture until mixture forms a soft dough and leaves the side of the bowl.

3 Lightly sprinkle flour over a cutting board or countertop. Place dough on floured surface; gently roll in the flour to coat. To knead dough, fold dough toward you. With the heels of your hands, lightly push dough away from you with a short rocking motion. Move dough a quarter turn and repeat 10 times. Dough will feel springy and smooth.

4 Place the dough on an ungreased cookie sheet. Roll dough with a rolling pin or pat dough with fingers into an 8-inch round. Using a sharp knife that has been dipped in flour, cut dough round into 8 wedges, but do not separate the wedges. Brush 1 tablespoon whipping cream over wedges, using a pastry brush. Sprinkle with sugar crystals.

5 Bake 14 to 16 minutes or until light golden brown. Immediately remove from cookie sheet to a cooling rack; carefully separate wedges. Serve warm.

High Altitude (3500–6500 ft): Decrease baking powder to 1½ teaspoons.

1 Scone: Calories 230; Total Fat 11g; Cholesterol 55mg; Sodium 370mg; Total Carbohydrate 27g (Dietary Fiber 0g); Protein 4g **% Daily Value:** Vitamin A 8%; Vitamin C 0%; Calcium 10%; Iron 8% **Carbohydrate Choices:** 2

Chocolate Chip Scones: Stir in ½ cup miniature semisweet chocolate chips with the egg, vanilla and whipping cream in step 2.

Currant Scones: Stir in ½ cup currants or raisins with the egg, vanilla and whipping cream in step 2.

Cutting Scones

Use a sharp knife that has been dipped in flour to cut the dough into wedges. Do not separate the wedges before baking.

Baking Powder Biscuits

PREP TIME: 10 Minutes • **START TO FINISH:** 25 Minutes

12 biscuits

2 cups all-purpose flour

1 tablespoon granulated sugar

3 teaspoons baking powder

1 teaspoon salt

½ cup shortening, butter or margarine

¾ cup milk

Drop Baking Powder Biscuits:
Spray the cookie sheet with cooking spray. Increase milk to 1 cup. Drop dough by 12 spoonfuls, about 2 inches apart, onto the cookie sheet.

1 Heat the oven to 450°F. In a medium bowl, stir the flour, sugar, baking powder and salt until mixed. Cut in the shortening, using a pastry blender or fork, until mixture looks like fine crumbs. Stir in the milk until mixture forms a soft dough and leaves the side of the bowl (dough will be soft and sticky).

2 Lightly sprinkle flour over a cutting board or countertop. Place dough on floured surface; gently roll in the flour to coat. To knead dough, fold dough toward you. With the heels of your hands, lightly push dough away from you with a short rocking motion. Move dough a quarter turn and repeat 10 times. Dough will feel springy and smooth.

3 On the floured surface, flatten dough evenly, using hands or a rolling pin, until dough is ½ inch thick.

4 Before cutting each biscuit, dip a 2½-inch round cutter into flour to lightly coat it so it will cut cleanly through the dough without sticking. To cut, push the cutter straight down through the dough without twisting or turning. Cut the biscuits as close together as possible. On an ungreased cookie sheet, place biscuits about 1 inch apart for biscuits with crusty sides, or place with sides touching for biscuits with soft sides.

5 Bake 10 to 12 minutes or until golden brown. Immediately remove from cookie sheet. Serve warm.

High Altitude (3500–6500 ft): No change.

1 Biscuit: Calories 160; Total Fat 9g; Cholesterol 0mg; Sodium 330mg; Total Carbohydrate 18g (Dietary Fiber 1g); Protein 3g **% Daily Value:** Vitamin A 0%; Vitamin C 0%; Calcium 8%; Iron 6%
Carbohydrate Choices: 1

Cutting Baking Powder Biscuits

To cut biscuits, push a round cutter dipped in flour straight down in the dough. Remove excess dough around biscuits. Using a turner, move each biscuit to a cookie sheet.

To cut remaining biscuits, gather the excess dough together and gently flatten dough until ½ inch thick. Use as little additional flour on the surface as possible to prevent tough, dry biscuits.

5 YEAST BREADS

YEAST BREADS 101

Making yeast bread isn't difficult; it just takes time. The irresistible aroma and fresh-baked results are well worth the wait! Making and shaping yeast dough does take a little practice, but even those slightly misshapen loaves of bread taste delectable.

Types of Yeast Breads

Yeast breads fall into two main categories: batter breads and kneaded breads.

BATTER BREADS are quick to prepare because they do not require kneading. The texture after baking is coarser than that of a kneaded bread, but it still has that great yeasty flavor. A batter bread may be a good way to start learning to make yeast breads because you just pour the batter into a greased pan and don't have to shape the loaf.

KNEADED BREADS require hands-on work, which can be very relaxing and enjoyable after you learn the knack of kneading. Bread dough can also be kneaded using an electric mixer and a dough hook, but you may want to try it by hand first because it can be very satisfying.

Kneaded breads get their fine texture and structure from developing the gluten during kneading. Gluten is a protein in flour that stretches as the dough rises after being developed during kneading and gives strength to the dough.

Yeast Bread Pans

Dull-finish loaf pans, including dull aluminum, tin and glass, absorb more heat, so yeast bread loaves brown more quickly and evenly and have a crisper crust.

Insulated pans and cookie sheets will not result in well-browned crusts. Cookie sheets without a rim or sides allow better heat circulation, so the breads baked on them will brown better.

For dinner rolls and sweet rolls with tender, golden brown crusts, use shiny pans, cookie sheets and muffin cups, which reflect heat.

Spray pans and cookie sheets with cooking spray or grease with shortening to help the crust brown and prevent bread and rolls from sticking to the pan.

Dark Nonstick Pans

Darker, nonstick pans are readily available, but they absorb more heat, so baked items may become too dark. Manufacturers of dark bakeware may recommend reducing the oven temperature by 25°F for some baked items to compensate for this.

MAKING YEAST DOUGH

The secret to a successful loaf of yeast bread is time and patience. It takes time to make the dough, knead it the correct length of time, let it rise, shape the loaf and let it rise again before baking. These steps may take patience and practice, but you will enjoy the journey and eating the results. The ideal yeast bread loaf has a uniformly golden or deeper brown top crust, good high volume and even shape, with an even interior texture with no large air holes.

After the first addition of flour has been beaten in, the dough will be very soft and fall in "sheets" off a rubber spatula.

Mix in only enough flour so dough leaves the side of the bowl and is easy to handle.

To knead, fold dough toward you. With heels of hands, push dough away with a rocking motion. Turn dough a quarter; repeat.

When dough is properly kneaded, it will feel elastic and the top will be smooth with some blisters appearing on the surface. Place dough in bowl.

Dough should rise until double in size. Press fingertips about ½ inch into dough. If indentations remain, the dough has risen enough.

Gently push fist into dough to deflate. This releases large air bubbles to produce a finer texture in traditional loaves.

Faster Dough Rising

Place the covered bowl on a cooling rack over a bowl of very warm water. Cover the bowl with a clean kitchen towel.

Or let dough rise in the microwave. Fill a measuring cup with water and microwave until the water boils. Place the covered bowl of dough in the microwave with the steaming water and let rise (but do not microwave the dough).

Shaping a Loaf

There's more than one way to shape the perfect loaf of bread. This is a classic technique for shaping a loaf that will be baked in a loaf pan. Roll the dough tightly to help prevent large air pockets.

Flatten dough with hands or rolling pin into 18 × 9-inch rectangle.

Tightly roll dough up toward you, beginning at a nine-inch side.

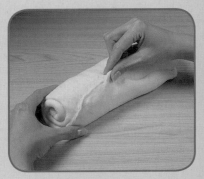

Press with thumbs to seal after each turn. Pinch edge of dough into roll to seal.

The "Upper Crust"

For some, the crust is the best part of a slice of homemade bread. Here are some "upper crust" treatments you may want to brush on the top of the bread just before baking.

Shiny crust: Brush with an egg or egg white beaten with a little water.

Softer, deep golden brown crust: Brush with softened butter or margarine.

Crisp crust: Brush or spray lightly with water.

Soft, tender crust: Brush with milk.

Misting and Creating Steam

Creating moisture in the oven or on a loaf of bread helps to give the finished loaf a crisp crust. Using a spray bottle with a fine spray, mist the loaf with water a few times during the first 10 minutes of baking. This slows down the formation of the top crust, so the loaf will rise higher as it bakes and form a crisp crust. Or add moisture by placing a metal pan with hot water in the oven with the bread. As the water evaporates, it dries the surface of the bread, forming a crisp crust.

BAKING YEAST BREAD

When the dough in the pan has almost doubled in size, it is time to heat the oven. Here are some tips for baking your bread loaf:

Move the oven rack to a low position so the top of the pan will be in the center of the oven or the position as directed in the recipe.

Heat the oven to the temperature directed in the recipe so it is hot when the pan is placed in the oven. This creates a last great rise of the dough called "ovenspring." This last rise continues for the first 5 to 10 minutes of baking or until the yeast gets so hot it dies.

Use an oven thermometer to check the temperature is correct because ovens can vary. If the oven is too hot the bread starts to bake before it has gone through its final rise or ovenspring. If the oven is too cold, the bread rises too slowly and the loaf will have lower volume.

Place the pan in the center of the rack. If baking more than one pan, place the pans far enough apart so they aren't touching each other or the sides of the oven. The air must circulate around the pans for even baking.

Bake the loaf until the top crust is a deep golden brown or test the doneness by tapping the top; it should sound hollow. Then tip the loaf out of the pan and tap the bottom and it should sound hollow. If not, return the loaf to the pan and bake a few minutes longer.

Immediately tip the finished loaf out of the pan to prevent it from steaming, which results in a soft or soggy crust.

Place the loaf, top side up, on a cooling rack and cool away from a direct draft to prevent the top from cracking.

For a softer crust, brush the top of the loaf with room-temperature butter or margarine using a pastry brush or piece of paper towel or waxed paper.

Cool the loaf at least 30 minutes before slicing. If the loaf is too warm it is difficult to cut and the slices won't hold their shape.

Check Doneness with a Thermometer

You can use an instant-read thermometer to test whether the loaf is done. Tip the loaf out of the pan and insert the thermometer directly in the center of the bottom and push it so the point is in the middle of the loaf. The loaf is done if the center is at least 200°F.

What Went Wrong?

Yeast Breads

This Happened	This Is Why
Not high	• water too hot for yeast • too little flour • not kneaded enough • rising time too short • pan too large
Coarse textured	• rising time too long • too little flour • not kneaded enough • oven too cool
Dry and crumbly	• too much flour • not kneaded enough
Full of large air pockets	• dough not rolled tightly when loaf was shaped
Yeasty flavored	• rising time too long • temperature too high during rising time

Fresh Herb Batter Bread

PREP TIME: 10 Minutes • **START TO FINISH:** 1 Hour 35 Minutes
1 loaf (20 slices)

Cooking spray to grease pan

3 cups all-purpose or bread flour

1 tablespoon granulated sugar

1 teaspoon salt

1 package regular or fast-acting dry yeast (2¼ teaspoons)

1¼ cups water

2 tablespoons shortening (or room-temperature butter or margarine)

2 tablespoons chopped fresh parsley

1½ teaspoons chopped fresh or ½ teaspoon dried rosemary leaves

½ teaspoon chopped fresh or ¼ teaspoon dried thyme leaves

1 tablespoon butter or margarine, room temperature, if desired

1 Spray the bottom and sides of an 8 × 4-inch or 9 × 5-inch loaf pan with the cooking spray.

2 In a large bowl, stir 2 cups of the flour, the sugar, salt and yeast with a wooden spoon until well mixed. In a 1-quart saucepan, heat the water over medium heat until very warm and an instant-read thermometer reads 120°F to 130°F. Add the water, shortening, parsley, rosemary and thyme to the flour mixture. Beat with an electric mixer on low speed 1 minute, stopping frequently to scrape batter from side and bottom of bowl with a rubber spatula, until flour mixture is moistened. Beat on medium speed 1 minute, stopping frequently to scrape bowl. With a wooden spoon, stir in remaining 1 cup flour until smooth.

3 Spread the batter evenly in the pan, using a rubber spatula to scrape batter from bowl. Round the top of the loaf by patting with floured hands. Lightly spray a sheet of plastic wrap with cooking spray; cover the pan loosely with the plastic wrap, sprayed side down. Let rise in a warm place about 40 minutes or until dough has doubled in size. Remove plastic wrap.

4 Move the oven rack to the middle of the oven. Heat the oven to 375°F.

5 Bake 40 to 45 minutes until top of loaf is light brown and loaf sounds hollow when tapped with a finger. Immediately remove the loaf from the pan to a cooling rack, placing the loaf top side up. For a softer crust, brush top of loaf with 1 tablespoon butter, using a pastry brush. Serve warm or cooled. Cut bread with a serrated knife.

High Altitude (3500–6500 ft): Bake 45 to 50 minutes.

1 Slice: Calories 90; Total Fat 2g; Cholesterol 0mg; Sodium 125mg; Total Carbohydrate 15g (Dietary Fiber 0g); Protein 2g **% Daily Value:** Vitamin A 0%; Vitamin C 0%; Calcium 0%; Iron 6% **Carbohydrate Choices:** 1

Shaping Batter Bread Loaf

Spread the batter evenly in the pan; shape a rounded top by patting the batter with floured hands.

Four-Grain Batter Bread

PREP TIME: 15 Minutes • **START TO FINISH:** 1 Hour 10 Minutes

2 loaves (16 slices each)

Cooking spray to grease pans

2 tablespoons cornmeal

4½ to 4¾ cups all-purpose or
   bread flour

2 tablespoons granulated sugar

1 teaspoon salt

¼ teaspoon baking soda

2 packages regular or
   fast-acting dry yeast
   (4½ teaspoons)

2 cups milk

½ cup water

½ cup whole wheat flour

½ cup wheat germ

½ cup quick-cooking oats

2 teaspoons cornmeal

1   Spray bottoms and sides of two 8 × 4-inch loaf pans with the cooking spray. Sprinkle 1 tablespoon cornmeal in each pan. Rotate pan so cornmeal is evenly spread over bottom and sides of pan, then turn pan over, tap bottom and shake excess cornmeal out of pan.

2   In a large bowl, stir 3½ cups of the all-purpose flour, the sugar, salt, baking soda and yeast until well mixed. In a 1-quart saucepan, heat the milk and water over medium heat, stirring occasionally, until very warm and an instant-read thermometer reads 120°F to 130°F. Add the milk mixture to the flour mixture. Beat with an electric mixer on low speed 1 minute, stopping frequently to scrape batter from side and bottom of bowl with a rubber spatula, until flour mixture is moistened. Beat on medium speed 3 minutes, stopping occasionally to scrape bowl. With a wooden spoon, stir in the whole wheat flour, wheat germ, oats and enough of the remaining all-purpose flour to make a stiff batter.

3   Divide the batter evenly between the pans, using a rubber spatula to scrape batter from bowl. Round the tops of the loaves by patting with floured hands. Sprinkle each loaf evenly with 1 teaspoon cornmeal. Cover the pans loosely with a sheet of plastic wrap. Let rise in a warm place about 30 minutes or until batter is about 1 inch below tops of pans. Remove plastic wrap.

4   Move the oven rack to the middle of the oven. Heat the oven to 400°F.

5   Bake about 25 minutes or until tops of loaves are light brown and loaves sound hollow when tapped with a finger. Immediately remove loaves from the pans to a cooling rack, placing the loaves top sides up. Serve warm or cooled. Cut bread with a serrated knife.

High Altitude (3500–6500 ft): Bake about 30 minutes.

1 Slice: Calories 100; Total Fat 1g; Cholesterol 0mg; Sodium 90mg; Total Carbohydrate 19g (Dietary Fiber 1g); Protein 3g **% Daily Value:** Vitamin A 0%; Vitamin C 0%; Calcium 2%; Iron 6% **Carbohydrate Choices:** 1

Whole Wheat–Raisin Batter Bread: Increase whole wheat flour to 2 cups. Omit wheat germ and oats. Stir in 1 cup raisins with the second addition of all-purpose flour.

Making Batter Bread

Stir in enough all-purpose flour to make a stiff batter that will be slightly sticky.

ic White Bread

6 to 7 cups all-purpose or bread flour

3 tablespoons granulated sugar

1 tablespoon salt

2 tablespoons shortening (or room-temperature butter or margarine)

2 packages regular or fast-acting dry yeast (4½ teaspoons)

2¼ cups water

Cooking spray to grease bowl and pans

2 tablespoons butter or margarine, melted

Additional butter or margarine, room temperature, if desired

1 In a large bowl, stir 3½ cups of the flour, the sugar, salt, shortening and yeast until well mixed. In a 1½-quart saucepan, heat the water over medium heat until very warm and an instant-read thermometer reads 120°F to 130°F. Add the water to the flour mixture. Beat with an electric mixer on low speed 1 minute, stopping frequently to scrape batter from side and bottom of bowl with a rubber spatula, until flour mixture is moistened. Beat on medium speed 1 minute, stopping frequently to scrape bowl. With a wooden spoon, stir in enough of the remaining flour, 1 cup at a time, until dough is soft, leaves side of bowl and is easy to handle (dough may be slightly sticky). (See Making Yeast Dough, page 161.)

2 Sprinkle flour lightly on a countertop or large cutting board. Place dough on floured surface. Knead by folding dough toward you, then with the heels of your hands, pushing dough away from you with a short rocking motion. Move dough a quarter turn and repeat. Continue kneading about 10 minutes, sprinkling surface with more flour if dough starts to stick, until dough is smooth and springy. Spray a large bowl with the cooking spray. Place dough in bowl, turning dough to grease all sides. Cover bowl loosely with plastic wrap; let rise in a warm place 40 to 60 minutes or until dough has doubled in size. Dough is ready if an indentation remains when you press your fingertips about ½ inch into the dough.

3 Spray the bottoms and sides of two 8 × 4-inch or 9 × 5-inch loaf pans with the cooking spray. Sprinkle flour lightly on a countertop or large cutting board. Gently push your fist into the dough to deflate it. Pull the dough away from the side of the bowl, and place it on the floured surface.

4 Divide the dough in half. (See Shaping Loaf, page 162.) Using your hands or a rolling pin, flatten each half into an 18 × 9-inch rectangle. Beginning at a 9-inch side, roll dough up tightly, pressing with thumbs to seal after each turn. Pinch edge of dough into the roll to seal edge. Pinch each end of roll to seal ends, then fold ends under the loaf. Place each loaf, seam side down, in a pan. Brush loaves lightly with the melted butter. Cover loosely

Kneading Yeast Dough

The dough will feel springy and be smooth with some blisters on the surface when it has been kneaded long enough.

with plastic wrap; let rise in a warm place 35 to 50 minutes or until dough has doubled in size. Remove plastic wrap.

5 Move the oven rack to a low position so that tops of the pans will be in the center of the oven. Heat the oven to 425°F.

6 Bake 25 to 30 minutes or until tops of loaves are deep golden brown and loaves sound hollow when tapped with a finger. Immediately remove the loaves from the pans to a cooling rack, placing the loaves top sides up. For a softer crust, brush tops of loaves with room-temperature butter, using a pastry brush. Cool 30 minutes before slicing; cut with a serrated knife.

High Altitude (3500–6500 ft): No change.

1 Slice: Calories 100; Total Fat 2g; Cholesterol 0mg; Sodium 230mg; Total Carbohydrate 19g (Dietary Fiber 0g); Protein 3g **% Daily Value:** Vitamin A 0%; Vitamin C 0%; Calcium 0%; Iron 6% **Carbohydrate Choices:** 1

Honey–Whole Wheat Bread

PREP TIME: 35 Minutes • **START TO FINISH:** 3 Hours 40 Minutes

2 loaves (16 slices each)

3 cups whole wheat flour

⅓ cup honey

¼ cup shortening (or room-temperature butter or margarine)

3 teaspoons salt

2 packages regular or fast-acting dry yeast (4½ teaspoons)

2¼ cups water

3 to 4 cups all-purpose or bread flour

Cooking spray to grease bowl and pans

2 tablespoons butter or margarine, melted

Additional butter or margarine, room temperature, if desired

Dough Rising in Pan

The dough should rise just to the top of the pan but not over the top because the dough will continue to rise as it bakes. If it rises too high before baking the loaf may be misshapen.

---

1   In a large bowl, beat the whole wheat flour, honey, shortening, salt and yeast with an electric mixer on low speed until well mixed. In a 1½-quart saucepan, heat the water over medium heat until very warm and an instant-read thermometer reads 120°F to 130°F. Add the water to the flour mixture. Beat on low speed 1 minute, stopping frequently to scrape batter from side and bottom of bowl with a rubber spatula, until flour mixture is moistened. Beat on medium speed 1 minute, stopping frequently to scrape bowl. With a wooden spoon, stir in enough of the all-purpose flour, 1 cup at a time, until dough is soft, leaves side of bowl and is easy to handle (dough may be slightly sticky). (See Making Yeast Dough, page 161.)

2   Sprinkle flour lightly on a countertop or large cutting board. Place dough on floured surface. Knead by folding dough toward you, then with the heels of your hands, pushing dough away from you with a short rocking motion. Move dough a quarter turn and repeat. Continue kneading about 10 minutes, sprinkling surface with more flour if dough starts to stick, until dough is smooth and springy. Spray a large bowl with the cooking spray. Place dough in bowl, turning dough to grease all sides. Cover bowl loosely with plastic wrap; let rise in a warm place 40 to 60 minutes or until dough has doubled in size. Dough is ready if an indentation remains when you press your fingertips about ½ inch into the dough.

3   Spray the bottoms and sides of two 8 × 4-inch or 9 × 5-inch loaf pans with the cooking spray. Sprinkle flour lightly on a countertop or large cutting board. Gently push your fist into the dough to deflate it. Pull the dough away from the side of the bowl, and place it on the floured surface.

4   Divide the dough in half. (See Shaping Loaf, page 162.) Using your hands or a rolling pin, flatten each half into an 18 × 9-inch rectangle. Beginning at a 9-inch side, roll dough up tightly, pressing with thumbs to seal after each turn. Pinch edge of dough into the roll to seal edge. Pinch each end of roll to seal ends, then fold ends under the loaf. Place each loaf, seam side down, in a pan. Brush loaves lightly with the melted butter. Cover loosely with plastic wrap; let rise in a warm place 35 to 50 minutes or until dough has doubled in size. Remove plastic wrap.

5   Move the oven rack to a low position so that tops of the pans will be in the center of the oven. Heat the oven to 375°F.

6   Bake 40 to 45 minutes or until tops of loaves are deep golden brown and loaves sound hollow when tapped with a finger. Immediately remove the loaves from the pans to a cooling rack, placing the loaves top sides up. For a softer crust, brush tops of loaves with room-temperature butter, using a pastry brush. Cool 30 minutes before slicing; cut with a serrated knife.

High Altitude (3500–6500 ft): Use two 9-inch loaf pans. Bake 42 to 47 minutes.

1 Slice: Calories 120; Total Fat 2.5g; Cholesterol 0mg; Sodium 230mg; Total Carbohydrate 20g (Dietary Fiber 2g); Protein 3g **% Daily Value:** Vitamin A 0%; Vitamin C 0%; Calcium 0%; Iron 6% **Carbohydrate Choices:** 1

Sunflower-Herb Whole Wheat Bread: Add 1 tablespoon dried basil leaves and 2 teaspoons dried thyme leaves with the salt. Stir in 1 cup unsalted sunflower nuts with the all-purpose flour.

Pull-Apart Bread

PREP TIME: 30 Minutes • **START TO FINISH:** 1 Hour 35 Minutes

1 loaf (12 servings)

Cooking spray to grease pan

3½ to 3¾ cups all-purpose or bread flour

2 tablespoons granulated sugar

½ teaspoon salt

1 package regular or fast-acting dry yeast (2¼ teaspoons)

1 cup milk

¼ cup butter or margarine (½ stick)

1 large egg

¼ cup butter or margarine (½ stick)

1   Spray a 12-cup fluted tube cake pan or 10-inch angel food (tube) cake pan with the cooking spray. In a large bowl, stir 1½ cups of the flour, the sugar, salt and yeast until well mixed.

2   In a 1-quart saucepan, heat the milk and ¼ cup butter over medium-low heat, stirring frequently, until very warm and an instant-read thermometer reads 120°F to 130°F. Add the milk mixture and the egg to the flour mixture. Beat with an electric mixer on low speed 1 minute, stopping frequently to scrape batter from side and bottom of bowl with a rubber spatula, until flour mixture is moistened. Beat on medium speed 3 minutes, stopping frequently to scrape bowl. With a wooden spoon, stir in enough of the remaining flour, 1 cup at a time, until dough is soft, leaves side of bowl and is easy to handle (dough may be slightly sticky). (See Making Yeast Dough, page 161.)

3   Sprinkle flour lightly on a countertop or large cutting board. Place dough on floured surface. Knead by folding dough toward you, then with the heels of your hands, pushing dough away from you with a short rocking motion. Move dough a quarter turn and repeat. Continue kneading about 5 minutes, sprinkling surface with more flour if dough starts to stick, until dough is smooth and springy.

4   Place ¼ cup butter in a small microwavable bowl; cover with a microwavable paper towel. Microwave on High 30 to 50 seconds or until melted.

5   Shape the dough into 24 balls. Dip each ball of dough into the melted butter. Layer evenly in the pan. Cover bowl loosely with plastic wrap; let rise in a warm place 20 to 30 minutes or until dough has doubled in size. Dough is ready if an indentation remains when you press your fingertips about ½ inch into the dough. Remove plastic wrap.

6   Move the oven rack to a low position so that tops of the pans will be in the center of the oven. Heat the oven to 350°F.

Making Pull-Apart Bread

Dip balls of dough into butter; place them evenly in two rows in pan.

7 Bake 25 to 30 minutes or until golden brown. Cool bread in pan 2 minutes. Place a heatproof serving plate upside down on pan; holding plate and pan with pot holders, turn plate and pan over together, then remove pan. Serve bread while warm, pulling it apart with 2 forks or your fingers.

High Altitude (3500–6500 ft): Bake 30 to 35 minutes.

1 Serving: Calories 230; Total Fat 9g; Cholesterol 40mg; Sodium 170mg; Total Carbohydrate 31g (Dietary Fiber 1g); Protein 5g **% Daily Value:** Vitamin A 6%; Vitamin C 0%; Calcium 4%; Iron 10% **Carbohydrate Choices:** 2

Pizza Dough

PREP TIME: 20 Minutes • **START TO FINISH:** 3 Hours

8 servings

½ **cup water**

1 package regular or fast-acting dry yeast (2¼ teaspoons)

1¼ to 1½ cups all-purpose or bread flour

1 teaspoon olive or vegetable oil

½ **teaspoon salt**

½ **teaspoon granulated sugar**

Cooking spray to grease bowl

1 can (8 oz) pizza sauce

Toppings for desired pizza (see opposite page)

Shaping Pizza Dough Crust

Push the dough from center to the edge to form a 12-inch circle, using floured fingertips. The edge should be slightly thicker than the center to help hold the filling.

1 In a 1-quart saucepan, heat the water over medium heat until warm and an instant-read thermometer reads 105°F to 115°F. In a large bowl, dissolve the yeast in the warm water. With a wooden spoon, stir in half of the flour and all of the oil, salt and sugar. Stir in enough of the remaining flour, ¼ cup at a time, until dough is easy to handle. (See Making Yeast Dough, page 161.)

2 Sprinkle flour lightly on a countertop or large cutting board. Place dough on floured surface. Knead by folding dough toward you, then with the heels of your hands, pushing dough away from you with a short rocking motion. Move dough a quarter turn and repeat. Continue kneading about 10 minutes, sprinkling surface with more flour if dough starts to stick, until dough is smooth and springy. Spray a large bowl with the cooking spray. Place dough in bowl, turning dough to grease all sides. Cover bowl loosely with plastic wrap; let rise in a warm place 20 minutes.

3 Gently push your fist into the dough to deflate it. Cover bowl loosely with plastic wrap; refrigerate at least 2 hours but no longer than 48 hours. (If dough should double in size during refrigeration, gently push fist into dough to deflate it.)

4 Move the oven rack to the middle position of the oven. Heat the oven to 425°F. Place dough on center of an ungreased cookie sheet or 12-inch pizza pan. Press the dough into a 12-inch round, using floured fingers. Press dough from center to edge so the edge is slightly thicker than the center. Spread the pizza sauce over the dough to within ½ inch of edge. Add the toppings for either cheese, hamburger, Italian sausage or pepperoni pizza.

5 Bake 15 to 20 minutes or until crust is golden brown and cheeses are melted and lightly browned.

High Altitude (3500–6500 ft): Bake about 23 minutes.

1 Serving (Crust and Sauce): Calories 80; Total Fat 1g; Cholesterol 0mg; Sodium 150mg; Total Carbohydrate 16g (Dietary Fiber 0g); Protein 2g **% Daily Value:** Vitamin A 0%; Vitamin C 0%; Calcium 0%; Iron 6% **Carbohydrate Choices:** 1

Cheese Pizza: Sprinkle pizza sauce with 3 cups shredded mozzarella cheese (12 oz) and ¼ cup grated Parmesan cheese.

Hamburger Pizza: In 10-inch skillet, cook 1 pound lean (at least 80%) ground beef, 1 cup chopped onion and 1 teaspoon Italian seasoning over medium heat 8 to 10 minutes, stirring occasionally, until beef is thoroughly cooked. Pour into paper towel–lined strainer to drain. Spread beef mixture over pizza sauce. Sprinkle with 2 cups shredded mozzarella cheese (8 oz) and ¼ cup grated Parmesan cheese.

Italian Sausage Pizza: In 10-inch skillet, cook 1 pound bulk Italian pork sausage and 1 cup chopped green bell pepper (if desired) over medium heat 8 to 10 minutes, stirring occasionally, until pork is no longer pink. Pour into paper towel–lined strainer to drain. Spread sausage mixture over pizza sauce. Sprinkle with 2 cups shredded mozzarella cheese (8 oz) and ¼ cup grated Parmesan cheese.

Pepperoni Pizza: Arrange 1 package (3 oz) sliced pepperoni over pizza sauce. Sprinkle with 2 cups shredded mozzarella cheese (8 oz) and ¼ cup grated Parmesan cheese.

Focaccia

PREP TIME: 30 Minutes • **START TO FINISH:** 1 Hour 50 Minutes

2 breads (12 slices or 8 wedges each)

2½ to 3 cups all-purpose or bread flour

2 tablespoons chopped fresh or 1 tablespoon dried rosemary leaves, crushed

1 tablespoon granulated sugar

1 teaspoon salt

1 package regular or fast-acting dry yeast (2¼ teaspoons)

1 cup water

3 tablespoons olive or vegetable oil

Cooking spray to grease bowl and cookie sheets

2 tablespoons olive or vegetable oil

¼ cup grated or finely shredded Parmesan cheese

1 In a large bowl, stir 1 cup of the flour, the rosemary, sugar, salt and yeast with a wooden spoon until well mixed. In a 1-quart saucepan, heat the water over medium heat until very warm and an instant-read thermometer reads 120°F to 130°F. Add the water and 3 tablespoons oil to the flour mixture. Beat with an electric mixer on medium speed 3 minutes, stopping frequently to scrape batter from side and bottom of bowl with a rubber spatula. With a wooden spoon, stir in enough of the remaining flour, ¼ cup at a time, until dough is soft, leaves side of bowl and is easy to handle (the dough may be slightly sticky). (See Making Yeast Dough, page 161.)

2 Sprinkle flour lightly on a countertop or large cutting board. Place dough on floured surface. Knead by folding dough toward you, then with the heels of your hands, pushing dough away from you with a short rocking motion. Move dough a quarter turn and repeat. Continue kneading 5 to 8 minutes, sprinkling surface with more flour if dough starts to stick, until dough is smooth and springy. Spray a large bowl with the cooking spray. Place dough in bowl, turning dough to grease all sides. Cover bowl loosely with plastic wrap; let rise in a warm place 30 minutes or until dough has almost doubled in size. Dough is ready if an indentation remains when you press your fingertips about ½ inch into the dough.

3 Spray 2 cookie sheets or 12-inch pizza pans with the cooking spray. Gently push your fist into the dough to deflate it. Divide dough in half. Shape each half into a flattened 10-inch round on a cookie sheet. Lightly spray 2 sheets of plastic wrap with cooking spray; cover the dough loosely with the plastic wrap, sprayed side down. Let rise in a warm place about 30 minutes or until dough has doubled in size. Remove plastic wrap.

4 Heat the oven to 400°F. Using your fingers, gently make ½-inch-deep depressions about 2 inches apart in dough. Carefully brush with 2 tablespoons oil, using a pastry brush; sprinkle with cheese. Bake 15 to 20 minutes or until golden brown. Serve warm or cooled.

High Altitude (3500–6500 ft): No change.

1 Slice: Calories 80; Total Fat 3.5g; Cholesterol 0mg; Sodium 120mg; Total Carbohydrate 11g (Dietary Fiber 0g); Protein 2g **% Daily Value:** Vitamin A 0%; Vitamin C 0%; Calcium 0%; Iron 4% **Carbohydrate Choices:** 1

Making Depressions in Focaccia Dough

Gently make ½-inch-deep depressions about two inches apart in dough, using fingers. If dough is sticky, dip your fingers in flour.

Dinner Rolls

PREP TIME: 30 Minutes • **START TO FINISH:** 2 Hours 15 Minutes

15 rolls

3½ to 3¾ cups all-purpose or bread flour

¼ cup granulated sugar

¼ cup butter or margarine (½ stick), room temperature

1 teaspoon salt

1 package regular or fast-acting dry yeast (2¼ teaspoons)

½ cup water

½ cup milk

1 large egg

Cooking spray to grease bowl and pan

1 tablespoon butter or margarine, melted

Additional butter or margarine, room temperature, if desired

1 In a large bowl, stir 2 cups of the flour, the sugar, ¼ cup butter, salt and yeast with a wooden spoon until well mixed. In a 1-quart saucepan, heat the water and milk over medium heat, stirring frequently, until very warm and an instant-read thermometer reads 120°F to 130°F. Add the water mixture and egg to flour mixture. Beat with an electric mixer on low speed 1 minute, stopping frequently to scrape batter from side and bottom of bowl with a rubber spatula, until flour mixture is moistened. Beat on medium speed 1 minute, stopping frequently to scrape bowl. With a wooden spoon, stir in enough of the remaining flour, about ½ cup at a time, until dough is soft, leaves side of bowl and is easy to handle (dough may be slightly sticky). (See Making Yeast Dough, page 161.)

2 Sprinkle flour lightly on a countertop or large cutting board. Place dough on floured surface. Knead by folding dough toward you, then with the heels of your hands, pushing dough away from you with a short rocking motion. Move dough a quarter turn and repeat. Continue kneading about 5 minutes, sprinkling surface with more flour if dough starts to stick, until dough is smooth and springy. Spray a large bowl with the cooking spray. Place dough in bowl, turning dough to grease all sides. Cover bowl loosely with plastic wrap; let rise in a warm place about 1 hour or until dough has doubled in size. Dough is ready if an indentation remains when you press your fingertips about ½ inch into the dough.

3 Spray the bottom and sides of a 13 × 9-inch pan with the cooking spray. Gently push your fist into the dough to deflate it. Divide dough into

Shaping Dinner Rolls

For dinner rolls, shape each piece of dough into a ball, pulling edges under to make a smooth top. Place balls, smooth side up, in greased pan.

For cloverleaf rolls, shape each piece of dough into a ball, pulling edges under to make a smooth top. Place three balls, smooth side up, in each muffin cup.

15 equal pieces. Shape each piece into a ball; place in pan. Brush with melted butter. Lightly spray sheet of plastic wrap with cooking spray; cover the pan loosely with the plastic wrap, sprayed side down. Let rise in a warm place about 30 minutes or until dough has doubled in size. Remove plastic wrap.

4 Move the oven rack to a low position so that top of the pan will be in the center of the oven. Heat the oven to 375°F. Bake 12 to 15 minutes or until golden brown. Remove from pan to a cooling rack. For a softer crust, brush tops of rolls with room-temperature butter, using a pastry brush. Serve warm or cooled.

High Altitude (3500–6500 ft): Bake 18 to 21 minutes.

1 Roll: Calories 160; Total Fat 4.5g; Cholesterol 25mg; Sodium 190mg; Total Carbohydrate 26g (Dietary Fiber 0g); Protein 4g **% Daily Value:** Vitamin A 4%; Vitamin C 0%; Calcium 0%; Iron 8% **Carbohydrate Choices:** 2

Cloverleaf Rolls: Grease 24 regular-size muffin cups with cooking spray. Make dough as directed except divide dough into 72 equal pieces. Shape each piece into a ball. Place 3 balls in each muffin cup. Brush with butter. Cover loosely with plastic wrap; let rise in a warm place about 30 minutes or until dough has doubled in size. Bake as directed.

Italian Breadsticks

PREP TIME: 35 Minutes • **START TO FINISH:** 1 Hour 20 Minutes

32 breadsticks

Cooking spray to grease cookie sheets

1 package regular or fast-acting dry yeast (2¼ teaspoons)

⅔ cup water

1 tablespoon granulated sugar

1 teaspoon salt

¼ cup olive or vegetable oil

2 to 2¼ cups all-purpose or bread flour

2 tablespoons olive or vegetable oil

1 large egg

1 tablespoon water

1½ teaspoons coarse salt or sesame seed

1 Spray cookie sheets with the cooking spray. In a large bowl, place the yeast. In a 1-quart saucepan, heat the water over medium heat until warm and an instant-read thermometer reads 105°F to 115°F. Pour water over yeast; stir until yeast is dissolved. Stir in the sugar, 1 teaspoon salt, ¼ cup oil and 1 cup of the flour. Beat with an electric mixer on medium speed until smooth. With a wooden spoon, stir in enough of the remaining flour, about ½ cup at a time, until dough is soft, leaves side of bowl and is easy to handle (dough may be slightly sticky). (See Making Yeast Dough, page 161.)

2 Sprinkle flour lightly on a countertop or large cutting board. Place dough on floured surface. Knead by folding dough toward you, then with the heels of your hands, pushing dough away from you with a short rocking motion. Move dough a quarter turn and repeat. Continue kneading about 5 minutes, sprinkling surface with more flour if dough starts to stick, until dough is smooth and springy. If dough is sticky, lightly flour your hands. Shape dough into a uniform roll that's 10 inches long. Cut roll crosswise into 32 equal parts. Roll each part into a pencil-like rope, 8 inches long for thick breadsticks or 10 inches long for thin breadsticks. Place 1 inch apart on cookie sheets. Brush with 2 tablespoons oil. Lightly spray sheets of plastic wrap with cooking spray; cover dough loosely with the plastic wrap, sprayed side down. Let rise in a warm place 20 minutes.

3 Place an egg separator over a small bowl. Crack open the egg, letting the yolk fall into the center of the separator and the egg white slip through the slots into the bowl. Cover and refrigerate egg yolk up to 4 days to use in another recipe.

Making Breadsticks

 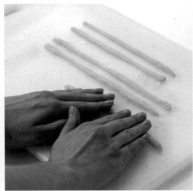

To get even pieces of dough, cut the 10-inch roll of dough in half. Continue cutting each piece in half until you have 32 pieces.

Roll each piece of dough into pencil-like rope, on a lightly floured surface if the dough is sticky. Make an eight-inch rope for thicker breadsticks and a 10-inch rope for thinner breadsticks.

4 Move the oven rack to the middle position of the oven. Heat the oven to 350°F. In a small bowl, beat the egg white and 1 tablespoon water slightly with a fork or wire whisk. Brush mixture over breadsticks, using a pastry brush; sprinkle with coarse salt. Bake 1 cookie sheet at a time 20 to 25 minutes or until breadsticks are golden brown. Remove from cookie sheets to cooling rack. Serve warm or cooled.

High Altitude (3500–6500 ft): No change.

1 Breadstick: Calories 50; Total Fat 2.5g; Cholesterol 0mg; Sodium 190mg; Total Carbohydrate 6g (Dietary Fiber 0g); Protein 1g **% Daily Value:** Vitamin A 0%; Vitamin C 0%; Calcium 0%; Iron 2% **Carbohydrate Choices:** ½

Soft Pretzels

PREP TIME: 35 Minutes • **START TO FINISH:** 1 Hour 15 Minutes
16 pretzels

3¾ to 4¼ cups all-purpose flour

1 tablespoon granulated sugar

1½ teaspoons salt

1 package regular or fast-acting
   dry yeast (2¼ teaspoons)

1½ cups water

2 tablespoons vegetable oil

Cooking spray to grease cookie
   sheets

1 cup water

2 teaspoons baking soda

2 teaspoons coarse salt

1   In a large bowl, stir 2 cups of the flour, the sugar, salt and yeast with a wooden spoon until well mixed. In a 1-quart saucepan, heat 1½ cups water over medium heat until very warm and an instant-read thermometer reads 120°F to 130°F. Add the warm water and oil to the flour mixture. Beat with an electric mixer on low speed 1 minute, stopping frequently to scrape batter from side and bottom of bowl with a rubber spatula. Beat on medium speed 1 minute, stopping frequently to scrape bowl. With a wooden spoon, stir in enough of the remaining flour, about ½ cup at time, until dough is soft, leaves side of bowl and is easy to handle (dough may be slightly sticky). (See Making Yeast Dough, page 161.)

2   Sprinkle flour lightly on a countertop or large cutting board. Place dough on floured surface. Knead by folding dough toward you, then with the heels of your hands, pushing dough away from you with a short rocking motion. Move dough a quarter turn and repeat. Continue kneading about 5 minutes, sprinkling surface with more flour if dough starts to stick, until dough is smooth and springy. Lightly spray a sheet of plastic wrap with cooking spray; cover the dough loosely with the plastic wrap, sprayed side down. Let rest 10 minutes.

3   Move the oven rack to the middle of the oven. Heat the oven to 425°F. Spray cookie sheets with the cooking spray. In a shallow bowl, stir 1 cup water and the baking soda to make pretzel "wash."

4   Divide dough into 16 equal pieces. With your hands, roll each piece into a 24-inch rope (dip hands in pretzel wash to make rolling dough easier). To make pretzel shape, form rope into a circle, crossing ends at top. Fold dough so crossed ends rest

Shaping Pretzels

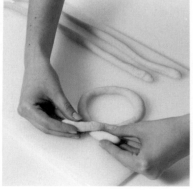

Bring ends of rope up and together to form a circle with about 1½ inches of the ends overlapping.

Fold overlapping ends down onto the center of the circle to form a pretzel.

on bottom of circle. Stir pretzel wash; brush over both sides of pretzel, using a pastry brush. Place pretzel on cookie sheet. Repeat with remaining dough. Reserve remaining pretzel wash. Cover pretzels loosely with plastic wrap. To make thin pretzels, let rest about 5 minutes or until very slightly puffed. To make thicker pretzels, let rise in a warm place 15 to 20 minutes or until puffed.

5 Just before baking, brush pretzels with reserved wash; sprinkle with coarse salt. Bake 1 cookie sheet at a time 10 to 13 minutes or until golden brown. Remove from cookie sheets to a cooling rack; cool at least 15 minutes. Serve warm or cooled.

High Altitude (3500–6500 ft): No change.

1 Pretzel: Calories 120; Total Fat 2g; Cholesterol 0mg; Sodium 670mg; Total Carbohydrate 23g (Dietary Fiber 0g); Protein 3g **% Daily Value:** Vitamin A 0%; Vitamin C 0%; Calcium 0%; Iron 8% **Carbohydrate Choices:** 1½

Parmesan-Herb Soft Pretzels: Mix 2 tablespoons grated Parmesan cheese, ½ teaspoon dried basil leaves and ¼ teaspoon garlic powder. Brush hot baked pretzels with melted butter; sprinkle with cheese mixture.

Monkey Bread

PREP TIME: 35 Minutes • **START TO FINISH:** 3 Hours 25 Minutes

16 servings

3½ to 4 cups all-purpose flour

⅓ cup granulated sugar

1 teaspoon salt

1 package regular or fast-acting dry yeast (2¼ teaspoons)

1 cup water

⅓ cup butter or margarine, room temperature

1 large egg

Cooking spray to grease bowl

Baking spray with flour to grease pan

¾ cup granulated sugar

½ cup finely chopped nuts

1 teaspoon ground cinnamon

½ cup butter or margarine (1 stick)

Lining Tube Pan with Foil

Remove the bottom of the pan. Turn the pan over and shape a piece of foil over the bottom. Turn the pan over and fit the foil in the pan. Place the bottom inside.

1 In a large bowl, stir 2 cups of the flour, ⅓ cup sugar, the salt and yeast with a wooden spoon until well mixed. In a 1-quart saucepan, heat the water and ⅓ cup butter over medium-low heat, stirring frequently, until very warm and an instant-read thermometer reads 120°F to 130°F. Add the water mixture and egg to the flour mixture. Beat with a wire whisk or an electric mixer on low speed 1 minute, stopping frequently to scrape batter from side and bottom of bowl with a rubber spatula, until smooth. Beat on medium speed 1 minute, stopping frequently to scrape bowl. With a wooden spoon, stir in enough of the remaining flour, 1 cup at a time, until dough is soft, leaves side of bowl and is easy to handle (dough may be slightly sticky). (See Making Yeast Dough, page 161.)

2 Sprinkle flour lightly on a countertop or large cutting board. Place dough on floured surface; roll ball of dough around 3 or 4 times to cover with flour. Knead by folding dough toward you, then with the heels of your hands, pushing dough away from you with a short rocking motion. Move dough a quarter turn and repeat. Continue kneading about 10 minutes, sprinkling surface with more flour if dough starts to stick, until dough is smooth and springy.

3 Spray a large bowl with the cooking spray. Place dough in bowl, turning dough to grease all sides. Cover bowl loosely with plastic wrap; let rise in a warm place 1 hour to 1 hour 30 minutes or until dough has doubled in size. Dough is ready if an indentation remains when you press your fingertips about ½ inch into the dough.

4 Spray 10-inch angel food (tube) cake pan or 12-cup fluted tube cake pan with the baking spray. (If angel food cake pan has removable bottom, line pan with foil before spraying to help prevent the sugar mixture from dripping in the oven during baking.) In a small bowl, mix ¾ cup sugar, the nuts and cinnamon. In a 1-quart saucepan, heat ½ cup butter over low heat until melted.

5 Gently push your fist into the dough to deflate it. Shape dough into about 25 balls, 1½ inches in diameter. Dip each ball into melted butter, then into the sugar-cinnamon mixture. Place a single layer of balls in the pan so they just touch. Top with another layer of balls. Cover pan loosely with plastic wrap; let rise in a warm place about 40 minutes or until dough has doubled in size. Remove plastic wrap.

6 Move the oven rack to a low position so that the top of the pan will be in the center of the oven. Heat the oven to 375°F. Bake 35 to 40 minutes or until golden brown. (If bread browns too quickly, cover loosely with foil.) Run a metal spatula or knife around the edge of the pan to loosen the bread. Place a heatproof serving plate upside down on pan; holding plate and pan with pot holders, turn plate and pan over together. Let pan remain 1 minute so butter-sugar mixture can drizzle over bread, then remove pan. Serve bread while warm, pulling it apart using 2 forks or your fingers.

High Altitude (3500–6500 ft): Bake 40 to 45 minutes.

1 Serving: Calories 270; Total Fat 13g; Cholesterol 40mg; Sodium 220mg; Total Carbohydrate 35g (Dietary Fiber 1g); Protein 4g **% Daily Value:** Vitamin A 6%; Vitamin C 0%; Calcium 0%; Iron 8%
Carbohydrate Choices: 2

Cinnamon Rolls

PREP TIME: 40 Minutes • **START TO FINISH:** 3 Hours 20 Minutes

15 rolls

ROLLS

3½ to 4 cups all-purpose flour
⅓ cup granulated sugar
1 teaspoon salt
2 packages regular or fast-acting dry yeast (4½ teaspoons)
1 cup milk
¼ cup butter or margarine (½ stick), room temperature
1 large egg
Cooking spray to grease bowl and pan

FILLING

½ cup granulated sugar
2 teaspoons ground cinnamon
¼ cup butter or margarine (½ stick), room temperature
½ cup raisins, if desired
¼ cup finely chopped nuts, if desired

GLAZE

1 cup powdered sugar
1 tablespoon butter or margarine, room temperature
½ teaspoon vanilla
1 to 2 tablespoons milk

Slicing Cinnamon Rolls

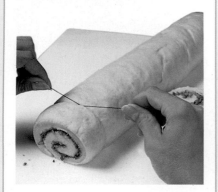

Place a piece of dental floss under the roll, bring ends of floss up and crisscross at top of roll, then pull ends in opposite directions.

1 In a large bowl, stir 2 cups of the flour, ⅓ cup granulated sugar, the salt and yeast with a wooden spoon until well mixed. In a 1-quart saucepan, heat the milk over medium heat until very warm and an instant-read thermometer reads 120°F to 130°F. Add the warm milk, ¼ cup butter and egg to the flour mixture. Beat with an electric mixer on low speed 1 minute, stopping frequently to scrape batter from side and bottom of bowl with a rubber spatula, until flour mixture is moistened. Beat on medium speed 1 minute, stopping frequently to scrape bowl. With a wooden spoon, stir in enough of the remaining flour, about ½ cup at a time, until dough is soft, leaves side of bowl and is easy to handle (dough may be slightly sticky). (See Making Yeast Dough, page 161.)

2 Sprinkle flour lightly on a countertop or large cutting board. Place dough on floured surface. Knead by folding dough toward you, then with the heels of your hands, pushing dough away from you with a short rocking motion. Move dough a quarter turn and repeat. Continue kneading about 5 minutes, sprinkling surface with more flour if dough starts to stick, until dough is smooth and springy. Spray a large bowl with the cooking spray. Place dough in bowl, turning dough to grease all sides. Cover bowl loosely with plastic wrap; let rise in a warm place about 1 hour 30 minutes or until dough has doubled in size. Dough is ready if an indentation remains when you press your fingertips about ½ inch into the dough.

3 In a small bowl, mix ½ cup sugar and the cinnamon; set aside. Spray the bottom and sides of a 13 × 9-inch pan with the cooking spray. Sprinkle flour lightly on a countertop or large cutting board. Gently push your fist into the dough to deflate it. Pull the dough away from the side of the bowl, and place it on the floured surface.

4 Using your hands or a rolling pin, flatten dough into a 15 × 10-inch rectangle. Spread ¼ cup butter over dough to within ½ inch of edges. Sprinkle with sugar-cinnamon mixture, raisins and nuts. Beginning at a 15-inch side, roll dough up tightly. Pinch edge of dough into the roll to seal edge. Stretch and shape roll until even and 15 inches long. Using a sharp serrated knife or length of dental floss, cut roll into 15 (1-inch) slices. Place slices slightly apart in the pan. Cover pan loosely with plastic wrap; let rise in a warm place about 30 minutes or until dough has doubled in size. Remove plastic wrap.

5 Move the oven rack to the middle position of the oven. Heat the oven to 350°F. Bake 30 to 35 minutes or until golden brown. Immediately remove rolls from pan, place right side up on a cooling rack. Cool 5 minutes.

6 In a small bowl, stir glaze ingredients until smooth, adding enough milk so glaze is thin enough to drizzle. Over the warm rolls, drizzle glaze from the tip of a tableware teaspoon, moving the spoon back and forth to make thin lines of glaze. Serve warm.

High Altitude (3500–6500 ft): No change.

1 Roll: Calories 260, Total Fat 8g; Cholesterol 35mg; Sodium 220mg; Total Carbohydrate 43g (Dietary Fiber 1g); Protein 4g **% Daily Value:** Vitamin A 6%; Vitamin C 0%; Calcium 4%; Iron 10% **Carbohydrate Choices:** 3

Do-Ahead Cinnamon Rolls: After placing slices in pan, cover tightly with plastic wrap or foil and refrigerate 4 to 24 hours. Before baking, remove from refrigerator; remove plastic wrap or foil and cover loosely with plastic wrap. Let rise in a warm place about 2 hours or until dough has doubled in size. If some rising has occurred in the refrigerator, rising time may be less than 2 hours. Bake as directed.

Caramel Sticky Rolls

PREP TIME: 40 Minutes • **START TO FINISH:** 3 Hours 15 Minutes

15 rolls

ROLLS

3½ to 4 cups all-purpose flour
⅓ cup granulated sugar
1 teaspoon salt
2 packages regular or
    fast-acting dry yeast
    (4½ teaspoons)
1 cup milk
¼ cup butter or margarine
    (½ stick), room temperature
1 large egg
Cooking spray to grease bowl

CARAMEL TOPPING

1 cup packed brown sugar
½ cup butter or margarine
    (1 stick), room temperature
¼ cup corn syrup
1 cup pecan halves, if desired

FILLING

½ cup chopped pecans, if desired
¼ cup granulated or packed
    brown sugar
1 teaspoon ground cinnamon
2 tablespoons butter or
    margarine, room temperature

Placing Roll Slices in Pan

Place rolls slightly apart, cut side down, on top of the pecan halves in the pan.

1   In a large bowl, stir 2 cups of the flour, ⅓ cup granulated sugar, the salt and yeast with a wooden spoon until well mixed. In a 1-quart saucepan, heat the milk over medium heat until very warm and an instant-read thermometer reads 120°F to 130°F. Add the warm milk, ¼ cup butter and egg to the flour mixture. Beat with an electric mixer on low speed 1 minute, stopping frequently to scrape batter from side and bottom of bowl with a rubber spatula, until flour mixture is moistened. Beat on medium speed 1 minute, stopping frequently to scrape bowl. With a wooden spoon, stir in enough of the remaining flour, about ½ cup at a time, until dough is soft, leaves side of bowl and is easy to handle (dough may be slightly sticky). (See Making Yeast Dough, page 161.)

2   Sprinkle flour lightly on a countertop or large cutting board. Place dough on floured surface. Knead by folding dough toward you, then with the heels of your hands, pushing dough away from you with a short rocking motion. Move dough a quarter turn and repeat. Continue kneading about 5 minutes, sprinkling surface with more flour if dough starts to stick, until dough is smooth and springy. Spray a large bowl with the cooking spray. Place dough in bowl, turning dough to grease all sides. Cover bowl loosely with plastic wrap; let rise in a warm place about 1 hour 30 minutes or until dough has doubled in size. Dough is ready if an indentation remains when you press your fingertips about ½ inch into the dough.

3   In a 2-quart saucepan, heat the brown sugar and ½ cup butter to boiling over medium-high heat, stirring constantly; remove from heat. Stir in the corn syrup. Pour into an ungreased 13 × 9-inch pan. Sprinkle with 1 cup pecan halves.

4   In a small bowl, mix ½ cup chopped pecans, ¼ cup sugar and the cinnamon; set aside.

5   Sprinkle flour lightly on a countertop or large cutting board. Gently push your fist into the dough to deflate it. Pull the dough away from the side of the bowl, and place it on the floured surface.

6   Using your hands or a rolling pin, flatten dough into a 15 × 10-inch rectangle. Spread 2 tablespoons butter over dough to within ½ inch of edges. Sprinkle with chopped pecan mixture. Beginning at a 15-inch side, roll dough up tightly. Pinch edge of dough into the roll to seal edge. Stretch and shape roll until even and 15 inches long. Using a sharp serrated knife or length of dental floss, cut roll into 15 (1-inch) slices. Place slices slightly apart in the pan. Cover pan loosely with plastic wrap; let rise in a warm place about 30 minutes or until dough has doubled in size. Remove plastic wrap.

7 Move the oven rack to the middle position of the oven. Heat the oven to 350°F. Bake 30 to 35 minutes or until golden brown. Let stand 2 to 3 minutes. Run a metal spatula or knife around the edge of the pan to loosen the rolls. Place a heatproof tray or serving plate upside down on pan; holding tray and pan with pot holders, turn tray and pan over together. Let pan remain 1 minute so caramel can drizzle over rolls, then remove pan. Serve warm.

High Altitude (3500–6500 ft): Bake 35 to 40 minutes.

1 Roll: Calories 320; Total Fat 12g; Cholesterol 45mg; Sodium 260mg; Total Carbohydrate 50g (Dietary Fiber 1g); Protein 4g **% Daily Value:** Vitamin A 8%; Vitamin C 0%; Calcium 4%; Iron 10% **Carbohydrate Choices:** 3

Do-Ahead Caramel Sticky Rolls: After placing slices in pan, cover tightly with plastic wrap or foil and refrigerate 4 to 24 hours. Before baking, remove from refrigerator; remove plastic wrap or foil and cover loosely with plastic wrap. Let rise in a warm place about 2 hours or until dough has doubled in size. If some rising has occurred in the refrigerator, rising time may be less than 2 hours. Bake as directed.

6 DESSERTS

DESSERTS 101

So what are desserts? They're all those other scrumptious baked treats that aren't cookies, cakes or pies. Here is where you will find cheesecake, cobbler, crisp, gingerbread—just to name a few.

Cheesecake

Creating a great cheesecake isn't difficult, but here are a few tips to keep in mind when baking your first cheesecake.

To check the doneness for most cheesecakes, touch the top lightly or gently shake the pan. If a small area in the center jiggles slightly or seems soft it is done and will become firm as the cheesecake cools.

Do not insert a knife to test for doneness because the hole could cause the cheesecake to crack.

Some recipes tell you to turn the oven off and let the cheesecake stand in the oven for at least 30 minutes to finish baking. Others may tell you to remove it from the oven and cool it at room temperature for a length of time before refrigerating. Follow the recipe for best results.

Refrigerate the baked cheesecake uncovered two to three hours or until chilled, before covering to prevent moisture from dripping onto the top of the cake.

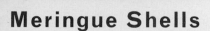

If the cheesecake has a side crust, after it has cooled for the recommended time, run a metal spatula or tableware knife between the crust and side of pan but don't remove the side of the pan. Loosening the crust keeps the cheesecake from pulling away, which may cause the top to crack.

Loosen the crust from the side of pan again before removing the side of the pan to loosen any parts that may have stuck again.

To cut cheesecake, dip the knife into water and clean it off after every cut.

Meringue Shells

Meringue, which is a froth of egg white, sugar and air, can be baked into a hard, crisp meringue shell such as the one for Cherry-Berry Meringue Torte (page 214).

Pick a cool, dry day to make meringue. If it's humid or rainy, the sugar in the meringue absorbs moisture from the air, making the meringue sticky and spongy.

Separate the eggs carefully, because even a speck of yolk in the whites will keep them from whipping up. Cold eggs separate most easily.

For the most volume, let the egg whites stand at room temperature for 30 minutes before beating.

Start with a clean, dry bowl and beaters so the egg whites will beat properly.

Beat sugar in gradually, about one tablespoon at a time, so that the meringue will be smooth and not gritty. Continue beating until the meringue stands in stiff, glossy peaks when you raise the beaters.

Cream Puffs

It's actually quite easy to make cream puffs successfully at home. They are made from the French *choux* pastry, which is cooked on top of the stove before it is baked.

Be sure to use a liquid measuring cup and measure the water accurately.

Add the flour as soon as the butter is melted so the water doesn't evaporate too quickly.

An electric mixer at medium speed can be used to beat in the eggs. Beat at least one minute after each addition until the pastry is smooth and glossy.

It is important not to underbeat the pastry. A rubber spatula pulled through the pastry should leave a clean path.

The puffs should be golden brown, crisp and dry when they are fully baked or they will collapse.

Fill the puffs with pudding or whipped cream no more than 30 minutes before serving to prevent the bottoms from becoming soggy.

Store unfilled puffs in an airtight container at room temperature overnight or freeze up to three months.

Sweetened Whipped Cream

Chill the bowl and beaters in the freezer or refrigerator for 10 to 20 minutes or until cold. If you don't use a chilled bowl and beaters, the cream will whip but it will take longer. Always start with cold cream from the refrigerator for the best volume. Beat all ingredients with an electric mixer on high speed until peaks form.

Whipping (Heavy) Cream	Granulated or Powdered Sugar	Vanilla	Makes
1 cup	2 tablespoons	1 teaspoon	2 cups
¾ cup	2 tablespoons	1 teaspoon	1½ cups
½ cup	1 tablespoon	½ teaspoon	1 cup

Whipped Cream

A dollop of whipped cream adds that luscious finishing touch to any dessert—whether the dessert is served warm or cold.

Soft Whipped Cream: Beat just until cream has thickened and small peaks form when beaters are lifted from cream. The cream will flow softly over the top of a dessert.

Soft Peak Whipped Cream: Beat cream long enough to form soft peaks when the beaters are lifted from the cream. The cream will hold its shape on top of a dessert.

Overbeaten Whipped Cream: When cream is beaten too long, it will curdle and begin to separate. It is still tasty and can be used to top desserts if you don't mind the appearance.

Hot Fudge Sundae Cake

PREP TIME: 20 Minutes • **START TO FINISH:** 1 Hour 10 Minutes

9 servings

1 cup all-purpose flour

¾ cup granulated sugar

2 tablespoons unsweetened baking cocoa

2 teaspoons baking powder

¼ teaspoon salt

½ cup milk

2 tablespoons vegetable oil

1 teaspoon vanilla

1 cup chopped nuts, if desired

1¾ cups water

1 cup packed brown sugar

¼ cup unsweetened baking cocoa

Ice cream, if desired

1 Heat the oven to 350°F. In an ungreased 9-inch square pan, stir the flour, granulated sugar, 2 tablespoons cocoa, the baking powder and salt with a spoon until mixed. Stir in the milk, oil and vanilla until smooth. Stir in the nuts. Spread the batter evenly in the pan.

2 In a 2-cup glass measuring cup, microwave the water uncovered on High 3 to 5 minutes or until boiling.

3 Meanwhile, sprinkle the brown sugar and ¼ cup cocoa over the batter. Pour the water evenly over the batter.

4 Bake about 40 minutes or until the top is dry. Cool 10 minutes on a cooling rack.

5 Spoon the warm cake into dessert dishes. Top with ice cream. Spoon sauce from the pan onto each serving.

High Altitude (3500–6500 ft): Bake about 45 minutes.

1 Serving: Calories 260; Total Fat 4g; Cholesterol 0mg; Sodium 190mg; Total Carbohydrate 54g (Dietary Fiber 1g); Protein 3g **% Daily Value:** Vitamin A 0%; Vitamin C 0%; Calcium 10%; Iron 10% **Carbohydrate Choices:** 3½

Making Sundae Cake

Sprinkle the sugar and baking cocoa over the batter in the pan. Pour the hot water evenly over the batter.

Gingerbread with Lemon Sauce

PREP TIME: 10 Minutes • **START TO FINISH:** 1 Hour 5 Minutes

9 servings

GINGERBREAD

Baking spray with flour to grease pan

¾ cup water

2⅓ cups all-purpose flour

½ cup butter or margarine (1 stick), room temperature

⅓ cup granulated sugar

1 cup mild-flavor or full-flavor molasses

1 teaspoon baking soda

1 teaspoon ground ginger

1 teaspoon ground cinnamon

¾ teaspoon salt

1 large egg

LEMON SAUCE

½ cup granulated sugar

2 tablespoons cornstarch

¾ cup water

1 tablespoon grated lemon peel

¼ cup lemon juice

2 tablespoons butter or margarine

Sweetened Whipped Cream (page 193), if desired

1 Heat the oven to 325°F. Spray the bottom and sides of a 9-inch square pan with the baking spray. In a 1-cup glass measuring cup, microwave the water uncovered on High 1 to 2 minutes or until hot.

2 In a large bowl, beat hot water and remaining gingerbread ingredients with an electric mixer on low speed 30 seconds, stopping frequently to scrape batter from side and bottom of bowl with a rubber spatula. Beat on medium speed 3 minutes, stopping occasionally to scrape bowl. Pour batter into the pan; use a rubber spatula to scrape batter from bowl. Spread batter evenly in pan and smooth top of batter.

3 Bake 50 to 55 minutes or until a toothpick inserted in center comes out clean. Cool in pan on a cooling rack about 30 minutes.

4 Meanwhile, in a 1-quart saucepan, stir ½ cup sugar and the cornstarch until mixed. Gradually stir in ¾ cup water. Cook over medium heat, stirring constantly, until mixture thickens and boils. Boil and stir 1 minute; remove from heat. Stir in the lemon peel, lemon juice and 2 tablespoons butter.

5 Make Sweetened Whipped Cream. Serve squares of warm gingerbread with warm or room-temperature lemon sauce and whipped cream. Store any leftover sauce in the refrigerator up to 10 days.

High Altitude (3500–6500 ft): No change.

1 Serving: Calories 440; Total Fat 14g; Cholesterol 55mg; Sodium 450mg; Total Carbohydrate 74g (Dietary Fiber 1g); Protein 4g **% Daily Value:** Vitamin A 8%; Vitamin C 2%; Calcium 10%; Iron 20% **Carbohydrate Choices:** 5

Squeezing Juice

When squeezing juice, place the juicer over a measuring cup. The juicer also strains out most of the seeds and pulp.

Pineapple Upside-Down Cake

PREP TIME: 15 Minutes • **START TO FINISH:** 1 Hour 20 Minutes

9 servings

¼ cup butter or margarine
(½ stick)

1 can (20 oz) sliced pineapple in
juice*

⅔ cup packed brown sugar

Maraschino cherries without
stems, if desired

1⅓ cups all-purpose flour

¾ cup granulated sugar

⅓ cup butter or margarine

½ cup milk

1½ teaspoons baking powder

½ teaspoon salt

1 large egg

Sweetened Whipped Cream
(page 193), if desired

1 Heat the oven to 350°F. Place ¼ cup butter in a 9-inch round cake pan or square pan, then place pan in the oven to melt the butter. Meanwhile, drain the pineapple in a strainer in the sink (or save pineapple juice if desired).

2 Carefully remove pan from oven. Sprinkle the brown sugar over the melted butter. Arrange the pineapple slices on the brown sugar, cutting one or more slices into pieces if necessary to fit. Place a cherry in the center of each pineapple slice.

3 In a large bowl, beat the flour, granulated sugar, ⅓ cup butter, the milk, baking powder, salt and egg with an electric mixer on low speed 30 seconds, stopping frequently to scrape batter from side and bottom of bowl with a rubber spatula. Beat on high speed 3 minutes, stopping occasionally to scrape bowl. Pour batter over pineapple; use a rubber spatula to scrape batter from bowl. Spread batter evenly in pan and smooth top of batter.

4 Bake round pan 45 to 50 minutes, square pan 50 to 55 minutes, or until a toothpick inserted in the center comes out clean.

5 To remove cake from pan, immediately place a heatproof plate upside down on pan; holding plate and pan with pot holders, turn plate and pan over together. Let the pan remain over the cake a few minutes so brown sugar topping can drizzle over cake. Remove pan. Cool 15 minutes.

6 Meanwhile, make Sweetened Whipped Cream. Serve warm cake with whipped cream.

*A 20-oz can of crushed pineapple in juice can be substituted for the rings. Drain the pineapple in a strainer and spoon it on the brown sugar. Arrange the cherries on the pineapple.

High Altitude (3500–6500 ft): Decrease granulated sugar to ½ cup and baking powder to 1 teaspoon.

1 Serving: Calories 350; Total Fat 14g; Cholesterol 40mg; Sodium 270mg; Total Carbohydrate 53g (Dietary Fiber 1g); Protein 3g **% Daily Value:** Vitamin A 4%; Vitamin C 2%; Calcium 8%; Iron 8% **Carbohydrate Choices:** 3½

Arranging Pineapple Rings

Place a pineapple ring in the center of the pan, and arrange rings around it. Cut any remaining rings into pieces to fill in the spaces.

Boston Cream Pie

PREP TIME: 35 Minutes • **START TO FINISH:** 2 Hours 35 Minutes

8 servings

CREAM FILLING
2 large eggs

1½ cups milk

⅓ cup granulated sugar

2 tablespoons cornstarch

⅛ teaspoon salt

2 teaspoons vanilla

CAKE
Baking spray with flour to grease pan

1¼ cups all-purpose flour or 1½ cups cake flour

1 cup granulated sugar

⅓ cup butter or margarine, room temperature

¾ cup milk

1½ teaspoons baking powder

1 teaspoon vanilla

½ teaspoon salt

1 large egg

CHOCOLATE ICING
3 tablespoons butter or margarine

3 oz unsweetened baking chocolate

3 to 4 tablespoons water

1 cup powdered sugar

¾ teaspoon vanilla

1 Place an egg separator over a small bowl. Crack open 1 egg over the egg separator to separate the yolk from the white; then separate the other egg. (Save the whites for another recipe.) In a small bowl, place the yolks. Beat the egg yolks with a fork or wire whisk until mixed. Stir in 1½ cups milk; set aside.

2 In a 2-quart saucepan, stir ⅓ cup granulated sugar, the cornstarch and ⅛ teaspoon salt until mixed. Gradually stir egg mixture into sugar mixture. Cook over medium heat, stirring constantly, until mixture thickens and boils. Boil and stir 1 minute; remove from heat. Stir in 2 teaspoons vanilla. Press plastic wrap on surface of filling to prevent a tough layer from forming on top. Refrigerate at least 2 hours until set but no longer than 24 hours. While filling is chilling, continue with recipe.

3 Heat the oven to 350°F. Spray just the bottom of a 9-inch round cake pan with the baking spray.

4 In a large bowl, beat all cake ingredients with an electric mixer on low speed 30 seconds, stopping frequently to scrape batter from side and bottom of bowl with a rubber spatula. Beat on high speed 3 minutes, stopping occasionally to scrape bowl. Pour batter into the pan; use a rubber spatula to scrape batter from bowl. Spread batter evenly in pan and smooth top of batter.

5 Bake about 35 minutes or until a toothpick inserted in the center comes out clean. Cool cake in pan on a cooling rack 20 minutes, then remove onto cooling rack to finish cooling completely, about 1 hour. (See Removing Round Cake from Pan, page 62.)

6 In a 1-quart saucepan, melt 3 tablespoons butter and the chocolate over low heat, stirring occasionally. Meanwhile, in 1-cup glass measuring cup, microwave the water uncovered on High 15 to 30 seconds or until hot. Remove chocolate mixture from heat. Stir in the powdered sugar and ¾ teaspoon vanilla. Stir in 3 tablespoons hot water. Stir in additional water, 1 teaspoon at a time, until icing is smooth and thin enough to spread.

7 To split cake horizontally in half, mark middle points around side of cake with toothpicks. Using toothpicks as a guide, cut through the cake with a long, sharp knife, using a back-and-forth motion. On a serving plate, place bottom layer with the cut side up. Spread filling over bottom layer. Top with top of cake, cut side down.

8   Spread glaze over top of cake, using a metal spatula or back of a spoon, letting some glaze drizzle down side of cake. Refrigerate uncovered until serving. Store any remaining cake covered in the refrigerator.

High Altitude (3500–6500 ft): Increase all-purpose flour to 1½ cups or cake flour to 1¾ cups. Decrease sugar in cake to ¾ cup and butter to ½ cup.

1 Serving: Calories 510; Total Fat 21g; Cholesterol 115mg; Sodium 400mg; Total Carbohydrate 72g (Dietary Fiber 2g); Protein 7g **% Daily Value:** Vitamin A 10%; Vitamin C 0%; Calcium 15%; Iron 15% **Carbohydrate Choices:** 5

Splitting Cake Layer

Using toothpicks as a guide, cut through the cake with a long, sharp knife, using a back-and-forth motion.

Bread Pudding with Whiskey Sauce

PREP TIME: 25 Minutes • **START TO FINISH:** 2 Hours 20 Minutes

12 servings

BREAD PUDDING

Cooking spray for greasing baking dish

12 oz French bread or other firm bread

5 large eggs

¾ cup granulated sugar

2½ cups milk

2½ cups whipping cream

1 tablespoon vanilla

1 teaspoon ground cinnamon

½ cup raisins, if desired

2 tablespoons butter or margarine

2 tablespoons granulated sugar

½ teaspoon ground cinnamon

WHISKEY SAUCE

½ cup butter or margarine (1 stick)

2 tablespoons water

1 large egg

1 cup granulated sugar

2 tablespoons whiskey or bourbon or 1 teaspoon brandy extract

Cutting Bread Pieces

Stack two or three slices of bread and cut lengthwise into 1½-inch strips. Cut across the strips to make 1½-inch pieces.

1 Heat the oven to 325°F. Spray the bottom and sides of a 13 × 9-inch (3-quart) glass baking dish with the cooking spray. Cut the bread into ½-inch slices. Stack 2 or 3 slices; cut in half lengthwise into 1½-inch strips, then cut across to make 1½-inch pieces. Continue with remaining bread slices to measure 10 cups; set aside.

2 Place an egg separator over a small bowl. Crack open 1 egg, letting the yolk fall into the center of the separator and the egg white slip through the slots into the bowl (separate just 1 egg). Cover and refrigerate the egg white up to 4 days to use in another recipe.

3 In a large bowl, beat the egg yolk, 4 whole eggs and ¾ cup sugar with a wire whisk until well mixed. Beat in the milk, whipping cream, vanilla and 1 teaspoon cinnamon until well mixed. Stir in 7 cups of the bread pieces and the raisins. Let stand 20 minutes. Pour into baking dish. Sprinkle remaining 3 cups bread pieces evenly over bread mixture in baking dish. Lightly press down with a rubber spatula or back of a spoon.

4 Place 2 tablespoons butter in a small microwavable bowl; cover with a microwavable paper towel. Microwave on High 30 to 50 seconds or until melted. In another small bowl, stir 2 tablespoons sugar and ½ teaspoon cinnamon until well blended. Brush top of bread mixture with melted butter, using a pastry brush; sprinkle with cinnamon-sugar.

5 Bake 55 to 65 minutes or until the top is puffed and light golden brown (the center will jiggle slightly). Cool on a cooling rack 30 minutes.

6 Meanwhile, in a 1-quart saucepan, melt ½ cup butter over low heat. Remove from heat; cool 10 minutes. In a small bowl, mix the water and 1 egg with a fork; stir into butter until mixed. Stir in 1 cup sugar. Cook over medium-low heat, stirring constantly, until sugar is dissolved and mixture begins to boil; remove from heat. Stir in the whiskey. Cool at least 10 minutes before serving.

7 Serve sauce over warm bread pudding. Store any remaining dessert and sauce covered in refrigerator.

High Altitude (3500–6500 ft): Heat oven to 350°F.

1 Serving: Calories 500; Total Fat 30g; Cholesterol 190mg; Sodium 300mg; Total Carbohydrate 50g (Dietary Fiber 0g); Protein 8g **% Daily Value:** Vitamin A 20%; Vitamin C 0%; Calcium 15%; Iron 8% **Carbohydrate Choices:** 3

Apple Crisp

PREP TIME: 20 Minutes • **START TO FINISH:** 1 Hour

6 servings

6 medium tart apples (such as Granny Smith, Jonathan, McIntosh or Rome)

¾ cup packed brown sugar

½ cup all-purpose flour

½ cup quick-cooking or old-fashioned oats

¾ teaspoon ground cinnamon

¾ teaspoon ground nutmeg

⅓ cup butter or margarine

Ice cream or half-and-half, if desired

1 Heat the oven to 375°F. Peel the apples if desired. Cut each apple into quarters; remove core. Cut the apple quarters into ¼-inch slices to measure 6 cups. Spread the slices in an ungreased 8-inch square pan.

2 In a medium bowl, mix the brown sugar, flour, oats, cinnamon and nutmeg. Cut in the butter with a pastry blender or fork until mixture is crumbly. Sprinkle mixture evenly over apples.

3 Bake 35 to 40 minutes or until the topping is golden brown and the apples are tender when pierced with a fork. Serve warm with ice cream or half-or-half.

High Altitude (3500–6500 ft): Bake 40 to 45 minutes.

1 Serving: Calories 350; Total Fat 11g; Cholesterol 25mg; Sodium 85mg; Total Carbohydrate 59g (Dietary Fiber 5g); Protein 3g **% Daily Value:** Vitamin A 8%; Vitamin C 6%; Calcium 4%; Iron 8% **Carbohydrate Choices:** 4

Blueberry Crisp: Substitute 6 cups of fresh or frozen blueberries for the apples. If using frozen blueberries, thaw and drain them first.

Making Apple Crisp

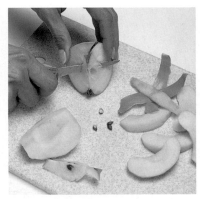

Cut the apple into quarters, and remove the core. Cut each quarter into slices.

Sprinkle the oat and brown sugar mixture, which will be crumbly, evenly over the apples.

Strawberry Shortcakes

PREP TIME: 15 Minutes • **START TO FINISH:** 1 Hour 15 Minutes

8 servings

STRAWBERRIES

2 pints (4 cups) strawberries

½ cup granulated sugar

SHORTCAKES

2 cups all-purpose flour

½ cup granulated sugar

3 teaspoons baking powder

½ teaspoon salt

½ cup cold butter or margarine
(1 stick)

1 large egg

⅔ cup milk

2 cups Sweetened Whipped
Cream (page 193)

1 Rinse the strawberries with cool water, and dry on paper towels. Cut out the hull, or "cap," from each strawberry with the point of a paring knife. Cut the strawberries lengthwise into slices. In a large bowl, stir the strawberries and ½ cup sugar until well mixed. Let stand about 1 hour so strawberries will become juicy.

2 Heat the oven to 425°F. In a medium bowl, stir the flour, ½ cup sugar, the baking powder and salt until mixed. Cut the butter into 1-tablespoon-size pieces; add to flour mixture. Cut in the butter, using a pastry blender or fork, until mixture looks like coarse crumbs. In a small bowl, beat the egg slightly with a fork. Stir the egg and milk into the flour mixture just until mixed.

3 Onto an ungreased cookie sheet, drop the dough by 8 spoonfuls about 2 inches apart. Bake 12 to 14 minutes or until golden brown.

4 Make Sweetened Whipped Cream. While the shortcakes are hot, split them in half horizontally, using a knife. Fill and top each shortcake with the strawberries and whipped cream.

High Altitude (3500–6500 ft): Heat oven to 400°F. In shortcakes, decrease sugar to ¼ cup and baking powder to 1½ teaspoons. Bake 14 to 16 minutes.

1 Serving: Calories 460; Total Fat 22g; Cholesterol 90mg; Sodium 440mg; Total Carbohydrate 60g (Dietary Fiber 2g); Protein 6g **% Daily Value:** Vitamin A 15%; Vitamin C 70%; Calcium 15%; Iron 10% **Carbohydrate Choices:** 4

Easy Strawberry Shortcake: Heat the oven to 375°F. Spray bottom and side of 8-inch or 9-inch round cake pan with baking spray with flour. Make dough as directed. Spoon into pan; spread evenly with a rubber spatula. Bake 30 to 35 minutes or until toothpick inserted in center comes out clean. Cool 10 minutes. Remove cake from pan and place on cutting board. To serve, cut shortcake into 6 wedges and top with strawberries and whipped cream.

Dropping Shortcake Dough

Drop dough by spoonfuls onto an ungreased cookie sheet. If dough is sticky, use a rubber spatula or another spoon to push the dough off the spoon.

Fresh Peach Cobbler

PREP TIME: 35 Minutes • **START TO FINISH:** 1 Hour 5 Minutes
6 servings

6 medium peaches*
½ cup granulated sugar
1 tablespoon cornstarch
¼ teaspoon ground cinnamon
1 teaspoon lemon juice
1 cup all-purpose flour
1 tablespoon granulated sugar
1½ teaspoons baking powder
½ teaspoon salt
3 tablespoons cold butter or
    margarine
½ cup milk
2 tablespoons granulated sugar
Sweetened Whipped Cream
    (page 193), if desired

1 Heat the oven to 400°F. Cut each peach in half, and remove the pit. Peel each peach half, using a paring knife. Cut peaches into slices to measure 4 cups.

2 In a 2-quart saucepan, stir ½ cup sugar, the cornstarch and cinnamon until mixed. Stir in the peaches and lemon juice. Cook over medium-high heat 4 to 5 minutes, stirring frequently, until mixture thickens and boils. Boil and stir 1 minute. Pour into an ungreased 2-quart casserole; keep peach mixture hot in oven while making dough.

3 In a medium bowl, stir flour, 1 tablespoon sugar, the baking powder and salt until mixed. Cut in the butter, using a pastry blender or fork, until mixture looks like fine crumbs. Stir in the milk. Drop dough by 6 spoonfuls onto the hot peach mixture. Sprinkle 2 tablespoons sugar over the dough.

4 Bake 25 to 30 minutes or until topping is golden brown. Meanwhile, make Sweetened Whipped Cream. Serve warm cobbler with whipped cream.

*You can substitute 4 cups frozen sliced peaches (from two 1-lb bags), thawed and drained, for the fresh peaches.

High Altitude (3500–6500 ft): No change.

1 Serving: Calories 280; Total Fat 7g; Cholesterol 15mg; Sodium 370mg; Total Carbohydrate 51g (Dietary Fiber 2g); Protein 4g **% Daily Value:** Vitamin A 10%; Vitamin C 6%; Calcium 10%; Iron 8% **Carbohydrate Choices:** 3½

Fresh Blueberry Cobbler: Substitute 4 cups blueberries for the peaches. Omit cinnamon.

Fresh Cherry Cobbler: Substitute 4 cups pitted fresh sour cherries (such as Early Richmond and Montmorency) for the peaches. Increase sugar in cherry mixture to 1¼ cups and cornstarch to 3 tablespoons. Substitute ¼ teaspoon almond extract for the lemon juice.

Slicing Peaches

Cut the peach lengthwise in half around the pit. Twist the peach halves in opposite directions to separate halves. Remove the pit. Peel the peach halves with a paring knife, and cut into slices.

Berry Cheesecake

PREP TIME: 30 Minutes • **START TO FINISH:** 9 Hours 35 Minutes

16 servings

Special Equipment: 9 × 3-inch springform pan

---

4 packages (8 oz each) cream cheese

About 38 thin chocolate wafer cookies (from 9-oz package)

¼ cup butter or margarine (½ stick)

⅔ cup granulated sugar

½ cup sour cream

1 tablespoon grated orange peel

4 large eggs

½ cup sour cream

2 tablespoons granulated sugar

2 cups assorted berries (such as blackberries, blueberries, raspberries and sliced strawberries)

Loosening Cheesecake from Pan

Run a metal spatula between the cheesecake and side of pan to loosen the baked cheesecake from the pan. It will be easier if you first dip the metal spatula into hot water and wipe off the water.

1 Place blocks of cream cheese on a plate, and let stand at room temperature about 30 minutes to soften slightly. Or to soften cream cheese in the microwave, remove foil wrappers and place in microwavable bowl; microwave on Medium (50%) 1 minute to 1 minute 30 seconds.

2 Heat the oven to 325°F. Place half of the cookies in a resealable food-storage plastic bag; seal the bag. Roll over cookies with a rolling pin or bottle, or press with bottom of small saucepan, to crush cookies into fine crumbs; place crumbs in a measuring cup. Crush the remaining cookies. You should have 2 cups of crumbs. Place crumbs in a medium bowl.

3 In a 1-quart saucepan, heat the butter over low heat until melted. Stir melted butter into cookie crumbs until well mixed. Using fingers, press crumb mixture firmly and evenly against the bottom and 2 inches up the side of an ungreased 9 × 3-inch springform pan to seal the bottom of the pan.

4 In a large bowl, beat the softened cream cheese, ⅔ cup sugar, ½ cup sour cream and the orange peel with an electric mixer on medium speed about 1 minute or until smooth. Add the eggs; beat on low speed until well blended. Pour mixture into crust; use a rubber spatula to scrape mixture from bowl. Spread evenly in pan and smooth top.

5 Bake 1 hour 10 minutes to 1 hour 20 minutes or until the center is set. Cool in pan on a cooling rack 15 minutes. Before removing the side of the pan, run a metal spatula or tableware knife between the cheesecake and inside of the pan. Remove side of pan, leaving cheesecake on pan bottom for serving. Refrigerate uncovered
3 hours, then cover and continue refrigerating at least 4 hours.

6 In a small bowl, stir ½ cup sour cream and 2 tablespoons sugar until mixed; spread over the top of the cheesecake. Top with berries.

High Altitude (3500–6500 ft): When baking, place pan of water on the oven rack below the rack with the cheesecake.

1 Serving: Calories 390; Total Fat 29g; Cholesterol 135mg; Sodium 290mg; Total Carbohydrate 24g (Dietary Fiber 1g); Protein 7g **% Daily Value:** Vitamin A 20%; Vitamin C 10%; Calcium 8%; Iron 8% **Carbohydrate Choices:** 1½

Cream Puffs

PREP TIME: 30 Minutes • **START TO FINISH:** 2 Hours 5 Minutes

12 cream puffs

PUFFS

½ cup butter or margarine
   (1 stick)

1 cup water

1 cup all-purpose flour

4 large eggs

CREAM FILLING

2 large eggs

⅓ cup granulated sugar

2 tablespoons cornstarch

⅛ teaspoon salt

2 cups milk

2 tablespoons butter
   or margarine, room
   temperature

2 teaspoons vanilla

Powdered sugar, if desired

Making Cream Puff Dough

Stir vigorously with a wooden spoon after adding the flour until the mixture forms a ball that does not separate.

1   Heat the oven to 400°F. Cut ½ cup butter into 1-tablespoon-size pieces. In a 2-quart saucepan, heat the butter and water over high heat, stirring occasionally, until boiling rapidly.

2   Stir the flour into the boiling mixture; reduce heat to low. With a wooden spoon, beat vigorously over low heat about 1 minute or until the mixture forms a ball; remove from heat.

3   With a wooden spoon, beat in 1 egg at a time, beating vigorously after each addition until mixture is smooth and glossy.* Onto an ungreased cookie sheet, drop the dough by slightly less than ¼ cupfuls in mounds about 3 inches apart.

4   Bake 35 to 40 minutes or until puffed and golden. Remove from cookie sheet to a cooling rack; prick side of each puff with the tip of a sharp knife to release steam. Cool puffs, away from drafts, for 30 minutes.

5   Meanwhile, place an egg separator over a small bowl. Crack open 1 egg, letting the yolk fall into the center of the separator and the egg white slip through the slots into the bowl. Place yolk in a medium bowl, then separate the other egg. Cover and refrigerate egg whites up to 4 days to use in another recipe.

6   Slightly beat the egg yolks with a wire whisk; set aside. In a 2-quart saucepan, stir the granulated sugar, cornstarch and salt until mixed. Gradually stir in the milk with a wire whisk. Cook over medium heat, stirring constantly, until mixture thickens and boils. Boil and stir 1 minute. Gradually stir at least half of the hot mixture into the egg yolks, then stir the egg mixture back into the hot mixture in the saucepan. Boil and stir 1 minute; remove from heat. Stir in 2 tablespoons butter and the vanilla. Press plastic wrap on surface of filling to prevent a tough layer from forming on top. Refrigerate at least 1 hour or until cool.

7   Cut off the top third of each puff, using a sharp knife; reserve tops. Pull out any strands of soft dough from puffs. Fill bottom of each puff with about 2 rounded tablespoons filling; replace the tops. Sprinkle with powdered sugar. Cover and refrigerate until serving. Store any remaining cream puffs covered in the refrigerator.

Ice-Cream Puffs: Omit the Cream Filling and fill cream puffs with your favorite flavor ice cream. Cover and freeze until serving. Serve with chocolate sauce or caramel sauce.

Whipped Cream Puffs: Omit the Cream Filling. In a chilled large bowl, beat 2 cups whipping cream and ¼ cup granulated or powdered sugar with electric mixer on high speed until soft peaks form. Fill cream puffs with whipped cream. Sprinkle with powdered sugar or serve with chocolate sauce.

*Or beat in eggs with an electric mixer on medium speed. Beat 1 minute after adding each egg.

High Altitude (3500–6500 ft): No change.

1 Cream Puff: Calories 210; Total Fat 13g; Cholesterol 135mg; Sodium 140mg; Total Carbohydrate 17g (Dietary Fiber 0g); Protein 6g **% Daily Value:** Vitamin A 10%; Vitamin C 0%; Calcium 6%; Iron 4% **Carbohydrate Choices:** 1

213

Cherry-Berry Meringue Torte

PREP TIME: 30 Minutes • **START TO FINISH:** 18 Hours

8 servings

MERINGUE SHELL

3 large eggs

¼ teaspoon cream of tartar

¾ cup granulated sugar

CREAM FILLING

1 package (3 oz) cream cheese

½ cup granulated sugar

½ teaspoon vanilla

1 cup whipping cream

1 cup miniature marshmallows

CHERRY-BERRY TOPPING

1½ cups fresh strawberries

1 can (21 oz) cherry pie filling

1 teaspoon lemon juice

Shaping Meringue Shell

Shape meringue with the back of a spoon into a round, building up the side.

1 About 30 minutes before making the meringue shell, place an egg separator over a small bowl. Crack open each egg over the egg separator to separate the white from the yolk. (Save egg yolks for another recipe.)

2 Place the egg whites in a clean medium bowl, and let stand at room temperature up to 30 minutes.*

3 Heat the oven to 275°F. Line a cookie sheet with a piece of foil or cooking parchment paper.

4 Add the cream of tartar to the egg whites; beat with an electric mixer on high speed until mixture looks foamy. Beat in ¾ cup sugar, 1 tablespoon at a time; continue beating about 5 minutes, stopping occasionally to scrape mixture from side and bottom of bowl with a rubber spatula, until mixture is glossy and forms stiff peaks when beaters are lifted. (Do not underbeat because the meringue shell won't hold its shape.) On the cookie sheet, shape the meringue into a 9-inch round with the back of a spoon, building up about a 1-inch side.

5 Bake 1 hour 30 minutes. Turn off oven; leave meringue in oven with door closed 1 hour. Remove from oven and cool on a cooling rack 2 hours longer.

6 Place a medium bowl and the beaters of electric mixer in refrigerator to chill. These will be used to beat the whipping cream, which beats better in a cold bowl.

7 Place block of cream cheese on a plate, and let stand at room temperature about 30 minutes to soften slightly. Or to soften cream cheese in the microwave, remove foil wrapper and place in microwavable bowl; microwave on Medium (50%) 45 to 60 seconds.

8 In a large bowl, stir together the softened cream cheese, ½ cup sugar and the vanilla until mixed; set aside.

9 Pour the whipping cream into the chilled bowl. Insert the chilled beaters in the electric mixer. Beat on high speed until whipped cream forms soft peaks when beaters are lifted. Gently fold the whipped cream and marshmallows into the cream cheese mixture.

10 Place the meringue on a serving plate, and spoon the filling onto the meringue. Cover and refrigerate at least 12 hours to blend the flavors but no longer than 24 hours.

11 Rinse the strawberries with cool water, and dry on paper towels. Cut out the hull, or "cap," from each strawberry with the point of a paring knife. Cut the strawberries lengthwise into slices to measure 1 cup. In a medium bowl, stir together the pie filling, strawberries and lemon juice.

12 To serve, spoon the berry mixture onto the filling. Or cut the meringue shell into serving pieces, and top each serving with the berry mixture.

*Egg whites will have better volume when beaten at room temperature in a bowl that is clean and dry.

High Altitude (3500–6500 ft): No change.

1 Serving: Calories 370 Total Fat 13g; Cholesterol 45mg; Sodium 70mg; Total Carbohydrate 59g (Dietary Fiber 1g); Protein 4g **% Daily Value:** Vitamin A 10%; Vitamin C 25%; Calcium 4%; Iron 2% **Carbohydrate Choices:** 4

Individual Cherry-Berry Meringue Tortes: Line a cookie sheet with a piece of foil or cooking parchment paper. Drop meringue by ⅓ cupfuls onto cookie sheet. Shape into about 4-inch rounds, building up about ½-inch sides. Bake 1 hour. Turn off oven; leave meringues in oven with door closed 1 hour 30 minutes. Finish cooling at room temperature, about 2 hours. Make Cream Filling as directed; divide among meringue shells. Cover; refrigerate at least 12 hours but no longer than 24 hours. Make Cherry-Berry Topping; serve with meringues.

7 YOU CAN BAKE IT!

YOU CAN BAKE IT 101

Now you're feeling comfortable baking butter-type cakes for a party, whipping up a batch of muffins for brunch or shaping a loaf of yeast bread. It's time to hone your baking skills and try some recipes that take a little more technique.

Angel Food Cake

Angel food cake is a type of foam cake. The trick to making an angel food cake is beating the egg whites properly and folding the flour mixture into the beaten egg whites so you don't break down the air. The ideal angel food cake should have a high volume with a golden brown rounded top with cracks. The interior should be soft, moist and delicate with a feathery, fine texture. Here are some guidelines for making an angel food cake you will be proud of.

Don't grease and flour pans for angel food cake unless directed to in the recipe. During baking, the batter has to cling to and climb up the side and tube of the pan.

If you're using an angel food cake pan (tube pan), move the oven rack to the lowest position so the cake will bake completely without getting too brown on top.

Start with a clean, dry bowl and beaters so the egg whites will beat properly. Even a speck of fat from an egg yolk will keep them from whipping up.

Beat the egg whites until stiff, straight peaks form when beaters are raised. Underbeating or underfolding the egg whites can result in coarse, low-volume cakes. Overbeating or overfolding can break down the egg whites and result in compact cakes.

Angel food cakes are done when the cracks feel dry and the top springs back when touched lightly. A cake that pulls away from the side of the pan and/or falls out of the pan is overbaked.

When the cake is done, immediately turn the pan upside down onto a heatproof funnel or bottle. Let it hang until the cake is completely cooled, about two hours.

To remove the cooled cake from the pan, slide a tableware knife or metal spatula between the cake and side of pan. Move the knife up and down, being careful not to tear the cake. Invert the pan. The cake will slip out.

What Went Wrong?

Angel Food Cake

This Happened	This Is Why
Low and compact	• underbeaten or extremely overbeaten egg whites • overfolded batter • incorrect cooling (not cooled upside down)
Coarse texture	• underfolded batter
Tough	• underbeaten egg whites • overfolded batter

Making Angel Food Cake

Beat egg whites and sugar until stiff and glossy peaks form when the beaters are removed from the egg whites.

Using a rubber spatula, cut down vertically through center of egg whites, across the bottom and up the side, turning egg whites over.

Using a metal spatula, cut through batter, pushing batter against side of pan to break large air pockets.

Melting Chocolate

Melting chocolate isn't as easy as it may seem. It can become thick and grainy, and you may not have a clue what went wrong.

Be sure the pan and utensils are dry because even a drop or two of water can cause chocolate to become stiff and grainy, which is known as "seizing."

Use a heavy pan on very low heat and stir frequently to avoid scorching or burning the chocolate. Heat that's too high will also cause the chocolate to seize.

Chopping the chocolate before melting helps the chocolate melt quicker.

Stir the chocolate occasionally to prevent scorching. Also, by blending the solid pieces with the melted chocolate, the pieces will melt faster.

Correcting Seized Chocolate

If the smallest amount of moisture, such as steam, condensation or a few drops of water, comes in contact with chocolate while it melts, the chocolate will "seize," or turn grainy and hard. If this happens, remove the pan from the heat. With a wire whisk, stir in a liquid (warm water or milk, melted butter or margarine, vegetable oil or shortening), 1 tablespoon at a time, until the chocolate is smooth.

Seized chocolate is thick, dull and grainy.

Stir in a small amount of warm water until smooth and shiny.

Melting Chocolate in the Microwave

Baking Chocolate: Place 1 to 3 ounces unwrapped squares in a microwavable glass dish or measuring cup. Microwave uncovered on Medium (50%) 1½ to 1½ minutes, stirring frequently, until melted.

Chocolate Chips: Place ½ to 1 cup chips in microwavable glass bowl or glass measuring cup. Microwave uncovered on Medium (50%) 2 to 3 minutes, stirring frequently because chips will not change shape until melted.

Almond Biscotti

PREP TIME: 25 Minutes • **START TO FINISH:** 1 Hour 45 Minutes

40 cookies

1 cup slivered almonds

1 cup granulated sugar

½ cup butter or margarine (1 stick), room temperature

1 teaspoon almond extract

1 teaspoon vanilla

2 large eggs

3½ cups all-purpose flour

1 teaspoon baking powder

½ teaspoon baking soda

Hazelnut Biscotti: Substitute 1 cup hazelnuts (filberts), coarsely chopped, for the almonds.

1 Heat the oven to 350°F. Spread the almonds in an ungreased shallow pan. Bake 6 to 10 minutes, stirring occasionally, until light brown; cool.

2 Meanwhile, in a large bowl, beat the sugar, butter, almond extract, vanilla and eggs with an electric mixer on medium speed (or with a wooden spoon) until mixed. With a wooden spoon, stir in the flour, baking powder and baking soda until mixed. Stir in the toasted almonds.

3 Lightly sprinkle flour over a cutting board or countertop. Place the dough on the floured surface. To knead dough, fold dough toward you. With the heels of your hands, gently push dough away from you with a short rocking motion. Move dough a quarter turn and repeat 2 to 3 minutes or until dough holds together and almonds are evenly distributed.

4 Divide the dough in half. On one side of an ungreased cookie sheet, shape half of dough into a 10 × 3-inch rectangle, rounding edges slightly, using hands. Repeat with remaining dough on same cookie sheet.

5 Bake about 25 minutes or until the center is firm to the touch. Cool on cookie sheet 15 minutes, then move to a cutting board. Cut each rectangle diagonally crosswise into ½-inch slices, using a serrated or sharp knife.

6 Place 20 of the slices, cut sides down, on ungreased cookie sheet. Bake about 15 minutes longer or until crisp and light brown. Immediately remove from cookie sheet to a cooling rack; cool. Cool cookie sheet 5 minutes, then repeat with remaining slices.

High Altitude (3500–6500 ft): Increase first bake time to about 27 minutes. Increase second bake time to about 20 minutes.

1 Cookie: Calories 100; Total Fat 4g; Cholesterol 15mg; Sodium 50mg; Total Carbohydrate 14g (Dietary Fiber 0g); Protein 2g **% Daily Value:** Vitamin A 0%; Vitamin C 0%; Calcium 0%; Iron 4% **Carbohydrate Choices:** 1

Making Biscotti

Shape the dough into a rectangle using hands. Round the edges slightly.

Cut the rectangle diagonally into ½-inch slices after the first baking, using a serrated or sharp knife. Place slices, cut sides down, on cookie sheet.

Spritz

PREP TIME: 1 Hour 50 Minutes • **START TO FINISH:** 2 Hours 20 Minutes
About 5 dozen cookies

Special Equipment: Cookie press

1 cup butter (2 sticks),
    room temperature*
½ cup granulated sugar
1 large egg
2½ cups all-purpose flour
¼ teaspoon salt
¼ teaspoon almond extract
    or vanilla
Few drops of food color, if desired
Colored sugars, red cinnamon
    candies, nonpareils, edible
    sprinkles, candy-coated mini
    baking bits, if desired

1 Heat the oven to 400°F. In a large bowl, beat the butter, sugar and egg with an electric mixer on medium speed (or with a wooden spoon) until mixed. Stir in the flour, salt, almond extract and food color until mixed.

2 Fit desired disc in the cookie press, following the manufacturer's directions. Place the dough in the cookie press barrel. On an ungreased room temperature aluminum cookie sheet,** form desired shapes. (It is important to press out the correct amount of dough; too little, and it sticks on the press. Too much, and the design of the cookie disappears during baking. It will take a little practice to press just the right amount of dough. It is best to do a test by forming a couple of cookies and baking them to be sure the consistency and amount of dough is correct.) Sprinkle cookies with colored sugar.

3 Bake 5 to 8 minutes or until set but not brown. Immediately remove from cookie sheet to a cooling rack. Cool completely, about 30 minutes.

*We recommend using only butter for the correct consistency of the dough and a rich flavor.

**Do not use a nonstick cookie sheet or a warm cookie sheet or line the cookie sheet with parchment paper because the dough will not stick.

High Altitude (3500–6500 ft): No change.

1 Cookie: Calories 50; Total Fat 3g; Cholesterol 10mg; Sodium 35mg; Total Carbohydrate 6g (Dietary Fiber 0g); Protein 0g **% Daily Value:** Vitamin A 0%; Vitamin C 0%; Calcium 0%; Iron 0% **Carbohydrate Choices:** ½

Chocolate Spritz: Stir 2 oz unsweetened baking chocolate, melted and cooled, into butter-sugar mixture. Omit food color.

Spicy Spritz: Stir in 1 teaspoon ground cinnamon, ½ teaspoon ground nutmeg and ¼ teaspoon ground allspice with the flour.

Making Spritz Cookies

Place the press upright on the cookie sheet. Turn the knob clockwise to press out enough dough to make a cookie. Give the knob a slight turn counterclockwise to help release the dough.

If the dough is too soft and is sticking to the cookie press, stir in a small amount of flour, 1 teaspoon at a time, until dough is no longer sticky. Or remove the cookie dough from the cookie press barrel and chill the cookie press.

German Chocolate Cake

PREP TIME: 30 Minutes • **START TO FINISH:** 2 Hours 20 Minutes

12 servings

CAKE
Cooking spray to grease pans

4 oz sweet baking chocolate

½ cup water

**2¼ cups all-purpose flour
or 2½ cups cake flour**

1 teaspoon baking soda

1 teaspoon salt

2 cups granulated sugar

**1 cup butter or margarine
(2 sticks), room temperature**

4 large eggs

1 teaspoon vanilla

1 cup buttermilk

COCONUT-PECAN FILLING
3 large eggs

**1 cup granulated sugar or
packed brown sugar**

**½ cup butter or margarine
(1 stick)**

**1 cup evaporated milk
(from 12-oz can)**

1 teaspoon vanilla

1⅓ cups flaked coconut

1 cup chopped pecans

Beating Sugar and Butter

**Beat the granulated sugar and
butter** until it is well combined
and has a light, fluffy appearance.

1 Heat the oven to 350°F. Spray the bottoms and sides of three 8-inch or 9-inch round cake pans with the cooking spray. Cut three 8-inch or 9-inch rounds of waxed paper or cooking parchment paper. Line bottoms of pans with the paper.

2 Coarsely chop the chocolate. In a 1-quart saucepan, heat the chocolate and water over low heat, stirring frequently, until chocolate is completely melted; remove from heat and cool.

3 Meanwhile, in a medium bowl, stir the flour, baking soda and salt until mixed; set aside. In another medium bowl, beat 2 cups sugar and 1 cup butter with an electric mixer on medium speed until light and fluffy; set aside.

4 Place an egg separator over a small bowl. Crack 1 egg over the egg separator to separate the yolk from the white. Separate 3 more eggs. Place yolks in a small bowl. (Save the white for another recipe.)

5 On medium speed, beat 1 egg yolk at a time into the sugar mixture until mixed. On low speed, beat in the melted chocolate and 1 teaspoon vanilla. On low speed, beat in ½ of the flour mixture just until smooth, then beat in ½ of the buttermilk just until smooth. Repeat beating in flour mixture alternately with the buttermilk just until smooth.

6 Wash and dry mixer beaters. In a small bowl, beat the eggs whites on high speed until beaten egg whites form stiff peaks when beaters are lifted. Add egg whites to the batter; to fold in, use a rubber spatula to cut down vertically through the batter, then slide the spatula across the bottom of the bowl and up the side, turning batter over. Rotate the bowl a quarter turn, and repeat this down-across-up motion. Continue folding until batter and egg whites are blended.

7 Pour batter into pans; use a rubber spatula to scrape batter from bowl, spread batter evenly in pans and smooth top of batter. (If batter is not divided evenly, spoon batter from one pan to another.) Refrigerate batter in third pan if not all pans will fit in oven at one time; bake third pan separately.

8 Bake 8-inch pans 35 to 40 minutes, 9-inch pans 30 to 35 minutes, or until a toothpick inserted in the center comes out clean.

9 Cool cakes in pans 10 minutes. To remove cake from pan, invert onto cooling rack, then invert right side up on second cooling rack. (See Removing Round Cake from Pan, page 62.) Cool completely, about 1 hour.

10 Separate the 3 eggs; save the egg whites for another recipe. In a 2-quart saucepan, stir the egg yolks, 1 cup sugar, ½ cup butter, the evaporated milk and 1 teaspoon vanilla until well mixed. Cook over medium heat about 12 minutes, stirring frequently, until thick and bubbly. Stir in the coconut and pecans. Cool about 30 minutes, beating occasionally with a spoon, until mixture is spreadable.

11 Place 1 cake layer, rounded side down, on a cake plate; using a metal spatula, spread ⅓ of the filling over the layer. Add second layer, rounded side down; spread with ⅓ of the filling. Add third layer, rounded side up; spread with remaining filling, leaving side of cake unfrosted. Store any remaining cake covered in the refrigerator.

High Altitude (3500–6500 ft): Heat oven to 375°F. In cake, decrease sugar to 1¾ cups and butter to ¾ cup.

1 Serving: Calories 730; Total Fat 40g; Cholesterol 190mg; Sodium 550mg; Total Carbohydrate 83g (Dietary Fiber 2g); Protein 9g **% Daily Value:** Vitamin A 20%; Vitamin C 0%; Calcium 10%; Iron 10% **Carbohydrate Choices:** 5½

Molten Chocolate Cakes

PREP TIME: 20 Minutes • **START TO FINISH:** 40 Minutes

6 servings

Shortening to grease cups

Unsweetened baking cocoa

6 large eggs

6 oz semisweet baking chocolate

½ cup (1 stick) plus 2 tablespoons butter or margarine

1½ cups powdered sugar

½ cup all-purpose flour

Additional powdered sugar, if desired

Do-Ahead Molten Chocolate Cakes: Prepare the batter and pour into custard cups as directed. Cover with plastic wrap and refrigerate up to 24 hours. You may need to bake the cakes 1 to 2 minutes longer.

Molten Cake Doneness

The center of the cake should be slightly thick and flowing. If underbaked the center will be too runny and if overbaked it will be cake-like in the center. Use an oven thermometer to check that the oven temperature is correct.

1 Heat the oven to 450°F. Grease the bottoms and sides of six 6-ounce custard cups with the shortening. Dust the cups with the cocoa by adding a small of amount of cocoa to each cup, then rotating the cup to cover the inside with cocoa; tap out excess cocoa over the sink.*

2 Place an egg separator over a small bowl. Crack 1 egg over the egg separator to separate the yolk from the white. (Save the white for another recipe.) Separate 2 more eggs; place yolks in a large bowl. Set egg yolks and 3 whole eggs aside.

3 Coarsely chop the chocolate. In a 2-quart saucepan, melt the chocolate and butter over low heat, stirring frequently; remove from heat. Cool slightly.

4 Add 3 whole eggs to the yolks in the large bowl; beat with a wire whisk until well mixed. Beat in 1½ cups powdered sugar until mixed. Beat in melted chocolate mixture and the flour until mixed. Divide the batter evenly among the custard cups. Place cups on a cookie sheet with sides.

5 Bake 12 to 14 minutes or until sides of cakes are set and centers are still soft (tops will be puffed and cracked). Let stand 3 minutes.

6 Run a small knife or metal spatula along sides of cakes to loosen. Immediately place a heatproof serving plate upside down onto each cup; holding plate and cup with pot holders, turn plate and cup over together, then remove cup. Sprinkle additional powdered sugar over cakes. Serve warm.

*Be sure to grease the custard cups with shortening, dust the cups with cocoa and bake the cakes at the correct oven temperature for the right time. These steps are critical to the success of this recipe. If the centers are too cake-like in texture, bake a few minutes less the next time; if they're too soft, bake a minute or two longer.

High Altitude (3500–6500 ft): Bake 14 to 16 minutes.

1 Serving: Calories 550; Total Fat 33g; Cholesterol 260mg; Sodium 170mg; Total Carbohydrate 56g (Dietary Fiber 2g); Protein 7g **% Daily Value:** Vitamin A 15%; Vitamin C 0%; Calcium 4%; Iron 10% **Carbohydrate Choices:** 4

Petits Fours

PREP TIME: 50 Minutes • **START TO FINISH:** 3 Hours 20 Minutes

About 54 pieces

WHITE CAKE
Baking spray with flour to grease pan

5 large eggs

2¼ cups all-purpose flour

1½ cups granulated sugar

⅔ cup butter or margarine, room temperature

1¼ cups milk

3½ teaspoons baking powder

1 teaspoon salt

1 teaspoon vanilla

ALMOND GLAZE
1 bag (2 lb) powdered sugar (about 7½ cups)

½ cup water

½ cup light corn syrup

2 teaspoons almond extract

1 to 3 teaspoons hot water

1 tube (4.25 oz) white decorating icing

Glazing Petits Fours

Spoon glaze evenly over cake piece so glaze covers top and sides of cake. Work quickly so glaze is smooth.

---

1 Heat the oven to 350°F. Spray the bottom and sides of a 15 × 10 × 1-inch pan with the baking spray.

2 Place an egg separator over a small bowl. Crack each egg over the egg separator to separate the yolk from the white. (Save the yolks for another recipe.)

3 In a large bowl, beat the egg whites and remaining cake ingredients with an electric mixer on low speed 30 seconds, stopping occasionally to scrape batter from side and bottom of bowl with a rubber spatula. Beat on high speed 3 minutes, stopping occasionally to scrape bowl. Pour the batter into the pan; use a rubber spatula to scrape batter from bowl. Spread batter evenly in pan and smooth top of batter.

4 Bake 25 to 30 minutes or until a toothpick inserted in the center comes out clean. Cool in pan 20 minutes on a cooling rack. To remove cake from pan, place a rectangular cooling rack upside down on pan; holding rack and pan with pot holders, turn rack and pan over together, then remove pan (leave top of cake down on rack). Cool completely, about 1 hour.

5 Place a piece of waxed paper or cooking parchment paper on the cake; top with an upside-down 15 × 10-inch cookie sheet. Holding cookie sheet and cooling rack, turn cookie sheet and rack over together so top of cake is facing up, then remove rack. Place cake in freezer 25 to 30 minutes or just until cake is firm (this makes it easier to cut into shapes). Cut cake into 1½-inch squares, rounds, diamonds or hearts; place in freezer until ready to glaze.

6 Line another cookie sheet with waxed paper or cooking parchment paper; place a cooling rack on the cookie sheet. In a 3-quart saucepan, stir the 7½ cups powdered sugar, ½ cup water, the corn syrup and almond extract until mixed. Heat over low heat, stirring frequently, until sugar is dissolved; remove from heat. Stir 1 teaspoon hot water at a time into glaze until glaze is smooth and pourable when poured from a spoon.

7 Place several cake pieces on the rack. Spoon enough glaze over top of each cake piece to cover top and sides. Repeat with remaining cake pieces. If glaze becomes too thick, it can be reheated over low heat, stirring constantly, until smooth and pourable. Any glaze on the paper-lined cookie sheet can be returned to the saucepan and reheated, stirring constantly, until glaze is smooth and pourable. Let cakes stand 15 minutes. With decorating icing, make a fun design on top of each petit four.

High Altitude (3500–6500 ft): Decrease baking powder to 2½ teaspoons.

1 Piece (Cake and Frosting): Calories 140; Total Fat 2.5g; Cholesterol 5mg; Sodium 100mg; Total Carbohydrate 29g (Dietary Fiber 0g); Protein 1g **% Daily Value:** Vitamin A 0%; Vitamin C 0%; Calcium 2%; Iron 0% **Carbohydrate Choices:** 2

229

Angel Food Cake

PREP TIME: 15 Minutes • **START TO FINISH:** 3 Hours 20 Minutes

12 servings

About 12 large eggs

1½ cups powdered sugar

1 cup cake flour or all-purpose flour

1½ teaspoons cream of tartar

1 cup granulated sugar

1½ teaspoons vanilla

½ teaspoon almond extract

¼ teaspoon salt

High Altitude (3500–6500 ft): Bake cake 40 to 45 minutes. Use paper baking cups when making cupcakes; recipe makes 36 cupcakes.

1 Serving: Calories 190; Total Fat 0g; Cholesterol 0mg; Sodium 105mg; Total Carbohydrate 41g (Dietary Fiber 0g); Protein 5g **% Daily Value:** Vitamin A 0%; Vitamin C 0%; Calcium 0%; Iron 4% **Carbohydrate Choices:** 3

Cooling Angel Food Cake

Immediately turn pan upside down onto a heatproof funnel or bottle. Let cake hang about two hours or until completely cool before removing from pan or it will collapse.

1 About 30 minutes before making the cake, place an egg separator over a small bowl. Crack each egg over the egg separator to separate the whites from the yolk. (Save the yolks for another recipe.) Transfer egg whites to a 2-cup measuring cup until there are 1½ cups of egg whites.

2 Place the egg whites in a clean large bowl, and let stand at room temperature up to 30 minutes.*

3 Move the oven rack to the lowest position; remove other oven rack. Heat the oven to 375°F. In a medium bowl, mix the powdered sugar and flour; set aside.

4 Add the cream of tartar to the egg whites; beat with an electric mixer on medium speed until mixture looks foamy. On high speed, beat in the granulated sugar, 2 tablespoons at a time; add the vanilla, almond extract and salt with the last addition of sugar. Continue beating until meringue is stiff and glossy. Do not underbeat.

5 Sprinkle the powdered sugar–flour mixture, ¼ cup at a time, over the meringue; to fold in, use a rubber spatula to cut down vertically through the batter, then slide the spatula across the bottom of the bowl and up the side just until sugar-flour mixture disappears. When all sugar-flour mixture has been folded in, spoon the batter into an ungreased 10 × 4-inch angel food (tube) cake pan. Using a metal spatula or knife, gently cut through the batter, spreading batter gently against side of pan and tube, to break large air pockets.

6 Bake 30 to 35 minutes or until cracks in cake feel dry and top springs back when touched lightly. Immediately turn pan upside down onto a heatproof funnel or bottle. Let cake hang about 2 hours or until completely cool.

7 Remove pan from funnel. Loosen the cake by running a knife or long metal spatula between the cake and side of pan. Place a serving plate upside down on pan; turn plate and pan over together and remove pan. (If pan has a removable bottom, remove side of pan, then carefully run a knife or long metal spatula between cake and pan bottom. Carefully remove bottom.) To cut cake, use a long serrated knife in a sawing motion, or use an electric knife.

*Egg whites will have better volume when beaten at room temperature in a bowl that is clean and dry.

Best-Ever Lemon Meringue Pie

PREP TIME: 50 Minutes • **START TO FINISH:** 3 Hours 35 Minutes

8 servings

**Pat-in-Pan Pastry (page 101)
or pastry for One-Crust Pie
(page 100)**

½ **cup granulated sugar**

4 **teaspoons cornstarch**

½ **cup cold water**

4 **large eggs**

1½ **cups granulated sugar**

⅓ **cup plus 1 tablespoon
cornstarch**

1½ **cups water**

3 **tablespoons butter or
margarine**

2 **teaspoons grated lemon peel**

½ **cup lemon juice**

2 **drops yellow food color,
if desired**

⅛ **teaspoon salt**

Spreading Meringue on Pie Filling

**Spread meringue evenly over
top** of pie filling and to the edge
of crust to seal the meringue to
the crust.

1   If making Pat-in-Pan Pastry, bake as directed for Prebaked Pie
Crust. If making One-Crust Pie, make as directed for Prebaked Pie
Crust; bake and cool as directed.

2   In a 1-quart saucepan, stir ½ cup sugar and 4 teaspoons
cornstarch until mixed. Stir in ½ cup cold water. Cook over
medium heat, stirring constantly, until mixture thickens and
boils. Boil 1 minute, stirring constantly; remove from heat. Let
cool completely, about 30 minutes, while continuing with the
recipe (mixture will be used in step 6).

3   Place an egg separator over a small bowl. Crack 1 egg over
the egg separator to separate the yolk from the white. Place yolk
in another small bowl. Separate 2 more eggs. When separating
fourth egg, place the yolk in another container to save for use in
another recipe. Set remaining 3 egg yolks aside (let stand at room
temperature no longer than 30 minutes).

4   Place the 4 egg whites in a clean large bowl, and let stand at
room temperature up to 30 minutes.*

5   Heat the oven to 350°F. Beat the egg yolks with a fork; set
aside. In a 2-quart saucepan, mix 1½ cups sugar and ⅓ cup plus
1 tablespoon cornstarch. Gradually stir in 1½ cups water. Cook
over medium heat, stirring constantly, until mixture thickens
and boils. Boil 1 minute, stirring constantly. Immediately stir at
least half of the hot mixture into the egg yolks, then stir yolks
back into hot mixture in saucepan. Boil 2 minutes, stirring
constantly, until very thick; remove from heat. Stir in the butter,
lemon peel, lemon juice and food color. Press plastic wrap on
surface of filling to prevent a tough layer from forming on top.

6   Add the salt to the egg whites; beat with an electric mixer on
high speed until egg whites just begin to form soft peaks when
beaters are lifted. Very gradually beat in the sugar mixture from
step 2 until stiff peaks form.

7 Pour hot lemon filling into pie crust. Spoon meringue onto hot lemon filling. Using a metal spatula, spread meringue over filling, carefully sealing meringue to edge of crust to prevent shrinking or weeping (little drops of moisture forming on the top of the meringue).

8 Bake about 15 minutes or until meringue is light brown. Cool pie away from drafts 2 hours. Refrigerate cooled pie until serving. Store remaining pie covered in refrigerator. (This pie is best served the day it is made. If refrigerated more than 1 day, the filling may become soft.)

*Egg whites will have better volume when beaten at room temperature in a bowl that is clean and dry.

High Altitude (3500–6500 ft): In step 1, bake One-Crust Pie 10 to 12 minutes. In step 8, bake 20 minutes.

1 Serving: Calories 460; Total Fat 15g; Cholesterol 90mg; Sodium 250mg; Total Carbohydrate 74g (Dietary Fiber 0g); Protein 5g **% Daily Value:** Vitamin A 4%; Vitamin C 4%; Calcium 0%; Iron 6% **Carbohydrate Choices:** 5

Popovers

PREP TIME: 10 Minutes • **START TO FINISH:** 45 Minutes

6 popovers

Shortening to grease pan

2 large eggs

1 cup all-purpose flour

1 cup milk

½ teaspoon salt

1 Heat the oven to 450°F. Generously spread shortening on the bottoms and sides of the cups in a 6-cup popover pan, using a paper towel or piece of waxed paper. Heat the popover pan in the oven 5 minutes.

2 Meanwhile, in a medium bowl, beat the eggs slightly with a fork or wire whisk. Beat in the flour, milk and salt just until smooth (do not overbeat or popovers may not puff as high). Remove popover pan from oven. Carefully fill the hot cups about half full with batter.

3 Bake 20 minutes. Reduce the oven temperature to 325°F. Bake 10 to 15 minutes longer or until popovers are deep golden brown. Remove from oven and immediately pierce each popover with the point of a knife to let the steam out. Remove popovers from cups. Serve hot.

High Altitude (3500–6500 ft): Use 1 cup plus 1 tablespoon flour. Heat oven to 400°F and bake for 20 minutes; reduce oven temperature to 325°F and bake 15 to 20 minutes longer.

1 Popover: Calories 130; Total Fat 3.5g; Cholesterol 75mg; Sodium 230mg; Total Carbohydrate 18g (Dietary Fiber 0g); Protein 6g **% Daily Value:** Vitamin A 4%; Vitamin C 0%; Calcium 6%; Iron 6% **Carbohydrate Choices:** 1

Do-Ahead Popovers: Bake popovers as directed. Remove from oven and immediately pierce each popover with the point of a knife to let the steam out. Cool completely on a cooling rack. Cover with a clean kitchen towel and store at room temperature up to 24 hours. Heat oven to 350°F. Place popovers on ungreased cookie sheet and bake 5 minutes or until hot.

Releasing Steam from Popovers

Remove popovers from oven and immediately pierce each popover with the point of a knife to let the steam out.

Cinnamon Swirl Raisin Bread

PREP TIME: 40 Minutes • **START TO FINISH:** 3 Hours 45 Minutes

2 loaves (16 slices each)

6 to 6½ cups all-purpose flour

½ cup granulated sugar

1 tablespoon salt

2 packages regular or fast-acting dry yeast (4½ teaspoons)

2 cups water

¼ cup vegetable oil

2 large eggs

Cooking spray to grease bowl and pans

1 cup raisins

1 tablespoon vegetable oil

½ cup granulated sugar

1 tablespoon ground cinnamon

2 tablespoons vegetable oil

1 tablespoon butter or margarine, room temperature, if desired

Kneading Raisins into Dough

Flatten the dough slightly and sprinkle with the raisins. Fold dough toward you, then push dough away from you with heels of hand. Continue kneading until the raisins are evenly distributed in the dough.

1 In a large bowl, stir 3 cups of the flour, ½ cup sugar, the salt and yeast until well mixed. In a 1½-quart saucepan, heat the water and ¼ cup oil over medium heat until very warm and an instant-read thermometer reads 120°F to 130°F. Add the water mixture and eggs to the flour mixture. Beat with a wooden spoon until smooth. Stir in enough of the remaining flour, 1 cup at a time, until dough is soft, leaves side of bowl and is easy to handle (dough may be slightly sticky). (See Making Yeast Dough, page 161.)

2 Sprinkle flour lightly on a countertop or large cutting board. Place dough on floured surface. Knead by folding dough toward you, then with the heels of your hands, pushing dough away from you with a short rocking motion. Move dough a quarter turn and repeat. Continue kneading 8 to 10 minutes, sprinkling surface with more flour if dough starts to stick, until dough is smooth and springy. Spray a large bowl with the cooking spray. Place dough in bowl, turning dough to grease all sides. (At this point, dough can be refrigerated up to 4 days.) Cover bowl loosely with plastic wrap; let rise in a warm place about 1 hour or until dough has doubled in size. Dough is ready if an indentation remains when you press your fingertips about ½ inch into the dough. (If using fast-acting yeast, omit 1 hour rising time; cover and let rest on floured surface 10 minutes.)

3 Spray two 9 × 5-inch loaf pans with the cooking spray. Sprinkle flour lightly on a countertop or large cutting board. Gently push your fist into the dough to deflate it. Divide the dough in half. On the floured surface, knead ½ cup of the raisins into each half. Using your hands or a rolling pin, flatten each half into an 18 × 9-inch rectangle. Brush 1 tablespoon oil over rectangles, using a pastry brush. In a small bowl, mix ½ cup sugar and the cinnamon; sprinkle each rectangle with half of sugar-cinnamon mixture. Beginning at a 9-inch side, roll dough up tightly, pressing with thumbs to seal after each turn. Pinch edge of dough into the roll to seal edge. Pinch each end of roll to seal ends, then fold ends under the loaf. (See Shaping Loaf, page 162.) Place each loaf, seam side down, in a pan. Brush 2 tablespoons oil over loaves. Cover loosely with plastic wrap; let rise in a warm place about 1 hour or until dough has doubled in size. Remove plastic wrap.

4 Move the oven rack to a low position so that tops of the pans will be in the center of the oven. Heat the oven to 375°F. Bake 30 to 35 minutes or until tops of loaves are deep golden brown and loaves sound hollow when tapped. Remove from pans to a cooling rack. To soften crust, brush butter over loaves. Cool 30 minutes before slicing; cut with a serrated knife.

High Altitude (3500–6500 ft): No change.

1 Slice: Calories 160; Total Fat 3.5g; Cholesterol 15mg; Sodium 230mg; Total Carbohydrate 28g (Dietary Fiber 1g); Protein 3g **% Daily Value:** Vitamin A 0%; Vitamin C 0%; Calcium 0%; Iron 8% **Carbohydrate Choices:** 2

Asiago Bread

PREP TIME: 25 Minutes • **START TO FINISH:** 4 Hours 20 Minutes
1 large loaf (24 slices)

Special Equipment: Clean spray bottle

3½ to 3¾ cups bread flour or all-purpose flour

1 teaspoon granulated sugar

1 package regular or fast-acting dry yeast (2¼ teaspoons)

1¼ cups water

2 tablespoons olive or vegetable oil

2 teaspoons dried rosemary or thyme leaves, if desired

1 teaspoon salt

1¼ cups diced Asiago, Swiss or other firm cheese

Cooking spray to grease bowl and cookie sheet

Sprinkling Flour on Loaf

Sprinkle the flour on the loaf using a small wire strainer. Shake it back and forth while moving it over the loaf.

1 In a large bowl, stir 1½ cups of the flour, the sugar and yeast until well mixed. In a 1½-quart saucepan, heat the water over medium heat until very warm and an instant-read thermometer reads 120°F to 130°F. Add the warm water to the flour mixture. Beat with a wire whisk or an electric mixer on low speed 1 minute, stopping frequently to scrape batter from side and bottom of bowl with a rubber spatula. Cover bowl tightly with plastic wrap; let stand about 1 hour or until bubbly.

2 Stir in the oil, rosemary and salt with a wooden spoon. Stir in enough of the remaining flour, ½ cup at a time, until dough is soft, leaves side of bowl and is easy to handle. Cover with plastic wrap; let stand 15 minutes.

3 Sprinkle flour lightly on a countertop or large cutting board. Place dough on floured surface. Knead by folding dough toward you, then with the heels of your hands, pushing dough away from you with a short rocking motion. Move dough a quarter turn and repeat. Continue kneading 5 to 10 minutes, sprinkling surface with more flour if dough starts to stick, until dough is smooth and springy. Knead in 1 cup of the cheese. Spray a large bowl with the cooking spray. Place dough in bowl, turning dough to grease all sides. Cover bowl tightly with plastic wrap; let rise in a warm place 45 to 60 minutes or until dough has doubled in size. Dough is ready if an indentation remains when you press your fingertips about ½ inch into the dough.

4 Lightly spray a cookie sheet with the cooking spray. Sprinkle flour lightly on a countertop or large cutting board. Gently push your fist into the dough to deflate it. Place dough on floured surface. Gently shape into football-shaped loaf, about 12 inches long, by stretching sides of dough downward to make a smooth top. Place loaf with smooth side up on the cookie sheet. Coat loaf generously with flour. Cover loosely with plastic wrap; let rise in a warm place 45 to 60 minutes or until dough has almost doubled in size.

5 Move oven racks to lowest and middle positions. Place an 8-inch or 9-inch square pan on the bottom oven rack; add hot water to the pan until about ½ inch from the top. Heat the oven to 450°F.

6 Pour a small amount of cool water into a clean spray bottle. Spray the loaf lightly with water; sprinkle with a small amount of flour. With a sharp serrated knife, carefully cut a ½-inch-deep slash lengthwise down the center of the loaf. Sprinkle the remaining ¼ cup cheese into the slash.

7 Bake 10 minutes. Reduce the oven temperature to 400°F. Bake 20 to 25 minutes longer or until loaf is deep golden and sounds hollow when tapped. Remove from cookie sheet to a cooling rack. Cool 30 minutes before slicing; cut with a serrated knife.

High Altitude (3500–6500 ft): No change.

1 Slice: Calories 110; Total Fat 3.5g; Cholesterol 10mg; Sodium 160mg; Total Carbohydrate 15g (Dietary Fiber 0g); Protein 4g **% Daily Value:** Vitamin A 4%; Vitamin C 0%; Calcium 6%; Iron 6% **Carbohydrate Choices:** 1

Apple Dumplings

PREP TIME: 25 Minutes • **START TO FINISH:** 1 Hour 5 Minutes

6 servings

2 cups all-purpose flour or whole wheat flour

1 teaspoon salt

⅔ cup plus 2 tablespoons cold butter or margarine

4 to 5 tablespoons cold water

6 baking apples, about 3 inches in diameter (such as Braeburn, Granny Smith or Rome)

3 tablespoons raisins

3 tablespoons chopped nuts

2½ cups packed brown sugar

1⅓ cups water

High Altitude (3500–6500 ft): Bake about 55 minutes.

1 Serving: Calories 830; Total Fat 27g; Cholesterol 65mg; Sodium 600mg; Total Carbohydrate 141g (Dietary Fiber 3g); Protein 6g **% Daily Value:** Vitamin A 15%; Vitamin C 4%; Calcium 10%; Iron 20% **Carbohydrate Choices:** 9½

1 Heat the oven to 425°F. In a large bowl, mix the flour and salt. Cut in the butter, using a pastry blender or fork, until particles are the size of small peas. Sprinkle with the cold water, 1 tablespoon at a time, mixing well with fork until all flour is moistened. Gather the dough together, and press it into a 6 × 4-inch rectangle.

2 Lightly sprinkle flour over a cutting board or countertop. Cut off ⅓ of the dough with a knife; set aside. On the floured surface, place ⅔ of the dough. Flatten dough evenly, using hands or a rolling pin, into a 14-inch square; cut into 4 squares. Flatten the remaining ⅓ of the dough into a 14 × 7-inch rectangle; cut into 2 squares. You will have 6 squares of dough.

3 Remove the stem end from each apple. Place the apple on a cutting board. Using a paring knife, cut around the core by pushing the knife straight down to the bottom of the apple and pull up. Move the knife and make the next cut. Repeat until you have cut around the apple core. Push the core from the apple. (Or remove the cores with an apple corer.) Peel the apples with a paring knife.

4 Place 1 apple on the center of each square of dough. In a small bowl, mix the raisins and nuts. Fill the center of each apple with raisin mixture. Moisten the corners of each square with small amount of water; bring 2 opposite corners of dough up over apple and press corners together. Fold in sides of remaining corners; bring corners up over apple and press together. Place dumplings in a 13 × 9-inch glass baking dish.

5 In a 2-quart saucepan, heat the brown sugar and 1⅓ cups water to boiling over high heat, stirring frequently. Carefully pour the sugar syrup around the dumplings.

Preparing Apple Dumplings

Cut around the apple core from the stem end using a paring knife. Then cut around the core from the bottom and push the core from the apple.

Moisten the corners of dough and bring opposite corners up over apple and press corners together. Repeat with remaining two corners.

6   Bake about 40 minutes, spooning syrup over apples 2 or 3 times, until crust is browned and apples are tender when pierced with a fork.

7   Serve warm or cooled with syrup from pan.

Peach Dumplings: Substitute 6 peaches, halved, pitted and peeled, for the apples. Substitute ¼ cup cranberry relish for the raisins and chopped nuts.

Chocolate Soufflé

PREP TIME: 20 Minutes • **START TO FINISH:** 1 Hour 25 Minutes
6 servings

Special Equipment:
6-cup soufflé dish

---

4 large eggs

2 oz unsweetened baking chocolate

½ cup granulated sugar

2 tablespoons cornstarch

1 cup milk

2 tablespoons butter or margarine, room temperature

1 teaspoon vanilla

About 2 teaspoons butter or margarine, room temperature, to grease soufflé dish

Additional granulated sugar for coating soufflé dish

½ teaspoon salt

¼ teaspoon cream of tartar

Sweetened Whipped Cream (page 193), if desired

1 Place an egg separator over a small bowl. Crack each egg over egg separator to separate the yolk from the white. Place yolk in another small bowl. Separate 2 more eggs. When separating fourth egg, place the yolk in another container to save for another recipe. Set remaining 3 egg yolks aside.

2 Place the 4 egg whites in a clean large bowl, and let stand at room temperature up to 30 minutes.*

3 Meanwhile, coarsely chop the chocolate. In a 1-quart saucepan, stir the sugar and cornstarch until mixed. Gradually stir in the milk. Add the chocolate. Cook over medium heat, stirring constantly, until chocolate is melted and mixture thickens and boils. Boil and stir 1 minute. Remove from heat.

4 In a small bowl, beat the egg yolks with an electric mixer on medium speed until very thick and lemon colored. Gradually beat in the chocolate mixture. With a wooden spoon, stir in 2 tablespoons butter and the vanilla. Cool to room temperature.

5 Heat the oven to 350°F. Spread 2 teaspoons butter on the bottom and side of a 6-cup soufflé dish, using a paper towel or piece of waxed paper. Sprinkle additional sugar over the butter. Make a 4-inch band of triple thickness of foil that is 2 inches longer than the circumference of the dish; butter one side of the band and sprinkle with sugar. Extend depth of dish by securing one end of foil band, buttered side in, to top outside edge of dish with masking tape. Bring foil band around edge of dish and secure with masking tape. (A buttered and sugared 2-quart casserole can be used instead of a soufflé dish and foil band.)

Preparing Soufflé Dish

Use a small wire strainer to sprinkle sugar evenly in the buttered soufflé dish. Move the strainer back and forth to sugar the bottom, then tilt and rotate the dish to sugar the side.

Extend the depth of the soufflé dish by securing a band of foil, buttered side in, with masking tape around top outside edge.

6 Add the salt and cream of tartar to the egg whites; beat with an electric mixer on high speed just until egg whites form stiff peaks when beaters are lifted. Stir about ¼ of the egg whites into the chocolate mixture. Add remaining egg whites; to fold in, use a rubber spatula to gently cut down vertically through the mixture, then slide the spatula across the bottom of the bowl and up the side, turning mixture over. Rotate the bowl a quarter turn, and repeat this down-across-up motion. Continue folding just until egg whites are blended into mixture. Carefully pour batter into the soufflé dish; use a rubber spatula to scrape batter from bowl, spread batter evenly in pan and smooth top of batter.

7 Bake 45 to 55 minutes or until a knife inserted halfway between the center and the edge comes out clean. Do not be alarmed if cracks appear on the top because they are characteristic of this soufflé.

8 Meanwhile, make Sweetened Whipped Cream. Serve soufflé immediately. Carefully remove foil band and divide soufflé into sections with 2 forks. Serve with whipped cream.

*Egg whites will have better volume when beaten at room temperature in a bowl that is clean and dry.

High Altitude (3500–6500 ft): No change.

1 Serving: Calories 230; Total Fat 12g; Cholesterol 115mg; Sodium 280mg; Total Carbohydrate 24g (Dietary Fiber 1g); Protein 6g **% Daily Value:** Vitamin A 6%; Vitamin C 0%; Calcium 8%; Iron 10% **Carbohydrate Choices:** 1½

Crème Brûlée

PREP TIME: 20 Minutes • **START TO FINISH:** 7 Hours

4 servings

Special Equipment: Four 6-ounce ceramic ramekins; kitchen torch

About 1 quart water

6 large eggs

2 cups whipping cream

⅓ cup granulated sugar

1 teaspoon vanilla

8 teaspoons granulated sugar

High Altitude (3500–6500 ft): No change.

1 Serving: Calories 570; Total Fat 45g; Cholesterol 450mg; Sodium 135mg; Total Carbohydrate 30g (Dietary Fiber 0g); Protein 12g **% Daily Value:** Vitamin A 35%; Vitamin C 0%; Calcium 10%; Iron 6% **Carbohydrate Choices:** 2

Caramelizing Sugar

Hold kitchen torch three to four inches from custard, move flame continuously over sugar in circular motion until sugar is melted and light golden brown.

1 Heat the oven to 350°F. Heat the water in a teakettle or covered 2-quart saucepan over high heat until boiling. The water will be used as a "water bath" when baking the custards.

2 Meanwhile, place an egg separator over a small bowl. Crack each egg over the egg separator to separate the yolks from the whites. (Save the whites for another recipe.)

3 Slightly beat the egg yolks with a wire whisk. In a large bowl, stir the whipping cream, ⅓ cup sugar and the vanilla until well mixed. Add egg yolks to cream mixture; beat with wire whisk until mixture is evenly colored and well mixed.

4 In a 13 × 9-inch pan, place four 6-ounce ceramic ramekins.* Pour the cream mixture evenly into the ramekins.

5 Pull out oven rack. Place pan with ramekins on the rack. Carefully pour just enough boiling water into the pan, being careful not to splash water into the ramekins, until water covers ⅔ of the height of the ramekins. Carefully push rack back into oven.

6 Bake 30 to 40 minutes or until tops are light golden brown and sides are set (the centers will be jiggly).

7 Using tongs or grasping tops of ramekins with a pot holder, carefully transfer ramekins to a cooling rack. Cool 2 hours or until room temperature. Cover tightly with plastic wrap; refrigerate until chilled, at least 4 hours but no longer than 2 days.

8 Uncover ramekins; gently blot any condensation on custards with a paper towel. Sprinkle 2 teaspoons sugar over each custard. Holding a kitchen torch 3 to 4 inches from custard, caramelize sugar on each custard by heating with torch about 2 minutes, moving flame continuously over the sugar in a circular motion, until the sugar is melted and light golden brown. (To caramelize sugar in the broiler, see Broiler Method below.) Serve immediately, or refrigerate up to 8 hours before serving.

*Do not use glass custard cups or glass pie plates; they cannot withstand the heat from the kitchen torch or broiler and may break.

Broiler Method: Sprinkle 2 teaspoons brown sugar over each chilled custard. Place ramekins in a 15 × 10 × 1-inch pan or on a cookie sheet with sides. Broil with tops of custards 4 to 6 inches from heat for 5 to 6 minutes or until the sugar is melted and forms a glaze.

MORE
BAKING BASICS
and BEYOND

Baking Terms

Baking has a vocabulary of terms and definitions of its own. This glossary isn't a complete list, but it will help you learn the most common terms you may see in cookbooks. For other helpful baking information, see Common Abbreviations (page 14), Measuring Equivalents (page 14), Know Your Baking Ingredients (page 9) and Baking Techniques (page 250).

BAKE: Cook in oven surrounded by dry heat. Bake uncovered for dry, crisp surfaces or covered for moistness.

BATTER: Uncooked mixture of flour, eggs and liquid in combination with other ingredients; thin enough to be spooned or poured (muffins, pancakes).

BLEND: Combine ingredients with spoon, wire whisk or rubber scraper until mixture is very smooth and uniform. A blender or food processor also may be used.

BOIL: Heat liquid until bubbles rise continuously and break on the surface and steam is given off. For rolling boil, the bubbles form rapidly.

CARAMELIZE: Melt sugar slowly over low heat or using a kitchen torch until it becomes golden brown, caramel-flavored syrup.

CHILL: Place food in the refrigerator until it becomes thoroughly cold.

COOL: Allow hot food to stand at room temperature for a specified amount of time. Placing hot food on a wire rack will help it cool more quickly. Stirring mixture occasionally also will help it cool more quickly and evenly.

COVER: Place lid, plastic wrap or foil over a container of food.

DISSOLVE: Stir a dry ingredient (yeast) into a liquid ingredient (warm water) until the dry ingredient disappears.

DOUGH: Mixture of flour and liquid in combination with other ingredients (often including a leavening) that is stiff but pliable. Dough can be dropped from a spoon (for cookies), rolled (for pie crust) or kneaded (for bread).

DRAIN: Pour off liquid by putting a food into a strainer or colander. When liquid is to be saved, place the strainer in a bowl or other container.

GARNISH: Decorate food with small amounts of other foods that have distinctive color or texture (nuts, fresh berries, whipped cream) to enhance appearance.

HEAT OVEN: Turn the oven control(s) to the desired temperature, allowing the oven to heat thoroughly before adding food. Heating takes about 10 minutes for most ovens. Also called preheat.

MELT: Turn a solid (chocolate, butter) into liquid by heating.

MICROWAVE: Melt, cook, reheat or thaw food in a microwave oven.

MINCE: Cut food into very fine pieces; smaller than chopped food.

PUREE: Mash or blend food until smooth and uniform consistency, using a blender or food processor or by forcing food through a sieve.

REDUCE HEAT: Lower heat to allow mixture to continue cooking slowly and evenly.

REFRIGERATE: Place food in refrigerator until it becomes thoroughly cold or to store it.

SCALD: Heat liquid to just below the boiling point. Tiny bubbles form at the edge. A thin skin will form on the top of scalded milk.

SIMMER: Cook in liquid at just below the boiling point. Usually done after reducing heat from a boil. Bubbles will rise slowly and break just below the surface.

SOFTEN: Let cold food stand at room temperature, or microwave at low power setting, until no longer hard (butter, cream cheese).

STIR: Combine ingredients with circular or figure-eight motion until uniform consistency. Stir once in a while for "stirring occasionally," stir often for "stirring frequently" and stir continuously for "stirring constantly."

STRAIN: Pour mixture or liquid through a fine sieve or strainer to remove larger particles.

TEAR: Break into pieces, using fingers.

TOAST: Brown lightly, using toaster, oven, broiler or skillet (bread, coconut, nuts).

TOSS: Tumble ingredients lightly with a lifting motion.

WHIP: Beat ingredients to add air and increase volume until ingredients are light and fluffy (whipping cream, egg whites).

ZEST: Outside colored layer of citrus fruit (oranges, lemons) that contains aromatic oils and flavor. Also, to remove outside colored layer of citrus fruit in fine strips, using knife, zester or vegetable peeler.

Baking Techniques

Beat: Combine ingredients vigorously with a spoon, fork, wire whisk or electric mixer until smooth or light and fluffy.

Chop: Cut into fine, medium or coarse irregular size pieces using a chef knife.

Core: To remove the center of a fruit (apple, pear, pineapple). Cores contain small seeds or are woody.

Crush: Press with side of chef knife blade, or use a meat mallet, rolling pin or bottom of heavy saucepan to smash food into small pieces.

Cube or Dice: Cut food into ½-inch or wider strips for cube or ½-inch or narrower strips for dice. Then cut across strips to make uniform size cubes.

Cut In: To work butter, margarine or shortening into dry ingredients until it forms crumbs. Use a pastry blender, lifting it up and down with a rocking motion. Or use a tableware fork and gently toss the dry ingredients.

Cut Up: Cut into small irregular size pieces using kitchen scissors or a knife.

Dot: Drop small pieces of ingredient (butter or margarine) randomly over food.

Drizzle: Pour in thin stream from a spoon, a squeeze bottle with a tip or a liquid measuring cup in an uneven pattern on food.

Dust: Sprinkle lightly with flour, granulated sugar, powdered sugar or baking cocoa. Can use a small strainer and move it back and forth or a spoon.

Flute: Squeeze the edge of a pastry to make a decorative pattern around edge of the pie crust.

Fold: Gently combine a light, airy mixture (beaten egg whites) with a heavier mixture (such as a batter). Use a rubber spatula to cut down through the mixture, then across the bottom and up and over.

Glaze: Brush, spread or drizzle an ingredient (jelly, frosting, melted chocolate) on hot or cold food, giving it a thin glossy coating.

Grate: Cut into tiny particles by rubbing food across the small rough holes of a grater.

Grease: Spray the bottom and sides of a pan with cooking spray. Or rub the bottom and sides with shortening, butter or margarine using a pastry brush, waxed paper or paper towel.

Grease and Flour: After greasing a pan with shortening, sprinkle with a small amount of flour and shake the pan to distribute it evenly. Turn pan upside down and tap bottom to remove excess flour.

Hull: Remove the stems and leaves from strawberries with a knife or huller.

Knead: Work dough into a smooth, springy mass, using your hands, to develop the gluten. Fold dough toward you and with heels of hands, push dough away with a short rocking motion.

Mix: Combine ingredients evenly, using any method.

Peel: Cut off outer covering with a knife or vegetable peeler, or strip off outer covering with fingers.

Roll: Flatten dough into a thin, even layer, using a rolling pin. Also to shape balls of cookie dough.

Roll Up: Roll a flat food that's spread with a filling beginning at one end until it is log-shaped.

Score: Cut shallow lines (about ¼ inch deep) on top of bread to decorate.

Separate Eggs: Place an egg separator over a bowl. Crack open the egg, letting yolk fall into center of separator and the egg white slip through the slots into the bowl.

Shred: Cut into long thin pieces by rubbing food across the large holes of a shredder. For finely shred, rub food across the smaller holes of a shredder.

Slice: Cut into flat, usually thin. pieces of the same width from a larger piece.

Snip: Cut small slits in surface of dough using a kitchen scissors. Also cut into very small pieces with kitchen scissors.

Soft Peaks: Egg whites or whipping creams beaten until the peaks curl when you lift the beater from the bowl.

Stiff Peaks: Egg whites or whipping creams beaten until the peaks stand up straight when you lift the beater from the bowl.

Baking Equipment and Gadget Wish List

Learning to bake can be enjoyable and fun whether you have just the basic essentials or a fully equipped kitchen. Here are some gadgets and equipment that you may want so you can expand your baking repertoire and help save time in the kitchen. These also make great gift suggestions!

Baking Mat: A silicone and fiberglass mat for lining baking pans. It has a non-stick surface, can be used over 2,000 times and is heat-resistant up to 480°F. It can also be used as a non-stick work surface for kneading dough and working with sticky batters or candies.

Biscuit Cutters: Round metal cutters used to cut baking powder biscuits and rolled cookies. Look for stainless-steel cutters with either a handle or rolled top edge to protect fingers. Available in graduated sizes from ¾ inch to three inches.

Cookie Dough Scoop: A spring-action scoop for making uniform-sized cookies that will bake evenly. A #70 scoop is equal to a level tablespoon and #16 is equal to ¼ cup. The large scoop is also good for filling muffin cups.

Cookie Press: Also called a cookie gun. It is a hollow tube fitted at one end with a decorative template or nozzle, and a plunger to force the soft dough out of the tube. Cookie presses come with a selection of interchangeable templates and tips. A cookie press is necessary to make spritz cookies.

Electric Mixer, Stand: A stand mixer is more powerful than a hand-held mixer and can be used for making thick cookie doughs and yeast bread doughs. Weight is important so it should be heavy so it doesn't move on the counter top when the machine is on high speed.

Fluted Tube Cake Pan: A fluted, round metal pan with a center tube for baking cakes and coffee cakes. It is also available in an array of interesting styles and shapes. A 10- or 12-cup size will work for most scratch recipes and cake mixes.

Food Processor, Mini: Also known as a mini chopper, it has a small plastic work bowl with a sharp S-shaped blade that easily chops small amounts of nuts, dried fruits and herbs.

Grater, Flat: Also known as a rasp grater, has rows of minute, ultra sharp holes that shredded or grate food precisely and cleanly without tearing. They are available with or without handles. You may need two; one for shredding and one for grating.

Kitchen Scissors: Also known as kitchen shears, are good for snipping dried or candied fruit and fresh herbs or for cutting up some soft candies and for all-purpose cutting and trimming ingredients.

Lemon Reamer: A wooden handheld reamer perfect for getting the juice out of a lemon, lime or orange. The point is good for removing seeds before you start juicing.

Pastry Blender: Used to cut shortening, butter or margarine into dry ingredients, such as flour and sugar, to make a crumbly mixture.

Pastry Scraper: A wide metal blade with a rolled handle used to scrape dough and flour from the work surface. It is also good for cutting dough or lifting and moving chopped ingredients from a cutting board to a bowl or pan.

Pizza Pan: A round metal pan with low sides for baking pizza. Some are perforated to help crisp the crust. Pans are available in 12-, 13-, 14- and 15-inch sizes.

Popover Pan: One metal pan with six deep cups, especially designed for baking popovers.

Soufflé Dish: Round dish with high sides and smooth interior, specifically designed for making soufflés.

Spatula, Medium Metal: Used to frost cakes or spread doughs in baking pans. A flexible metal blade is best for spreading frosting.

Spatula, Offset Small or Medium Metal: Also called an angled blade spatula because the blade is bent at a 45° angle. It is excellent for spreading batters and doughs in pans and frosting cakes and bars baked in rectangular or square pans.

Springform Pan: Round, deep pan with a spring-release removable side. Perfect for cheesecakes and desserts that shouldn't be turned upside down to remove from the pan. The cake can be served from the bottom of the pan. Pans are available in 8, 9, 10 or 11 inches.

Tart Pan: A round or rectangular pan, often with a removable bottom, that has scalloped edge. Pans are available in 10 or 11 inches. Individual-size pans are called tartlets.

Yields and Equivalents

How many apples do you need if a recipe calls for four cups sliced apples? Here are some guidelines to help determine how much you will need.

FOOD	IF YOUR RECIPE CALLS FOR	YOU WILL NEED APPROXIMATELY
APPLES	1 cup sliced or chopped	1 medium (6 ounces)
	1 pound	3 medium
APRICOTS, dried, halves	1 cup	5 ounces
BANANAS	1 cup sliced	1 medium or 2 small
	1 cup mashed	2 medium
BREAD, white	1 cup soft crumbs	1½ slices
	1 cup dry crumbs	4 to 5 slices, oven-dried
BUTTER OR MARGARINE	2 cups	1 pound
	½ cup	1 stick (¼ pound)
CARROTS	1 cup shredded	1½ medium
	1 cup ¼-inch slices	2 medium
CHEESE		
Hard, shredded or crumbled	1 cup	4 ounces
Cream	1 cup	8 ounces
CHOCOLATE		
Chips	1 cup	6 ounces
Unsweetened or semisweet baking	1 square or bar	1 ounce
COCONUT	1⅓ cups shredded or flaked	3 ounces
CRANBERRIES, dried	1 cup	4 ounces
CREAM		
Sour	1 cup	8 ounces
Whipping (heavy)	1 cup (2 cups whipped)	½ pint
CRUMBS, finely crushed		
Chocolate wafer	1½ cups	About 30 cookies
Graham cracker	1½ cups	About 20 squares
Vanilla wafer	1½ cups	About 38 cookies
DATES	2 cups whole pitted	12 ounces
	1 cup chopped	6 ounces
EGGS, large		
Whole	1 cup	4 large eggs
	1 egg	¼ cup fat-free cholesterol-free egg product
Whites	1 cup	7 to 8 large eggs (use only dry meringue powder or pasteurized liquid egg whites for recipes that call for raw egg white)
Yolks	1 cup	8 or 9 large eggs

continues on next page

Yields and Equivalents *(continued)*

FOOD	IF YOUR RECIPE CALLS FOR	YOU WILL NEED APPROXIMATELY
FLOUR		
All-purpose	3¾ cups	1 pound
Whole wheat	3⅓ cups	1 pound
LEMONS OR LIMES	1½ to 3 teaspoons grated peel	1 medium
	2 to 3 tablespoons juice	1 medium
NUTS (without shells)		
Chopped	1 cup	4 ounces
Whole or halves	3 to 4 cups	1 pound
ORANGES	1 to 2 tablespoons grated peel	1 medium
	⅓ to ½ cup juice	1 medium
PEACHES OR PEARS	2 cups sliced	3 medium (1 pound)
PINEAPPLES, fresh	4 cups cubed	1 medium
POMEGRANATES	1⅓ cups seeds	1 medium
PUMPKIN	1 cup mashed cooked	1 pound uncooked or 1 cup canned pumpkin
RHUBARB	3 cups 1-inch pieces	1 pound
SHORTENING	2⅓ cups	1 pound
	1 cup	1 stick
STRAWBERRIES	4 cups sliced	1 quart
SUGAR		
Brown	2¼ cups packed	1 pound
Granulated	2¼ cups	1 pound
Powdered	4 cups	1 pound
YEAST, regular or quick active dry	2¼ teaspoons	1 package (.25 ounce)

Emergency Substitutions

Using the ingredients recommended in a recipe is best. But if you have to substitute, try the following:

INSTEAD OF		AMOUNT	USE
BAKING POWDER		1 teaspoon	½ teaspoon cream of tartar plus ¼ teaspoon baking soda
BROWN SUGAR, packed		1 cup	1 cup granulated sugar plus 2 tablespoons molasses or dark corn syrup
BUTTERMILK OR SOUR MILK		1 cup	1 tablespoon lemon juice or white vinegar plus enough milk to make 1 cup; let stand 5 minutes before using. Or 1 cup plain yogurt.
CHOCOLATE	Semisweet baking	1 ounce	3 tablespoons semisweet chocolate chips or 1 ounce unsweetened baking chocolate plus 1 tablespoon sugar or 1 tablespoon baking cocoa plus 2 teaspoons sugar and 2 teaspoons shortening
	Semisweet chips	1 cup	6 ounces semisweet baking chocolate, chopped
	Unsweetened baking	1 ounce	3 tablespoons baking cocoa plus 1 tablespoon melted shortening or margarine
CORN SYRUP	Light	1 cup	1 cup sugar plus ¼ cup water
	Dark	1 cup	1 cup light corn syrup; ¾ cup light corn syrup plus ¼ cup molasses; or 1 cup maple-flavored syrup
CORNSTARCH		1 tablespoon	2 tablespoons all-purpose flour or 4 teaspoons quick-cooking tapioca
EGG		1 large	2 egg whites; ¼ cup fat-free cholesterol-free egg product; 2 egg yolks (for custards or puddings); or 2 egg yolks plus 1 tablespoon water (for cookies or bars)
FATS, solid		Any amount	Butter, margarine, shortening or vegetable oil
FLOUR	All-purpose	1 cup	1 cup plus 2 tablespoons cake flour or ½ cup whole wheat and ½ cup all-purpose
	Cake	1 cup	1 cup minus 2 tablespoons all-purpose flour
	Bread	1 cup	1 cup all-purpose flour or ½ cup all-purpose and ½ cup whole wheat flour
	Whole wheat	1 cup	1 cup all-purpose or ½ cup whole wheat and ½ cup all-purpose flour
GINGERROOT, grated or finely chopped		1 teaspoon	¾ teaspoon ground ginger
HERBS, chopped fresh		1 tablespoon	¾ to 1 teaspoon dried herbs
HONEY		1 cup	1¼ cups sugar plus ¼ cup water or apple juice
LEMON JUICE, fresh		1 tablespoon	1 tablespoon bottled lemon juice or white vinegar
LEMON PEEL, grated		1 teaspoon	1 teaspoon dried lemon peel
MILK, regular or low-fat		1 cup	½ cup evaporated milk plus ½ cup water; or nonfat dry milk prepared as directed on package
PUMPKIN OR APPLE PIE SPICE		1 teaspoon	Mix ½ teaspoon ground cinnamon, ¼ teaspoon ground ginger, ⅛ teaspoon ground allspice and ⅛ teaspoon ground nutmeg.
RAISINS		½ cup	½ cup currants, dried cherries, dried cranberries, chopped dates or chopped dried plums
YEAST, regular or quick active dry		1 package (.25 ounce)	2¼ teaspoons regular or quick active dry; or 1 package (.6 ounce) compressed cake yeast
YOGURT, plain unsweetened		1 cup	1 cup sour cream

Freezing Baked Items

Baked items can be frozen indefinitely; however, the quality will begin to deteriorate. The times below estimate how long frozen baked items will retain their quality. Be sure to wrap or store in moisture-proof freezer containers, seal and label to maintain flavor and quality.

FOOD	TO FREEZE	FREEZER (0°F OR BELOW)	TO SERVE
Breads, coffee cakes, muffins, scones, quick breads and yeast breads—baked	Cool completely. Do not frost or decorate. Place coffee cake on foil-wrapped cardboard before wrapping.	3 months	Unwrap slightly, thaw at room temperature 2 to 3 hours. To serve warm, wrap in foil and heat in 350°F oven for 15 to 20 minutes.
Cakes, unfrosted	Remove layer cakes or tubed cake from pan; cool completely. Place in sturdy freezer container and cover. Cool cakes baked in square or rectangular pan in the pan. Wrap pan with foil. Angel cakes are best put back in pan after cooling, wrap in foil, or place in sturdy freezer container.	4 months	Thaw, covered, at room temperature 2 to 3 hours.
Cakes, frosted	Place cake in freezer to harden frosting. Place in sturdy freezer container and cover.	3 months	Thaw, loosely covered, overnight in refrigerator.
Cheesecake, baked	Cool completely in pan and wrap with foil.	5 months	Thaw wrapped in refrigerator 4 to 6 hours.
Cookies, baked	If frosted or decorated, freeze on cookie sheet, then layer cookies in between pieces of waxed paper in a freezer container.	12 months—unfrosted 3 months—frosted	Thaw covered in container at room temperature. Remove cookies that should be crisp from the container.
Pies, baked pumpkin pies, pecan or fruit pies. Recommend not freezing custard, cream or pies with meringue topping.	Cool baked pie completed, then wrap in foil.	4 months	Heat unwrapped in 325°F oven for 45 minutes or until thawed and warm.
Pies, unbaked fruit pies.	Brush bottom crust with egg white before filling to prevent sogginess; do not cut slits in top crust. Cover with inverted foil or paper plate, then wrap in foil.	3 months	Unwrap, cut slits in top crust. Bake in 425°F oven for 15 minutes. Reduce temperature to 375°F and bake for 30 to 45 minutes or until center is hot.

High Altitude Baking

If you live at elevations of 3,500 feet or higher, you have some unique baking challenges. The decrease in air pressure at higher altitudes changes the way foods bake. Unfortunately, no set rules apply to all recipes so sometimes, trial and error is the best way to have baking success.

The following is affected when baking at high altitude:

- Gases expand more from the leavening
- Liquids boil at a lower temperature
- Liquids evaporate more quickly

These changes can translate into longer bake times, collapse of structure, drier finished products and possible overbrowning.

Most baked goods made with baking powder or baking soda (but not yeast) can be improved with one or more of the following changes:

- Increase the oven temperature by 25°F
- Increase the liquid
- Decrease the baking powder or baking soda
- Decrease the sugar and/or use a larger pan
- Decrease the fat in very rich recipes, such as pound cakes
- Quick breads and cookies usually need fewer adjustments

Yeast dough rises faster at high altitudes and can easily overrise. Let dough rise for a shorter time (just until it is double in size). Flour dries out more quickly at high altitudes, too, so use the minimum amount in the recipe or decrease the amount by ¼ to ½ cup.

For answers to your high altitude baking questions, call your local U.S. Department of Agriculture (USDA) Extension Service office, listed in the phone book under "County Government." Or write to Colorado State University, Department of Food Science and Human Nutrition Cooperative Extension, Fort Collins, CO 80523-1571. Also check your library for additional information.

Helpful Nutrition and Cooking Information

Nutrition Guidelines

We provide nutrition information for each recipe that includes calories, fat, cholesterol, sodium, carbohydrate, fiber, protein and % daily value and carbohydrate choices. Individual food choices can be based on this information.

RECOMMENDED INTAKE FOR A DAILY DIET OF 2,000 CALORIES AS SET BY THE FOOD AND DRUG ADMINISTRATION

Total Fat	Less than 65g
Saturated Fat	Less than 20g
Cholesterol	Less than 300mg
Sodium	Less than 2,400mg
Total Carbohydrate	300g
Dietary Fiber	25g

Criteria Used for Calculating Nutrition Information

- The first ingredient was used wherever a choice is given (such as ⅓ cup sour cream or plain yogurt).

- The first ingredient amount was used wherever a range is given (such as 3 to 4 cups all-purpose flour).

- The first serving number was used wherever a range is given (such as 4 to 6 servings).

- "If desired" ingredients and recipe variations were not included (such as sprinkle with brown sugar, if desired).

Ingredients Used in Recipe Testing and Nutrition Calculations

- Ingredients used for testing represent those that the majority of consumers use in their homes: large eggs, 2 percent milk, cooking spray and regular or fast-acting dry yeast.

- Fat-free, low-fat or low-sodium products were not used, unless otherwise indicated.

- Solid vegetable shortening, cooking sprays or spray with flour was used to grease pans, unless otherwise indicated.

Equipment Used in Recipe Testing

We use equipment for testing that the majority of consumers use in their homes. If a specific piece of equipment (such as a wire whisk) is necessary for recipe success, it is listed in the recipe.

- Cookware and bakeware without nonstick coatings were used, unless otherwise indicated.

- No dark-colored, black or insulated bakeware was used.

- When a pan is specified in a recipe, a metal pan was used; a baking dish or pie plate means ovenproof glass was used.

- An electric hand mixer was used for mixing only when mixer speeds are specified in the recipe directions. When a mixer speed is not given, a spoon or fork was used.

Metric Conversion Guide

VOLUME

U.S. Units	Canadian Metric	Australian Metric
¼ teaspoon	1 mL	1 ml
½ teaspoon	2 mL	2 ml
1 teaspoon	5 mL	5 ml
1 tablespoon	15 mL	20 ml
¼ cup	50 mL	60 ml
⅓ cup	75 mL	80 ml
½ cup	125 mL	125 ml
⅔ cup	150 mL	170 ml
¾ cup	175 mL	190 ml
1 cup	250 mL	250 ml
1 quart	1 liter	1 liter
1½ quarts	1.5 liters	1.5 liters
2 quarts	2 liters	2 liters
2½ quarts	2.5 liters	2.5 liters
3 quarts	3 liters	3 liters
4 quarts	4 liters	4 liters

WEIGHT

U.S. Units	Canadian Metric	Australian Metric
1 ounce	30 grams	30 grams
2 ounces	55 grams	60 grams
3 ounces	85 grams	90 grams
4 ounces (¼ pound)	115 grams	125 grams
8 ounces (½ pound)	225 grams	225 grams
16 ounces (1 pound)	455 grams	500 grams
1 pound	455 grams	½ kilogram

MEASUREMENTS

Inches	Centimeters
1	2.5
2	5.0
3	7.5
4	10.0
5	12.5
6	15.0
7	17.5
8	20.5
9	23.0
10	25.5
11	28.0
12	30.5
13	33.0

TEMPERATURES

Fahrenheit	Celsius
32°	0°
212°	100°
250°	120°
275°	140°
300°	150°
325°	160°
350°	180°
375°	190°
400°	200°
425°	220°
450°	230°
475°	240°
500°	260°

NOTE: The recipes in this cookbook have not been developed or tested using metric measures. When converting recipes to metric, some variations in quality may be noted.

How-Tos

Index

Page numbers in *italics* indicate illustrations

Complete your cookbook library with these *Betty Crocker* titles

Betty Crocker Baking for Today

Betty Crocker's Best Bread Machine Cookbook

Betty Crocker's Best Chicken Cookbook

Betty Crocker Christmas Cookbook

Betty Crocker's Best of Baking

Betty Crocker's Best of Healthy and Hearty Cooking

Betty Crocker's Best-Loved Recipes

Betty Crocker's Bisquick® Cookbook

Betty Crocker Bisquick® II Cookbook

Betty Crocker Bisquick® Impossibly Easy Pies

Betty Crocker Celebrate!

Betty Crocker's Complete Thanksgiving Cookbook

Betty Crocker's Cook Book for Boys and Girls

Betty Crocker's Cook It Quick

Betty Crocker Cookbook, 10th Edition—
The **BIG RED** *Cookbook*®

Betty Crocker Cookbook, Bridal Edition

Betty Crocker Cookbook, Heart Health Edition

Betty Crocker Cookie Book

Betty Crocker Cooking Basics

Betty Crocker's Cooky Book, Facsimile Edition

Betty Crocker Decorating Cakes and Cupcakes

Betty Crocker's Diabetes Cookbook

Betty Crocker Dinner Made Easy
with Rotisserie Chicken

Betty Crocker Easy Everyday Vegetarian

Betty Crocker Easy Family Dinners

Betty Crocker's Easy Slow Cooker Dinners

Betty Crocker's Eat and Lose Weight

Betty Crocker's Entertaining Basics

Betty Crocker's Flavors of Home

Betty Crocker 4-Ingredient Dinners

Betty Crocker Grilling Made Easy

Betty Crocker Healthy Heart Cookbook

Betty Crocker's Healthy New Choices

Betty Crocker's Indian Home Cooking

Betty Crocker's Italian Cooking

Betty Crocker Just the Two of Us Cookbook

Betty Crocker Kids Cook!

Betty Crocker's Kitchen Library

Betty Crocker's Living with Cancer Cookbook

Betty Crocker Low-Carb Lifestyle Cookbook

Betty Crocker's Low-Fat, Low-Cholesterol
Cooking Today

Betty Crocker More Slow Cooker Recipes

Betty Crocker's New Chinese Cookbook

Betty Crocker One-Dish Meals

Betty Crocker's A Passion for Pasta

Betty Crocker's Picture Cook Book,
Facsimile Edition

Betty Crocker Quick & Easy Cookbook

Betty Crocker's Slow Cooker Cookbook

Betty Crocker 30-Minute Meals for Diabetes

Betty Crocker Ultimate Bisquick® Cookbook

Betty Crocker's Ultimate Cake Mix Cookbook

Betty Crocker Whole Grains Cookbook

Betty Crocker Why It Works

Betty Crocker Win at Weight Loss Cookbook